LIVE EACH SEASON as it passes; breathe
the air, drink the drink, taste the fruit, and
resign yourself to the influences of each.

Henry David Thoreau

"Her primer for 'green' witchcraft—i.e., witchcraft in tune with seasonal elements—is a gold mine of concepts and resources for the novice to intermediate practitioner. Chock-full of relevant wisdom and lively humor, this is a valuable addition to any avid pagan's personal reference library."—*Library Journal*

Book of Witchery "This treasury of enchantments and spells will keep you conjuring seven days a week!" —*Prediction Magazine*

Practical Protection Magick "A solid work…Beginners and experienced practitioners alike will benefit from this information and from the author's affirmation of the reader's own personal empowerment." —*Witches & Pagans magazine*

"The book is written in her usual direct and lively style and contains those garden touches we love. This just might be my favorite Ellen Dugan [book] to date." —*New Age Retailer Fine Print Online*

about the
Author

Ellen Dugan, also known as the Garden Witch, is a psychic-clairvoyant who lives in Missouri with her husband and three children. A practicing Witch for over twenty-five years, Ellen also has many years of nursery and garden center experience, including landscape and garden design. She received her Master Gardener status through the University of Missouri and her local county extension office. Look for other articles by Ellen in Llewellyn's annual *Magical Almanac*, *Witches' Companion*, and *Herbal Almanac*, and visit her website at:

www.ellendugan.com

FROM THE AUTHOR OF *GARDEN WITCHERY*

seasons of witchery

CELEBRATING THE SABBATS WITH THE GARDEN WITCH

ELLEN DUGAN

LLEWELLYN PUBLICATIONS
woodbury, minnesota

FIRST EDITION
First Printing, 2012

Book design and edit by Rebecca Zins
Cover design by Ellen Lawson
Cover photo © Stacy Bass Photography
Interior artwork by Wen Hsu

Llewellyn is a registered trademark of Llewellyn Worldwide Ltd.

Library of Congress Cataloging-in-Publication Data

Dugan, Ellen, 1963–
    Seasons of witchery : celebrating the sabbats with the garden witch / Ellen Dugan.—1st ed.
        p. cm.
    Includes bibliographical references (p.   ) and index.
    ISBN 978-0-7387-3078-3
    1. Sabbat. 2. Religious calendars—Wicca. I. Title.
    BF1572.S28D84 2012
    133.4´3—dc23

                                                                                                    2012010678

Llewellyn Worldwide Ltd. does not participate in, endorse, or have any authority or responsibility concerning private business transactions between our authors and the public.

    All mail addressed to the author is forwarded, but the publisher cannot, unless specifically instructed by the author, give out an address or phone number.

    Any Internet references contained in this work are current at publication time, but the publisher cannot guarantee that a specific location will continue to be maintained. Please refer to the publisher's website for links to authors' websites and other sources.

Llewellyn Publications
A Division of Llewellyn Worldwide Ltd.
2143 Wooddale Drive
Woodbury, MN 55125-2989
www.llewellyn.com

Printed in the United States of America

other books by
ELLEN DUGAN

Garden Witchery: Magick from the Ground Up
(Llewellyn, 2003)

Elements of Witchcraft: Natural Magick for Teens
(Llewellyn, 2003)

Cottage Witchery: Natural Magick for Hearth and Home
(Llewellyn, 2005)

Autumn Equinox: The Enchantment of Mabon
(Llewellyn, 2005)

The Enchanted Cat: Feline Fascinations, Spells & Magick
(Llewellyn, 2006)

Herb Magic for Beginners: Down-to-Earth Enchantments
(Llewellyn, 2006; also available in Spanish as *Magia con las hierbas*)

Natural Witchery: Intuitive, Personal & Practical Magick
(Llewellyn, 2007)

How to Enchant a Man: Spells to Bewitch, Bedazzle & Beguile
(Llewellyn, 2008)

Garden Witch's Herbal: Green Magick, Herbalism & Spirituality
(Llewellyn, 2009)

Book of Witchery: Spells, Charms & Correspondences for Every Day of the Week
(Llewellyn, 2009)

Practical Protection Magick: Guarding & Reclaiming Your Power
(Llewellyn, 2011)

This book is dedicated to my children: Kraig, Kyle, and Erin. I am so proud of each of you, not only for what you have accomplished with your lives but for the amazing adults you have become. Be sure to always follow your dreams and reach for the stars—and there'll be no stopping you.

Love you,

Mom

table of
CONTENTS

Introduction xvii

What You Will Find in This Book xix

Beginning the Journey on the Longest Day of the Year xxi

Chapter 1: Midsummer/Summer Solstice 1

Midsummer, Summer Solstice, and Litha 4

Faeries in the Summer Flower Garden 6

The Garden Witch's List of Faerie Herbs 10

Midsummer Faerie Garden Blessing 18

Musings of a Garden Witch: Herbal Allies or Plant Familiars 20

A Call to Find Your Herbal Ally or Plant Familiar 25

Ellen's Garden of Witchery Journal: A Peek at My Garden 26

Personal Lessons for Midsummer: Fire Magick Equals Transformation 28

Midsummer Sangria Slush 30

Reflections on Midsummer: A Time of the Sun and the Moon 32

A Summer Spell to Bless Your Family or Coven 33

Chapter 2: Lughnasadh/Lammas 35

A Little History: The First Harvest Festival 36

Dog Days of Summer—Then and Now 38

Loaf Mass: Celebrating the Sabbat with Breads 40

Zucchini Bread Recipe 41

Ellen's Garden of Witchery Journal: Steamy Days and Butterflies 43

Butterfly Magick 45

Late Summer Gardening 49

Full Wort Moon in August 51

Personal Lesson for Lughnasadh: Change Is Constant 53

How I Spent My Summer Vacation… A Witch in a Trout Stream 56

Reflections on Lughnasadh: The Final Days of Summer 62

Earth Mother Candle Spell for Late August 63

Chapter 3: Autumn Equinox/Mabon 65

A Little History: The Autumn Equinox 66

The Autumn Equinox Officially Heralds the Fall Season 68

Autumn Holidays: Decorating the Magickal Home 69

Harvest Moon Magick 76

Full Harvest Moon Spell for Blessings 79

Pagan Pride Day: Or How to Go to a Pagan Festival and Still Enjoy Yourself 80

Rule Number One: Follow the Festival Rules and Be Polite 81

Rule Number Two: You Are Responsible for Your Children and/or Pets 81

Rule Number Three: Meeting Authors 82

Rule Number Four: Dress Weather Appropriate 86

Ellen's Garden of Witchery Journal: September Projects   88

Personal Lesson for the Autumn Equinox: Messages and Appreciation   90

Reflections on the Autumn Equinox: The Season of the Witch   95

Chapter 4: Samhain/Halloween   97

A Little History: A Fire Festival   98

Death and Transformation: Death takes a Holiday   100

Masks, Guisers, and Trick-or-Treaters   103

Colorful Signs of the Season   105

Cauldron Magick   106

  An Elemental Cauldron-Blessing Ritual   108

A Touch of Nature's Magick at Samhain   109

The Jack-o'-Lantern   110

  Jack-o'-Lantern Spell   112

Apples: The Magickal Fruit of Samhain   113

The Enchanting Apple: A Victorian Halloween Tradition   115

  A Halloween Apple Spell for Love Divination   116

  A Samhain Apple Muffin Recipe   117

Ellen's Garden of Witchery Journal: October Garden Magick   119

Samhain Flower Magick with the Chrysanthemum   121

  The Magick of Chrysanthemum Colors   122

  A Samhain Night Flower Fascination to Ward Off Ghosts   123

Personal Lesson for Samhain: Plan Ahead and Enjoy the Celebrations   124

Reflections on Samhain: Embracing the Darkness   129

Chapter 5: Yule/Winter Solstice   133

A Little History: Here Comes the Sun   135

Saturnalia   136

Santa: Shaman or Shapeshifter?   138

The Wild Hunt at Yuletide   142

Lucy and St. Lucia   144

A Candle Spell for Lucy and Little Yule   147

Decking the Halls   148

Ellen's Garden of Witchery Journal: The Plants of Yuletide   151

Evergreen   152

Holly   153

Ivy   154

Mistletoe   155

Herbal Charm for Yuletide   158

Gingerbread at Yuletide   159

Gingerbread People Cookies   161

Personal Lesson for Yuletide: The Witch Meets Santa   162

Reflections on Yuletide: The Real Reason for the Season   165

Chapter 6: Imbolc/Candlemas   169

A Little History: A Festival of Candlelight and Inner Light   171

Candlemas and Imbolc   174

The Goddess Brigid   178

An Imbolc Spell to Celebrate the Goddess Brigid   180

Herbal Magick at Imbolc   182
    Hellebore Herbal Spell for Protection and Hex-Breaking   184

An Imbolc Recipe to Warm Your Heart   185
    Blueberry Scones for Imbolc   186

The Value of a Coven Sister   187

Ellen's Garden of Witchery Journal: Greenhouse Therapy   191
    Greenhouse Charm   193

Personal Lesson for Imbolc: Relax, Rest, and Recharge   194

Reflections on the Season of Imbolc: February Thaw   198
    A Winter to Spring Psychic Protection Spell   199

Chapter 7: Vernal Equinox/Ostara   201

A Little History: The Vernal Equinox   203

Goddess Magick with Eostre: A Blessing for Your Home   205

Ostara's Hare of Fertility and Eggs   207

Perfect Eggs for Ostara   209
    Natural Egg Dyes   210
    Vernal Equinox Quiche   211

Springtime Decorating: Your Magickal Home   212

Full Moon in March: A Spell for Balance   213

Personal Lesson for the Vernal Equinox: Growth and Rebirth   215

A Spell for March 31: The Festival of Luna   218
    Directions and Supplies   218

Ellen's Garden of Witchery Journal: The April Planter's Moon   220

And Now for Something Completely Different: Palm-Reading Sunday   222

A Few Rules of Etiquette for Divination and Palm-Reading Basics   223

The Four Main Shapes of the Hand   224

The Four Major Lines of the Palm   227

Divination Is the Theme of the Day: So Have Fun!   230

Reflections on the Spring Season   231

Chapter 8: Beltane   237

Symbols of the Season: The Maypole and Flowers   239

Deities of Beltane: Flora the May Queen and the Green Man   240

A Lusty Beltane Day Spell   244

Honor the Green Man: Plant Green Flowers   245

Herbal Bouquets and Tussie-Mussies   248

The Language of Flowers and Fragrant Herbs   250

The Styles of Tussie-Mussies   255

An Enchanting History: The Bridal Bouquet   257

The Magick of Color for Floral Bouquets   260

Creating Your Own Herbal Tussie-Mussie Bouquet   262

Full Moon in May: The Dryad Moon   266

A Dryad Full Moon Spell to Protect Your Garden and Favorite Wild Places   267

Ellen's Garden of Witchery Journal: Secret Gardens   268

Personal Lesson for Beltane: Laugh, Damn It!   270

Afterword: Reflections on the Past Year   273

Acknowledgments   275

Appendix: Sabbat Correspondences   277

   Summer Solstice/Midsummer   277

   Lughnasadh/Lammas   278

   Autumn Equinox/Mabon   279

   Samhain/Halloween   279

   Yule/Winter Solstice   280

   Imbolc/Candlemas   281

   Vernal Equinox/Ostara   281

   Beltane   282

Glossary   285

Bibliography   295

   Websites   300

Index   301

Introduction

HOPE SMILES ON the threshold of the year
to come, whispering that it will be happier.

Lord Alfred Tennyson

The idea for this book popped into my mind on a late spring afternoon in 2010. I was cleaning out my computer, purging some old files, when I stumbled across a list of book ideas. Interestingly enough, the list of ideas was dated from 2004. I had not looked at this file in years, and then I had to laugh when I realized that out of the six possible books I had listed, five of them were now, in fact, published books.

A book on psychic abilities and the Craft became *Natural Witchery*. An outline for a cheeky and fun book on love magick was now *How to Enchant a Man*. A more in-depth book of shadows and an expansion of *7 Days of Magic* had turned into my largest book to date, which was now called *Book of Witchery*. A book outline with the working title of *Garden Witchery* II had become *Garden Witch's Herbal*, and a book idea that was entitled *A Darker Shade of Witchery* had been finished just a few months ago, in February of 2010, and was soon to become *Practical Protection Magick*.

Of the possible book ideas that remained, I felt a very strong tug at my solar plexus for the book outline on the magickal year. I thought about it for a few hours and realized

yes, indeed, I did still want to write that book. Honestly, the idea was still as fresh in my mind as it was the day I had sat and conjured up an outline for it so many years ago… So off to the local library I trekked to see what sort of reference material I could find. I came home loaded with a dozen reference books and tons of fresh ideas for the sabbats swirling in my brain.

Happily I decided, since Midsummer was just a week away, that I would work on this new book over the course of the calendar year, writing each chapter as the Wheel of the Year turned—documenting the changes in the garden and in my magickal life as they occurred. It was a challenge, it was fun, *and* it was different!

What You Will Find in This Book

> If one cannot enjoy reading
> a book over and over again, there
> is no use in reading it at all.
> *Oscar Wilde*

This is an intimate look at how I, the "Garden Witch," celebrated the Wheel of the Year. I have found that my readers are particularly interested in how I live, celebrate, and work my magick; they always enjoy the personal stories. And what better way to mix the two together than to write about the seasons and the magick I experienced as I lived and worked my way through them? In this book are my musings on the Wheel of the Year, my personal lessons for the sabbat, and stories about my own coven and how we celebrated, changed, and grew over the course of the year.

In this book you will also find a bit of history and lore on each sabbat, as well as simple and enjoyable suggestions for celebrating each one. There are decorating ideas and recipes. For fun, I thought an interesting addition to this book would be allowing you into my gardens, so you can take a peek at my magickal gardening journal throughout the year. Of course, each of the eight chapters will contain seasonal rituals and all sorts of natural magick, such as herbal and candle spells aligned with the eight Witch's holidays and with the four seasons.

Seasons of Witchery is a fresh take on the eight sabbats. A completely different look at the Wheel of the Year, it offers ideas and magickal ways to celebrate the sabbats simply and in tune with nature, both as a magickal gardener and as a Witch. My goal here is to share a more relaxing, inspiring, and personal take on the seasons and the sabbats. It is my hope that you will enjoy your time with me and use this book all throughout the magickal year.

Beginning the Journey on the Longest Day of the Year

> Wherever you go, no matter what the
> weather, always bring your own sunshine.
>
> *Anthony J. D'Angelo*

As I write this, it is sunrise on Midsummer Day. Here in Missouri the temperatures have been in the high nineties, and it has been extremely hot and humid. When I woke up just before dawn today I was full of energy and enthusiasm, with plans to officially begin this book project—right after lunch. (I'm a Virgo. I always have a plan, a list, and a schedule.)

I was also looking forward to giving myself an entire morning of blissful solitude, working in my gardens and gathering and tending my flowers and magickal herbs, celebrating the day as the sun rose, with only the flowers, trees, birds, and the cat for company. This is my own personal tradition for celebrating the Midsummer sabbat.

But perhaps the Goddess was already having a hand in this book, for as I pulled on my gardening shoes and walked to the back door with my little calico cat, Brie, hot on my heels, I heard a rumble of thunder and realized that a pop-up rain shower had moved in. So my sunrise gardening session was delayed for a few hours until the rain showers stopped and things dried out. I stood at that back door, surprised and frowning at the clouds and the rain, and feeling a bit annoyed at having my gardening plans thwarted.

My cat meowed pitifully as if she, too, were complaining at the rain and her being unable to go play in the gardens with me. I muttered under my breath and let loose a disgusted sigh, thinking how my perfectly planned-out morning had just been shot to hell by the weather.

Telling myself the rain was good for the flowers, I turned away from the back door and wondered what to do now, since I was up and raring to go…and then my gaze fell on my computer desk and all those reference books. I thought to myself, *no time like the present.* I kicked off my beat-up gardening shoes and set my gathering basket down—which the cat immediately climbed into—and booted up the computer and dove in. I could always work in the gardens after lunch.

This book begins its journey and the first chapter at Midsummer—completely different (and, I am sure, shocking) to some folks—but I am a gardener, after all. If we are celebrating a solar calendar and the natural Wheel of the Year, then let's start with a bang! What better time to kick off this book than when my garden is in full swing and all around me is nothing but growth and possibilities?

Midsummer

Summer Solstice

JUNE 20–23

THE SUMMER NIGHT is like
a perfection of thought.

Wallace Stevens

Midsummer, or Litha, is a celebration of light. This is a solar/fire festival that marks the astrological day of the summer solstice, which occurs on or around June 21, when the sun enters the sign of Cancer, the crab. Cancer is the only astrological sign that is associated with the moon. If you combine that lunar influence with the ultimate strength of the sun, you have quite the magickal wallop.

The day of the summer solstice has the longest daylight hours and the shortest nighttime hours of the year. As the sun reaches its highest position in the sky, we are at the climax of the sun's power. This is the greatest day of the sun's magick, even though it is bittersweet—for as soon as the day after the summer solstice, the sun's power gradually begins to decline, with nighttime hours slowly and inexorably increasing. After today, we are in the dark half of the Wheel of the Year, which may seem confusing, but truly the daylight hours are decreasing now, and the sun will start to reach its zenith at a lower point in the sky from now until December and the winter solstice.

The sabbat of Midsummer is a potent and magickal date. This is a great time for fire magick, bonfires, garden witchery, herbal and green magicks, and the best night of the year to commune with the elemental kingdom and the faeries. This is a time of celebration in nature: everything is green and growing. Nature is celebrating her achievement!

Fire festivals and fireworks are complementary; it all goes with that theme of fire magick for summer. At this time of year, your spellworking themes may include asking for the blessing and assistance of the faeries or working green magick with the garden. Prosperity, health, and abundance spells are appropriate at this point in time as well, since the light is at its peak and all of nature is at its most lush, vibrant, and green.

If you like to work with the more traditional fire theme of this sabbat, consider building a small ritual fire in your outdoor fire pit or chiminea. Bonfires on Midsummer have been lit by people from all over the world, from many magickal customs, for centuries. The bonfires were classically lit at sundown on Midsummer's Eve. So set up your fire and get ready to go! If you like, you can toss a few herbs or oak leaves into the flames as an offering to the Old Gods.

If you are unable to safely have an outdoor fire, then light several bright yellow candles and group them together inside of a cauldron, and enjoy the effect that several flickering flames make inside of that cauldron. Another idea that I started with my coven years ago was to pass out sparklers; after our rituals are complete, we light up the sparklers and dance around the gardens with the lightning bugs. When the sparklers are finished, we drop them into a bucket of water. Celebrate the summer solstice and put your own personal spin on things!

The magickal correspondences for Midsummer are simple and natural ones. Colors are gold and green—gold to celebrate the might of the sun and green to symbolize the leaves on the trees, all of nature, and the Faerie realm, which are all at their peak of influence and magickal power. Some eclectic magickal traditions may choose a celestial theme of deep blue and golden suns and stars. I like to think of those celestial decorations as symbols that represent the best influences of the moon, from the zodiac sign of Cancer, and the strength of the sun at the Solstice.

Also, just to keep things interesting, there is a watery theme to Midsummer as well. People did make journeys to sacred wells for cures at Midsummer. Wells, springs, and the life-giving summer rain are just as important to the crops and your own garden as the sunshine, so keep that in mind.

If you want to try something different for Midsummer, you could play up the beach/water/summer theme. I have seen a "magickal mermaid" ocean theme successfully used for Midsummer. It was hauntingly different, ethereal, and gorgeous—think of lots of starfish and sand dollars cleverly arranged on an altar, with iridescent seashells and blue beach glass scattered around the base of off-white candles and crystal-clear bowls of water. Again, these could be links to the zodiac sign of Cancer the crab. However, a beach-inspired Midsummer celebration sounds enchanting, doesn't it? If you live along the ocean or coast, I imagine that this would be gorgeous Midsummer altar décor and a distinctive theme for any ritual performed on a shore, beach, or in your own back yard.

Animals and insects that are traditionally linked to Midsummer festivals are creatures such as honeybees, eagles, hawks, goldfinches (a favored faerie bird), butterflies, dragonflies—oh, and don't forget those lightning bugs!

Lightning bugs, or fireflies, have long been associated with the fae and the elemental kingdom. On soft nights in June the lightning bugs are out in force, putting on quite the show for children—and for any magickally minded, young-at-heart adults who care to watch.

MIDSUMMER, SUMMER SOLSTICE, AND LITHA

WHAT'S IN A name? That which we call a
rose by any other name would smell as sweet.

William Shakespeare

Truly, there are more labels and names for this summer sabbat than you can shake a golden bough at. Everyone has an opinion and a theory about why there are so many titles for this sabbat, and of course everyone has an argument as to why the name they choose is correct. Today many Pagans, Wiccans, and Witches refer to the summer solstice sabbat as Litha or Midsummer.

If you are wondering where the usage of the name *Litha* came from in more modern times, you can thank Tolkien and the Lord of the Rings trilogy of books. In his classic books he called a Midsummer festival Litha, thus making the term romantically popular. Also, it should be pointed out that according to tradition, the ancient Anglo-Saxons called the month of June *Litha*. I would imagine that's probably how the title Litha caught on.

For me it has always felt correct to call this sabbat simply Midsummer, and I encourage you, the reader, to go with whatever title you choose to be correct for yourself for the summer solstice sabbat. Whether you call it Litha, Midsummer, or the summer solstice, it is an enchanting date in our magickal year and a phenomenal time for faerie magick and ritual.

Midsummer is a most opportune time to harvest your June-blooming magickal herbs and flowers for drying. Take a good look around your magickal gardens right now and see what can be gathered and stored away for use in your own future spells, enchantments, and charms. Also keep in mind that any strongly scented flower is rumored to be a faerie favorite, so incorporate your favorite scented summer flowers in your Midsummer rituals and spells with the faeries.

One of my favorite magickal themes for Midsummer is, of course, faeries. (Blame it on me seeing the play A *Midsummer Night's Dream* when I was a teenager many moons ago.) Faerie magick and green magick are perennially popular topics, and they do go well together. After all, where else are you going to encounter the faeries but in a Witch's magickal garden?

FAERIES IN THE SUMMER FLOWER GARDEN

I DO WANDER everywhere, swifter than
the moon's sphere; and I serve the Fairy
Queen, to dew her orbs upon the green.

William Shakespeare

Here are a few tips that you'll need to know when it comes to attracting the faeries to your property and for working successfully with them this Midsummer. Faeries in your garden will boost both your magick and your plants' growth. How do I know that these will work? Well, I have been using these techniques myself for over twenty years.

RULE NUMBER ONE: Be respectful and polite. Oh, yes, indeed. A certain amount of reverence and a good dose of common sense is required when working any magick or spell with the faerie realm. Be careful what you ask for, as you probably will get it. I would recommend adding a tagline to the end of all your faerie spells, to ensure that the magick doesn't go astray or that you are "pixied" (a term used to describe faerie trickery). Faerie trickery is sometimes silly and harmless—and sometimes it is much darker. Tag on a final line to your faerie spells with something like the following:

With help from the friendly faeries, this spell is sung
For the good of all, this magick brings harm to none.

Finally, if you can't take faerie magick seriously, then don't attempt it. Trust me— you do *not* want a bunch of ticked-off nature spirits on your property.

RULE NUMBER TWO: Know the faerie days and times. These days are all eight sabbats, at dusk the evening before the sabbats, and at all of the full moons throughout the year. However, it is possible to work with the faeries all year long. Traditionally you work faerie magick at a 'tween time—in other words, a "between time" such as dawn, noon, twilight, or midnight. These times of the day are neither one or the other, and it's precisely this quality that links it to the faerie realm. Think about it.

Twilight is neither day nor night, it is somewhere in between. Same with dawn, noon, or midnight. Dawn is between the night and day, noon is neither morning or afternoon, and midnight is on the cusp of a new day. They are between one and the other. At these moments—and during solar and lunar eclipses or the occasional blue moon—you will often encounter the most faerie activity and sense the strongest faerie energy. According to tradition, you will also have good luck contacting the faeries while the first spring flowers bloom in the garden, when the first leaves begin to fall in the autumn, and during the first snowfall of the season. These are also all great times to work magick with the faeries throughout the year.

RULE NUMBER THREE: Keep the spirits of nature, the elementals, and the faeries happy by taking care of your gardens and the flowers, trees, and herbs on your property to the best of your abilities. Water the plants regularly and keep them healthy. Pull the weeds and keep up the maintenance on your yard. Use your common sense; try to keep chemical usage to the bare minimum for ornamental plants, shrubs, and trees. For your herbs and magickal plants, try your hand at organic gardening (especially for culinary herbs and veggies).

Plus, if you lay off the chemicals, you'll have more beneficial insects and pollinators such as bees and butterflies in your garden. A healthy and natural garden is the best way to encourage the faeries to make their home on your property and to dwell happily in your garden.

RULE NUMBER FOUR: Encourage the fae to your property by making it a place filled with birds, butterflies, and bees. Hang up hummingbird feeders in the garden this summer. Plant flowers and blooming shrubs that attract the butterflies and hummingbirds with nectar and the birds with seeds and fruit. (There are many varieties of dogwood and viburnum which produce tiny berries that the songbirds will happily gobble up.)

Plant drought-tolerant native plants and readily available perennials such as the purple coneflower and brown-eyed Susans. Look for "grow native" plant tags at the local nurseries—you will have better luck with native plants and flowers, and the nature spirits are drawn to them quicker. Also, I suggest planting annual sunflowers. These plants will bloom reliably all though the summer months and into early fall. As September draws near, their cones dry up, and the goldfinches and other birds land on the flower heads for a snack.

Also, put up bird feeders in the garden. Nope, not kidding. Fill up your feeders with a good-quality songbird birdseed mix—something with dried fruit, safflower, and sunflower seeds. This will attract the largest variety of birds into the garden. Also hang up a bird feeder with thistle seeds in it. Goldfinches are sacred to the Faerie kingdom, and a thistle feeder will help to bring them into the garden. Then, once they find your other flowers, they keep coming back.

RULE NUMBER FIVE: Garden wherever and however you can! Container gardens, window boxes, and hanging baskets on a porch, deck, or balcony *do* count as a garden. When cleverly arranged and lushly planted, these become an enchanting container garden. You can easily add a small birdfeeder out there. Trust me, the nature spirits are everywhere. They are in the city and the suburbs and the country. If you lovingly tend your mini garden in the heart of the city with magickal intention, they will find you.

RULE NUMBER SIX: Do bless your magickal garden and your property (a ritual to do just that is on pages 18–20). Stamping your own magickal energy onto the property will only add to the atmosphere and encourage other elementals and faeries to wander through the area and see what's going on in your yard or garden.

THE GARDEN WITCH'S LIST OF FAERIE HERBS

THERE IS NOTHING new under the sun
but there are lots of old things we don't know.

Ambrose Bierce

I couldn't resist this topic. Maybe it's because at the moment my gardens are in their glory and I want to share my enthusiasm, but honestly—this is the perfect time of year to try your hand at a little garden witchery!

The following blooming herbs have a great deal of tradition and folklore behind them. Some of these herbs are culinary, and some are strictly ornamental. Several of these herbs, such as the violet, dandelion, and clover, may already be lurking unappreciated in your lawn, so look closely. Or you may already be growing a few ornamental varieties of herbs in your gardens. Any herb or strongly scented flower will attract the faeries, so make sure you tuck some of those plants into your gardens as well. Peruse the list below and see what plants grab your attention. Maybe you'll want to slip some of these plants into your herbal gardens to add to the enchanting atmosphere.

Also, depending on where you live and your climate or cold hardiness zone, you may or may not have some of these herbs in bloom for your personal Midsummer celebration. I live in the Midwestern United States. My cold hardiness zone is 5. By Midsummer my lilacs, pansies, iris, and peonies are finished blooming for the year. But if you live in a cooler, northern climate, those peonies, iris, pansies, and lilacs may still be blooming away. Peruse the following list and take a look at the many options you have available to you for your Midsummer's magick and what you have in bloom in your climate at the summer solstice.

NOTE: An herb may be classified today as a plant that is used for its medicinal, savory, or aromatic qualities. Any part of the plant—the roots, stem, bark, leaves, fruits, seeds, or flowers—may be used for such purposes. An herb may be a tree, shrub, woody perennial, flower, annual, or fern.

Also, please note that these meanings and associations are based in legend and folklore. Enjoy their magick and history, but remember this is not a medicinal guide by any means. The common name is listed first, followed by the botanical name in Latin, then the magickal information.

ANGELICA (*Angelica archangelica*)—This gorgeous and stately biennial herb encourages inspiration, protection, and healing, all with the help of the faeries. Sprinkle a bit of dried angelica leaves at the four corners of your property to surround you and your loved ones with protection and love.

CHAMOMILE (*Chamaemelum nobile*)—This plant soothes the spirit and can be a magnet for gentle nature spirits. It attracts prosperity and love, and the flower faeries enjoy its tiny flowers.

CLOVER (*Trifolium pratense*)—Red or white clover is traditionally a faerie favorite. Take a good look at your yard—clover is probably growing happily in your own lawn. It brings good luck and the blessings of "the little people." Holding clover in your hand is thought to gain you "faerie sight" (the ability to see the faeries).

DANDELION (*Taraxacum sect. Ruderalia* spp.)—The bane of many suburban lawns, this bright yellow flower is, however, a favorite of children and the faeries. Some faerie texts suggest plucking a dandelion puffball on the night of the full moon. Then you are to make an unselfish wish and blow the seeds to the wind. This way, the faeries of the element of air, the sylphs, are sure to answer your request.

FOXGLOVE (*Digitalis purpurea*)—Foxglove is a toxic plant and should be kept out of reach of small children. Foxglove has many enchanting folk names and is a favorite faerie plant. The name foxglove is thought to come from a corruption of the term "folks' gloves," as the faeries, or the folks, were thought to use the bell-shaped blossoms for hats and gloves. Magickally it may be used for protection. Today you can find many new varieties and cultivators for the garden in shades of purple, pink, white, and yellow.

IRIS (*Iris germanica var. florentina*)—The iris was named after the Greek goddess of the rainbow. A gorgeous faerie plant, iris is indeed available in all the colors of the rainbow. The iris boasts incredible scents, color combinations, and a variety of bloom times; definitely add these enchanting perennials to your gardens. According to plant folklore, the iris gifts you with communication, wisdom, knowledge, and eloquence.

LADY'S MANTLE (*Alchemilla mollis*)—Lady's mantle is a beautiful perennial herb to grow in a faerie garden. It has soft, pleated leaves that collect dew drops, earning it the folk name dewdrop. It blooms chartreuse-green delicate flowers in late May that currently are very popular in floral design.

The flowers hold for weeks and will grace your Midsummer gardens. This faerie herb is aligned to women's magick and the Goddess.

LAVENDER (*Lavandula* spp.)—There are many varieties of lavender. Some of my favorite varieties that do well in my gardens are 'Hidcote' and 'Munstead'. These two varieties love the heat and full sun and will survive a cold Midwestern winter with a lot of dramatic swings in temperature. Growing lavender in the garden brings good luck, and it is a protective, healing plant long believed to be a faerie favorite due to its incredible scent. I like to grow lavender in my rose garden, at the feet of the rose bushes. Lavender adds fragrance and texture.

LILAC (*Syringa vulgaris*)—The lilac is classified as an herb, as they do extract oil from the flowers to make perfume. The common lilac is actually a deciduous twiggy shrub that represents a first love. The scent of lilacs is also very protective. Growing one of these fragrant beauties in your garden ensures the blessings of the faeries and protection for your property. If you bring a few of the blossoms into your house, the scent will protect your home as well.

MARJORAM (*Origanum onites*)—This faerie herb is incorporated into charms and spells to draw love and fertility. It is also rumored to help keep a married couple happily together. For culinary purposes, marjoram is considered to be milder than oregano. The flowers of this herb attract pollinators, such as honeybees and butterflies, to your garden.

MEADOWSWEET (*Filipendula ulmaria*)—Also known as bridal wort, this sweetly scented faerie flower was used in Medieval times as a strewing herb and was popular in bridal bouquets. Its charming uses include love, joy, and—you guessed it—a beautiful wedding day and a happy marriage. Gorgeous and fragrant, this is a fantastic semi-shady herb for the home garden.

PANSY (*Viola* spp.)—The sweet, sunny faces of pansies are a popular faerie flower. They are available in a rainbow of colors (including black varieties) and are perfect both in containers and clustered together in the home garden. The cool weather–loving pansy can be incorporated into charms for healing, to bring about a sunny disposition, to mend a broken heart after a breakup, or to calm feuding friends.

PEONY (*Paeonia officinalis*)—The peony is—surprise!—considered an herb. This gorgeous shrub produces amazingly fragrant flowers in the late spring. A popular faerie plant, tuck a peony blossom or two in a vase and set it in the bedroom to ward off bad dreams. Wearing a peony blossom pinned to your blouse or tucked in your hair protects you from bad luck and negativity.

PURPLE CONEFLOWER (*Echinacea purpurea*)—An herb and a wildflower, the purple coneflower is full of magickal properties, including health, strength, and healing. Goldfinches love this tall, hardy flower, and so do the faeries. Purple coneflowers grow best in full to part sun and are drought tolerant once they are established. Grow these

perennials in a sunny spot in your garden, then sit back and enjoy the butterflies, who use them for landing pads, and the gold-finches as they flock to them to snack on the thistle in the cones. Remember: attract wildlife into the garden, and the faeries are sure to notice and check your garden out.

ROSE (*Rosa* spp.)—The rose is an herbal symbol for love and devotion. A popular faerie flower, roses are magical no matter what variety or color they happen to be. But to attract the faeries, the stronger the scent of the rose, the more attention the garden will receive. Use rose petals in charm bags or herbal spells to help speed things up. Also, you may scatter fresh rose petals on the ground to mark the boundaries of a ritual circle.

ROSEMARY (*Rosmarinus officinalis*)—Rosemary is for remembrance. This piney-scented, edible herb is sacred to the faeries and elves, and it is a wonderful plant to add to any herb garden for its texture, form, beauty, and scent. An old name for rosemary was elf-leaf. Rosemary is grown as an annual in colder winter climates. It will not survive being outdoors in temperatures below freezing. In my gardens, I can keep the rosemary plants alive until after Yuletide, then the cold temperatures finish it off. But it is inexpensive to purchase, and I enjoy growing several new plants every year.

SAGE (*Salvia officinalis*)—Sage, in all of its many wondrous varieties, brings wisdom. The classic garden sage (*Salvia officinalis*) is another culinary herb that will winter over nicely in your garden. During the late spring and summer months, be sure to clip back the purple blossoms to help the plant produce more leaves. It is a faerie herb of cleansing, knowledge, and protection.

ST. JOHN'S WORT (*Hypericum perforatum*)—This protective herb blooms once a year, typically right around June 20—just in time for the summer solstice, or Midsummer. It is also known as the "leaf of the blessed." Keeping this herb growing in your garden will protect you from faerie trickery. Carrying a few stems of the foliage was an old way to avoid being "faerie led," or lost and confused while wandering through the local enchanted forest. A word of warning: this is an aggressive herb; it grows like mint and can be difficult to control. I use it for a groundcover in my gardens under the shrubs I have planted as a hedgerow. It does fine there, but I work hard to keep it in check.

THYME (*Thymus vulgaris*)—This culinary herb is wonderful to grow in your garden, as it attracts the faeries and encourages health, love, and courage. According to legend, anyplace where thyme grows wild is a spot that has been blessed by the faeries.

VALERIAN (*Valeriana officinalis*)—A gorgeous garden plant with ferny-looking foliage that is topped off by tall, honey-scented flowers at Midsummer. The flowers are used in charm bags or tucked under the pillow to aid in a restful night's sleep. Valerian encourages love, protection, and sleep. In my cold hardiness zone, valerian blooms in early June and lasts through Midsummer.

VIOLETS (*Viola odorata*)—A traditional faerie wildflower, violets are thought to guard against faerie mischief and are a sweet and protective little blossom. Transplanting violets around your home is a clever and inexpensive way to use a bit of faerie magic to protect your home, property, and family.

YARROW (*Achillea* spp.)—An all-purpose wise woman's herb. Save a spot in your sunny garden for blooming yarrow. Today yarrow is available in a wide variety of colors: yellow, red, pink, white, and purple, so there is something for everyone to enjoy! The blossoms of the yarrow are very easy to dry; they maintain their color well and may be used for all sorts of positive spells and enchantments.

The faeries of the herb garden will make their presence known to you in subtle ways. If you truly wish to work with the nature spirits, then the most important thing you'll need is an open mind and a loving heart. Once upon a time, faeries were thought to whisper healing charms and recipes to the wise folks. By working together with this elemental energy in the creation and care of an herb garden, you will assist all of the plants that grow there.

Remember: you are more than just an herb gardener or a garden Witch. You are a caretaker and a steward of the land. Pass down this folklore and what plant tips you know to new gardeners and to the children in your life. When you open up your mind to the possibilities of the nature spirits and faeries, then you can reap the benefits in both your herb garden and in your life.

Midsummer Faerie Garden Blessing

Work this ritual at dawn on Midsummer Day. You will need only yourself and a small crystal point, which you are going to leave in the gardens for the faeries. Stand outside in your garden and hold your hands up and out to your sides. Keep the crystal point in the palm of one of your hands. (You can hold the crystal in place by tucking your thumb over it.) As you cup your hands up toward the sky, imagine them filling up with your personal power and your desire to invite the benevolent faeries onto your property.

You may call the quarters, if you like, according to your own magickal tradition or by using the following quarter calls.

Begin in the east:

Element of air, I call you to join me here
As I celebrate the longest day of the year.

Now turn to the right to face the south:

Element of fire, please join me on this day
Bringing warmth, magick, and light in mystical ways.

Right turn again to face the west:

Element of water, come now to bless this place
I am washed by love in this magick garden space.

Finally, turn right for the last time to face north:

Element of earth, I mark one of your holy times

Gift me with strength, growth, and joy with this bewitching rhyme.

Now move to the center, cast your circle, and say:

As above, now so below

The elemental powers spin, and my magick holds.

Now continue on with the spell verse while you stand in the garden:

I call the kindly faeries into my garden and yard

If you are friendly, then you are welcome from near and far.

Bless this land, protect these herbs and flowers

Fill them up with your magickal powers.

Now hear my request as these words are spoken

In thanks, I offer you this crystal token.

By the might of the Midsummer's sun

So must it be, and let it harm none.

When the spell verse is finished, turn your hands palms down over the garden and let the crystal fall where it may into the plants. Now envision the energy flowing out from your hands and into the garden.

Finally, crouch down and place both hands on the earth. Ground and center yourself. If necessary, you can tuck the crystal deeper into the garden and leave it for the fae.

If you called the quarters, be sure to release them. Here is a way to open the quarters without a lot of fuss.

Say:

Four elements, I release you to combine and swirl about
Allow for growth and love in the garden, and keep bad luck out!

Close up this magickal act as you normally do. Be sure to spend some time out in the gardens today—plant some new flowers or tend the ones you already have. Enjoy the beauty and magick of nature on one of her brightest and holiest of days.

Musings of a Garden Witch
HERBAL ALLIES OR PLANT FAMILIARS

HERBS ARE SPECIAL ambassadors
to the magic and miracle of nature.

Clea Danaan

A few days before the summer solstice this year, I changed my typical sunrise walking routine. Instead of a two-mile walk up to the park and back home, I took a three-and-a-half-mile hike. As it turned out, it was a good impulse.

While I was walking along the Missouri River on the Katy Trail, which is a recreational trail that runs all throughout the state of Missouri, the sweet scent of elderberry in bloom kept wafting my way. I am sure the other folks riding, jogging, and walking along the trail thought I was a bit strange, sniffing the air and slowing down to follow my nose and to look carefully at the vegetation growing wild between the trail and the river.

Sure enough, I soon saw small elderberry trees in bloom and setting fruit at various spots along the hiking trail. The scent is incredible, and some of the creamy-white blossom clusters were as big as dinner plates. Enchanted, I stepped off the trail and stopped to sniff them over—and ended up getting showered with fading tiny white petals from a nearby elder when a breeze wafted through. Laughing, I thanked the elder trees, and after a reverent stroke of their foliage and flowers, I continued happily along the trail to finish my walk. When I arrived home an hour later, I still had perfumed, tiny elderflower petals all over my hair.

The elder is a very magickal tree. It is sacred to the Crone Goddess and is a protected tree when it comes to magick. While it is small in stature, the local variety of elderberry (*Sambucus canadensis*) is classified as a tree, not a shrub. A part of the honeysuckle family, the white umbrella-shaped clusters of flowers are followed by dark, wine-colored berries in late summer, and the flower heads have been used for many things over the years. There are some old recipes that call for dipping the flower heads in batter and deep-frying them. Also, the flowers are used to make an elderflower cordial. The berries themselves have been pressed into tonics and cordials and brewed into champagnes and wine. The ripe berries are still popular for jellies, jams, syrups, and pies, and the elderberry fruit may also be used to create dyes.

According to folklore, the small elder tree is a Witch tree, supposed to mark the doorways to the faerie realm, and it wards off negative magick and baneful spells. Also, it was forbidden to cut down an elder tree or to burn its wood, which would explain the old rhyme *Elder is the Lady's tree, burn it not or cursed you'll be…* The mother of the elder tree was called Hyldemoer; it was rumored that she was, in fact, a dryad, or some say a goddess of both life and death. According to the old classic book *Teutonic Mythology*, this herbal tree was also called "ellorn" or "ell horn," and it was considered a holy and sacred plant. Even with all of the dire warnings of what would occur should you harm an elder tree, it is considered to be a friendly tree to conscientious magickal folks.

I have always felt especially drawn to the elder. I can smell them and spot them long before other folks. I always feel a tug on my solar plexus that lets me know when they are close by. I discovered long ago that the elder tree, with its gorgeous flowers and berries, is one of my plant familiars.

Plant familiar? I'll explain. Just like a totem animal, each of us also has specific plants that we are drawn to. These plants have a vibration that is harmonious with our own personal energies, and we can "link up," or work well together. Just like the psychic partnership you can have with your cat or dog that makes them your magickal familiar, so too can you have a working energetic relationship with a living plant.

Some folks will refer to this as a power plant, a plant totem, an herbal ally, or a plant familiar. But no matter how you describe this relationship, everyone has several herbal allies. You may have wild plant allies and garden plant allies. Oh—and yes, you may have tree allies as well. Yes, indeed, you will discover over the years that your plant allies, or tree and herb familiars, may expand or change. For me personally, my wild plant familiar is the elderberry, my tree ally is the oak, and my garden plant familiar is yarrow.

My coven sister has discovered that her wild plant familiar is the wood violet. She always finds them and is drawn to violets (especially the white ones) in wild places. When I gave her some transplanted perennials out of my own gardens this spring, she was thrilled to discover that a few wild violets had hitched along for the ride. She is babying those violets along, the way another gardener would watch their roses.

Now, her herb familiar/garden plant ally is definitely the foxglove. (She cheerfully admits to being a bit obsessed with this particular garden plant.) As nature photography is her hobby, she has taken many beautiful photographs of foxgloves in bloom over the years—the kind of ethereal photography that just makes your jaw drop. I was fortunate to receive one of the magickal photos framed as a gift this year. I immediately hung it in my kitchen, next to a large framed poster of herbs. Her plant obsession turned into my good luck!

It's also interesting to note that as my coven sister and I discussed the idea of her plant totems and allies, she suddenly realized that she owned many pieces of art and knickknacks in her home that featured violets and foxgloves. She started laughing once she realized that she did indeed have an herbal ally/wildflower totem. All she had to do to discover what they were was to check her home's decor and her own magickal gardens for the clues.

So ask yourself: do you have one favorite species of flower growing all over your own gardens? Which garden herb and flower are you typically attracted to? This is an easy answer for serious gardeners, because no matter what particular plant they are shopping for, it always gets pushed to the side when they get sidetracked and find themselves looking at their "favorite" plant instead. If this happens to you a lot, then you probably have just identified one of your herbal familiars, or plant allies.

Now take that a step further. Ask yourself, what is your favorite tree? Do you have a wildflower or wild plant that you always seem to find whenever you go out? Take some time this summer and check this out for yourself. Take a trip to a state park, take a walk through the woods, go visit a lovely botanical garden, and really look carefully at the gardens. What did you find? What drew you in?

Go to a local nursery or garden center and check out the plants for sale. See what calls to you. What captivated you and made you smile? Worlds of magick and plenty of green opportunities await you. All you have to do is get out there this summer and take the time to look.

A Call to Find Your Herbal Ally
or Plant Familiar

Here is a call to help you find your herbal ally, or plant familiar. I suggest doing this call while out in nature, perhaps sitting outside in your garden or a park or while you quietly peruse a nursery, garden center, or public botanical garden. Repeat the verse softly to yourself and put some feeling into the words.

The green world does call to those who know how to hear

Herbal allies surround me now from far and near.

Please partner with me in my magick so true

Strengthen and guide all herbal spells that I do.

The magick of Midsummer strengthens my plant familiar's call

May we work well together come winter, spring, summer, and fall.

Once you have finished the verse, go look around and see what plants you are drawn to. Happy hunting! Keep notes on what you discover while working with your plant allies/herbal familiars and see what sort of working relationship you develop.

Ellen's Garden of Witchery Journal
A Peek at My Garden

Gardens are not made
by sitting in the shade.
Rudyard Kipling

There is still plenty of work to be done in the garden in the summertime—deadheading and weeding and mulching. With gardens as extensive as we have, there is no such thing as letting the gardens go in summer. You have to stay on top of them.

I try to get outside in the mornings while it is still cool. Mornings or evenings are the best time to water the gardens as well. Lately I've been lucking out and we've had plenty of rain, so I have not had to water too much—just the window boxes and containers.

The tiger lilies are really blooming earlier than normal this year. Actually, the tiger lilies are just finishing up their bloom cycles at Midsummer this June. We did have a warmer, mild spring. I believe that has pushed all of the bloom times forward by about three weeks.

These orange lilies are a Missouri wildflower and are technically identified as a day-lily (*Hemerocallis fulva*) but are known to the locals with great affection as "tiger lilies."

How can you resist such cheerful and bright orange flowers? My daughter loves these flowers. I am betting they are actually *her* plant familiar. She has already asked if, when she gets a place of her own in a few years, she can have some tiger lilies to transplant into her own yard. Of course I am happy to share.

Also, my 'Moonshine' variety of yellow yarrow is finishing its bloom cycle this week, and the purple coneflowers are just beginning their seasonal display. I dead-headed the lavender today…It made me a little sad, but this will encourage another cycle of blossoms in late July and early August. So with bumblebees for company, I clipped away and neatened the plants up. This made the plants look cleaner, and now they can put their energy back into more flowers instead of seeds. Right now I smell like lavender, and it is bracing and comforting. Plus, as I worked in the yard earlier, the lingering scent helped to keep the mosquitoes away.

The tall garden phlox is also blooming early this year—typically it does not bloom until July. It is so fragrant in the late afternoon and evening hours. Oh, and the Queen Anne's lace has gone crazy. I'll have to be ruthless in a few weeks and cut it back hard. It's taller than I am this year.

My angelica has put on its big show, faded, and then had to be pulled out. A true biennial, it takes two years to bloom, and then it dies. The blossoms have stood a good five feet tall since mid May, but they managed to hold on for my editor to see when she came to visit, and then a week or so after, until late June. No worries. I'll hunt for another angelica plant next spring. I find those cycles of the garden comforting. Besides, the thrill of the hunt for plants or something new to try is part of the fun of gardening.

My coven is not meeting until early July for Midsummer celebrations this year. Seems that everyone (including me) is out of town the weekend closest to the sabbat for something or another. Still, I wanted to mark the day of the sabbat and to celebrate the official first day of summer, so one of my coven sisters who lives in my neighborhood is coming over, and we are going to sit in the back yard and have some raspberry wine. Ravyn and I will walk around the gardens, check out what is blooming, and then light a fire in the fire pit and probably roast marshmallows and make a couple of s'mores. We plan to read each other's tarot cards and just hang out and relax. The official full coven gathering won't be until the weekend after next. But the good news is that the firework stands will be open by then, so we can bring sparklers to the celebration!

Personal Lessons for Midsummer
FIRE MAGICK EQUALS TRANSFORMATION

> A GOOD RELATIONSHIP is like
> fireworks: loud, explosive, and liable to
> maim you if you hold on too long.
>
> Jeph Jacques

This year our theme for the sabbat was transformation and fire magick. Our hostess, Ember, and her husband had just completed a back yard patio, and she was raring to try out her new fire pit. The coven ladies were more than eager to see her gardens and the new patio.

It ended up only being four of us that Friday night having a belated celebration of the sabbat. One coven member was recovering from a recent surgery; she was doing well at home but was unable to drive. Honestly, we were more concerned about her recovering fully than missing the sabbat. And another member had a friend surprise her with tickets for the musical *Wicked*. We all jokingly said that this gave her a "pass," as she was at a cultural event where Witches were involved. Ahem.

And at the last minute, our final coven member was unable to attend, which made us all wonder if this particular member was going to be leaving the coven soon. We had all seen the signs. We wondered if this would be a quiet parting on good terms or an explosive, drama-filled situation. It ended up that we would not have long to wait to find out.

So those of us who were able gathered together and prepared to have a coven celebration with magick, ritual, food, wine, and fun. Since most of us came directly from work that evening, we decided to eat dinner first. To keep things festive we had some fantastic Midsummer seasonal sangria. This is simple to make with red wine and fruit juice. Here is the recipe, courtesy of Ember Grant.

Midsummer Sangria Slush

1 (8 ounce) can crushed pineapple

2½ cups dry red wine

1½ cups orange juice

½ cup lemon juice

½ cup sugar

Blend all ingredients in a blender for 20–30 seconds, making sure sugar is dissolved. (This amount of liquid barely fit in my blender, so I mixed it in batches.) Pour into a baking dish or something similar (I used a 9 x 12 glass dish). Freeze for several hours. Depending on how long you freeze it, allow it to sit at room temperature before serving. Ember let it sit on the counter for half an hour, then chopped it up with a fork and dumped it back into the blender to make it smooth. Enjoy!

• • • •

After dinner that night, the coven members decided to head outside, take a tour of our hostess's perennial gardens, settle in on that new fancy patio, and watch the sun set and get ready for our ritual. As it was only a few days away from the Fourth of July, there were plenty of neighborhood fireworks going off, which was fun and actually helped with the fire magick theme. As darkness fell, the fire pit was fired up and the four of us gathered around it to work our Midsummer ritual.

The ritual focused on transformation and releasing the things that no longer served us. We were each to write down an obstacle or problem and then fold it up, and one by one surrender the problem to the flames. The fire would transform the issues for us and make room for newer, more positive things in our lives. We finished up the lovely ritual, released the quarters, and then one of the ladies whipped out a big bag of fancy red, blue, and green sparklers, which we pounced upon.

So picture, if you will, four grown women running around a back yard giggling and playing with large sparklers. Our hostess's husband came out on the deck to watch the four of us run around like schoolkids with the sparklers, which were the fancy kind that shot sparks out of the end in pulses. Fiona started shouting out "It's a shooter!" which we all found hysterically funny—or it may have been the couple glasses of sangria that made it funnier…

After the sparklers were finished, we sat back on the patio and chatted about the coven, our missing members, and how they were doing. We talked and laughed about our lives and wondered what the future would hold for all of us as a group. As the night was exceptionally clear and the moon was waning, it was a good night for star gazing—I even found the constellation of Scorpio. It was a laid-back evening, and we all left feeling relaxed and mellow and happy at the magick we had worked together to transform our lives and any negativity we were experiencing into something positive.

Interestingly enough, when I got up the next morning, I had a hell of a magickal hangover—and not from drinking a couple glasses of sangria. Nope, this is the wiped-out feeling you get after you work big magick, which I found odd as it had been a mellow and fun night, with a relaxing, quiet ritual. Out of curiosity, I checked in with my coven sisters to see how they all felt.

Everyone felt wiped out and, for lack of a better term, magickally hung over. We all wondered at that and figured that between the Midsummer ritual, the fire, and the sparklers, we must have generated a lot of fire magick.

It wasn't until later that it began to sink in. Fire is the element of transformation... and sometimes you can be reminded of this fact in big ways. If I have learned anything over the years about running a coven, it is this: that the circle of members sometimes grows and expands, bringing opportunities for new growth and lessons—and sometimes it will contract inwards and grow smaller, which can create a focusing of energy and a consolidation, or tightening up, of the group energy.

The only thing that is constant is change.

Reflections on Midsummer
A Time of the Sun and the Moon

> The stars, the moon and the sun...
> so old, so wise. Think of what they've seen.
>
> E. Paluszak

As we are in a magickal time of the sun and the moon, I decided to close up this chapter with a spell that works with both the power of the summer solstice and the lunar influence of the zodiac sign of Cancer, the crab. Classically, any occasion where both the sun and the moon are present and visible together in the sky is an auspicious time

to cast a spell, as it is a time of great power. (Such as mornings during the waning moon and at sunset with the new moon.)

The sign of Cancer brings creativity and emotion. Zodiac energies prevalent at this time of year are loving sentiments, inspiration, the family unit, close-knit groups, and home life. I thought that a seasonal spell to bless your family or coven mates would be very appropriate.

A Summer Spell to Bless Your Family or Coven

For this spell you will want to incorporate a representation of the sun and moon together, something like the illustration above.

You may also use a lunar silver candle and a gold solar candle. You could even float silver and gold candles outdoors in your garden fountain or in a large cauldron, which would make a wonderful effect at night.

If you decide to use traditional candles, take a moment and engrave the silver candle with a crescent moon and the gold with a sun symbol. Place them in their holders on either side of the moon/sun image, and light the candles. If you like, jazz this up even more with fresh white flowers (for the moon) and fresh yellow flowers (for the sun).

When you are ready, repeat the charm below:

The enchanting season of summer has now begun
By the combination of sun and moon, this spell is spun.
In this time of the summer solstice, great magick is all around
The lunar energy of Cancer the Crab will also be found.
Bless my family and coven with this celestial energy
Bring happiness and love to all, and as I will it, so mote it be.

Allow the candles to burn in a safe place until they go out on their own. Blessed be and happy summer!

CHAPTER 2

Lughnasadh

Lammas

AUGUST 1

THE SUN, THE hearth of affection and life,
pours burning love on the delighted earth.

Arthur Rimbaud

The first harvest festival of Lughnasadh occurs at the halfway point of the summer solstice and the autumn equinox. It celebrates the gathering of the early grains and the harvesting of vegetables and fruits. This is a cross-quarter day, a fire festival, and one of the four major sabbats along with Samhain at the end of October, Imbolc in early February, and Beltane on the first of May.

Natural symbols for this sabbat include summer flowers (such as marigolds, yellow daisies, green herbs, and, of course, those bright, happy sunflowers), the classic sheaves of wheat, golden loaves of bread, fresh herbs, and summer vegetables and fruits from the garden. Colors to incorporate into your celebrations are white, yellow, green, and gold.

Lughnasadh is a time of wonderful abundance. The gardens are filled with fruits and veggies and herbs. The weather tends to be blisteringly hot at this time of year, and all of that sunshine goes into the crops. This is a good time to carefully consider what projects and goals you need to begin harvesting when bounty is all around you. What talents do you have that need to be put to use? The natural energy of abundance is here and all around us at Lughnasadh. All you have to do is be willing to tap into it.

A *Little History*
THE FIRST HARVEST FESTIVAL

THE ACT OF putting into your mouth
what the earth has grown is perhaps your
most direct interaction with the earth.

Frances Moore Lappé

This first harvest festival, the festival of Lugh, was known as Lughnasadh (pronounced loo-nah-sa) to the Celts. You may see many alternate spellings, as well as different names altogether, for this sabbat, and there is also the Irish alternate spelling Lunasa. In Gaelic, Lunasa is the name for the month of August. In addition, this festival was known as Lammas to the Anglo-Saxons. *Lammas* is considered to be roughly translated as "loaf mass."

Lugh is a Celtic solar god. This deity is a talented, handsome craftsman and master of myriad skills. One of his titles is Lugh Long Arm, as he holds a magick spear of thunderstorms; another is Lugh "the bright and shining one" who brings the crops to ripeness.

It is interesting to note that Lugh is aligned with the Roman Mercury, who is a trickster god. Both of the gods were considered to be multi-talented deities as they are both healers, blacksmiths, magicians, poets, and warriors. Lugh was considered the inventor of all of the arts. Artisans, bards, and crafters can call upon Lugh when they need help. Lugh's consort is the nature goddess Rosmerta.

Legend says Lugh started the harvest festival that bears his name in honor of his foster mother, and it was traditionally held on August 1. The harvest season was vitally important during medieval times, as a successful harvest would ensure that your family survived the coming winter. If the harvest was abundant, part of it could be sold or traded for goods and other supplies. It was, in effect, currency. As a modern Witch this notion may seem a little antiquated to you, but honestly it should not. The harvest is still vital to today's world and economy. Think about it the next time you go to the grocery store to select your fresh produce. Depending on the success of the fruit and vegetable crops, the prices may be higher or more reasonable.

According to oral history, this first harvest festival of Lugh lasted for weeks during the harvesting season, and activities included horseracing, fairs, crafts, and, of course, food. From the traditions of this old community first-harvest tradition came one of the modern eight sabbats that we celebrate today.

Occasionally you can find references to Lugnasa Sunday, or Garden Sunday linked in to this holiday. In keeping with the Anglo-Saxon loaf mass theme, in days past folks were thought to leave offerings of harvested grain, or of bread to their gods, and as Christianity took hold, they would bring in a loaf of bread to be blessed at their church that was freshly made from the newly harvested grain crop.

Lughnasadh was also a popular time for visiting sacred wells, fertility magick, marriages and divination. As the harvest season begins, we come to realize that summer is fading into autumn. The sun's power is on its annual descent and the daylight hours are starting to decrease.

Astrologically speaking the sun has entered the "power point" of the zodiac and is in the mid-point of Leo.

DOG DAYS OF SUMMER—THEN AND NOW

DOG DAYS BRIGHT and clear indicate a happy year, but when accompanied by rain, for better times our hopes are vain.

Traditional English Proverb

August tends to be brutally hot, and rain is all-important. While working on this chapter, here the temperatures have been in the 100-degree Fahrenheit range. Yesterday it topped out at 103 degrees. The dog days are definitely here.

According to tradition, these dog days are the scorching, sluggish weeks that begin in early July and continue throughout early September. These are some of the hottest days of the summer months; they tend to run in cycles, and their times may vary, of course, depending upon the region in which you live. So where did the term "dog days" originate from? From the Pagan Greeks and Romans.

The ancient people believed that when the dog star Sirius rose with the sun during this time of the year that it added its own light and power to the summer heat. The star Sirius gets its name from the Greek word *seirios* and means "glowing" or "scorcher." However, the Greco-Romans weren't the only ancient people to notice this star. To the ancient Egyptians, the star Sirius showed up just before the start of the Nile's flooding season and the beginning of the sacred year. This was a vitally important time to them, as the floods brought new, fertile soil to the valleys.

Meanwhile, back in ancient Rome, the dog days were marked between July 23 and August 23. Apparently the word on the street was only a dog would be crazy enough to go out in the heat in old Rome at that time. This star's extra power was thought to make plants wilt and the flaming passions of humans to run amok—which is where the term "star struck" may have originated from.

Even *The Old Farmer's Almanac* says the traditional time of the dog days is from July 3 to August 11. They stick to this date because, interestingly, these dates match the ancient timing of the rising of the dog star Sirius over the eastern horizon.

Sirius is still the brightest star in the heavens, next to the sun. Now, before someone starts to hop up and down, thinking they have found a mistake, keep in mind we are saying *stars*, not planets. So, yes, Venus and Jupiter may be brighter in the heavens—but they are planets, not stars.

Now to the technical bit: Sirius is found within the constellation of Canis Major, or Big Dog. This constellation is thought to represent one of Orion's hunting dogs. By following an imaginary line to the southeast (or to your left and slightly down) from the three stars of Orion's belt, the brilliant star Sirius can be found in the night sky.

The months of July and August are typically hot, steamy, and intense. I always figured it was summer's way of getting the last word in before the autumn season swept in. Some folks will claim it's due to climate changes…I'm betting it is a combination of both the summer and a dose of Sirius's power.

Loaf Mass
CELEBRATING THE SABBAT WITH BREADS

RELIGION IS MEANT to be bread for
daily use, not cake for special occasions.
Author Unknown

One of the classic activities for this particular sabbat is baking bread, which strikes terror in the hearts of many. While it can be fun to work with yeast, you have to respect it. To knead your own bread dough and to let it rise can also be tricky, as humidity will affect your bread baking. I have a bread-making machine—yes, I know it's like cheating, but it's easier and almost idiot-proof: you pop the mix, the water, and the yeast into the upright pan. Plug the machine in. Program it to the proper setting, press a button, and voilà! In a couple of hours you've got bread. Well, in a perfect world, anyway…

depending on the humidity levels the day you make the bread, it might be a huge, light, and beautiful loaf or it could be short, dense, and tough.

Which is why I prefer to make quick breads. That way, I can have more control over the finished product. Besides, it's more fun if it is made with seasonal fruits or vegetables. To me, the best part of this time of year is the bounty of affordable fruits and vegetables: peaches, blueberries, raspberries, blackberries, tomatoes, peppers, squash, zucchini…

…as in zucchini bread! If you'd like to enjoy the first harvest bread theme, consider making some quick bread for your family. I love zucchini bread. My challenge was to find a recipe that was lowfat, easy to make, and healthier than the traditional version but still delicious. It took a couple of tries, and I had to call on my inner Kitchen Witch, but after some experimentation I conjured up a winner.

Zucchini Bread Recipe

The following is a lowfat quick bread recipe, and unless you tell someone, they will never know the difference. It is easy and delicious, and it yields two regular-sized loaves or six mini loaves.

I like to use the food processor to shred the zucchini; it is so much faster. However, you can use a hand-held grater—just be sure to measure the three cups of shredded zucchini. Don't guess or eyeball that shredded zucchini. Measure it.

In a large bowl, mix the following ingredients together by hand:

3 cups shredded fresh zucchini
   (about 2 regular-sized zucchini squash)
2 cups sugar
1 cup unsweetened applesauce
2 teaspoons vanilla extract
½ cup egg substitute (such as Egg Beaters)
3⅓ cups all-purpose flour
2 teaspoons baking soda
1 teaspoon baking powder
2 teaspoons cinnamon
½ teaspoon salt
½ teaspoon nutmeg
½ teaspoon cloves

Spray two 8 x 4-inch bread pans or six mini pans with nonstick cooking spray, then pour the mixed batter evenly into the loaf pans. (If you are using the mini loaf pans, set these on a large baking sheet, then pour the batter into them.) Set the baking sheet holding the pans into the oven and bake.

For two regular-sized loaves of bread, bake at 325 degrees for 60–80 minutes. If you are doing mini loaves, you may have to shorten the baking time, so keep an eye on them.

Test for doneness when a toothpick inserted in the center comes out clean or with only a few crumbs.

Allow bread to cool for ten minutes before removing from large bread pans, then leave them to cool completely on a wire rack. (Allow mini loaves to cool in their little foil pans.)

This bread freezes well. Once it is completely cool, put inside a ziplock-type freezer bag and freeze.

Variations: This bread recipe can be made into lowfat pumpkin bread as well. Just switch out the fresh zucchini for one can of solid-pack pumpkin. It's a winner!

• • • •

Ellen's Garden of Witchery Journal STEAMY DAYS AND BUTTERFLIES

WATER AND PROTECT the root;
Heaven will watch the flower and fruit.

Chinese Proverb

Yes, it's hot. However, the plants turn all that sunshine and summer rain into energy to produce fruits and vegetables. For example, here in the Midwest, peaches are in season. Just yesterday I saw several stands and even pickup trucks pulled into parking lots selling local peaches. The grocery stores have huge, eye-catching displays of local peaches along with peach wine at the moment. Some of the early varieties of apples are ready to go. Grapes are almost ready to be harvested in the wine country.

My tomato and pepper plants are going crazy, to the point where we are giving away tomatoes to friends and family…oh, and the squirrels steal a few tomatoes too. Yesterday I went out to discover that my prized purple-striped heirloom tomato I had been watching come to ripeness had been vandalized by a snacking squirrel. On a funny note, he left the half-eaten tomato on top of a six-foot-tall fence post as a sort of warning, I suppose. You have to laugh at that. A sign of squirrel terrorist activity, for sure.

A fellow gardener told me that if you leave out a water supply for the squirrels, they will leave your tomatoes alone. Supposedly they go after them for the moisture, which is why they bite into them but rarely eat the whole tomato. Next year I'll put a little clay saucer of water out for the squirrels throughout the summer and see if that helps.

Last week I enjoyed a waning moon overhead while I took a walk at sunrise. It was a muggy, hot, and misty morning in the park. At the end of my walk through the park, I always cut through a formal sunken garden. While walking through it I admired the full explosion of annuals. The summer perennials were doing well, too, such as the black-eyed Susans, the roses, and the daisies. I stopped to sniff a purple butterfly bush and enjoyed the salmon-colored blossoms of the crepe myrtles. It was so humid that all of the plants were covered in dew—even the elephant ears looked silver from the heavy condensation. While the mist crawled along the ground, I felt like I was the only person in the park as I enjoyed the silent garden.

I perused the local nursery yesterday and purchased some great clearance plants for a bargain. Believe it or not, if you watch carefully, you can still find healthy and good plants on sale, especially at the end of the summer! I added some tall yellow daisies and a butterfly bush to my perennial garden. I love butterfly bushes, and in a week or so lots of butterflies are going to hit the gardens even though the temperatures are brutal and it's a fight to keep everything going until September's rains and cooler temperatures.

August is the time of year in Missouri where we see tons of butterflies as they follow the yearly migration south. If you have host plants and feeder plants such as coneflowers, Joe-Pye weed, lantana, petunias, and tall garden phlox, the butterflies won't just pass through—they will detour and flutter about in your own garden for a while. Lately, every time I go out in the garden, I am surrounded by butterflies.

BUTTERFLY MAGICK

HAPPINESS IS AS a butterfly which, when pursued, is always beyond our grasp, but which if you sit down quietly, may alight upon you.

Nathaniel Hawthorne

The butterfly is a classic natural symbol of the element of air and also of magickal transformation and change. To many ancient cultures it was a symbol of the human soul. According to folklore, if a butterfly flies into the house, it is the spirit of a loved one who has passed over coming in for a visit. Also, it's interesting to note that wherever there are butterflies, it is believed that there is also a healthy population of faeries and nature spirits.

The butterfly reminds you that a metamorphosis is occurring. It may be physical or spiritual, but change is here. So you have to ask yourself what stage of change are you currently in? Organize your thoughts and routine a bit, and let go of old ideas and habits that no longer serve you.

The butterfly is a symbol of joy. After all, butterflies rarely sit still when they feed. They dance across the flower petals with energy and enthusiasm. Did you know that butterflies actually taste the flowers through their feet? Yes, indeed; now, if *that* does not make you smile, I don't know what will.

If the butterfly is dancing and flitting through your world at the moment, it is probably asking about how much joyfulness you actually allow in your life. How would you answer? Do you allow yourself to laugh and to be joyful? No matter what dramas may be happening around you, can you still smile and take pleasure in simple things?

Even with all the intensity of a sultry August afternoon, don't fight it; relax and see how your life and world transforms if you just let go. Remember: do not be afraid of change. It does not always have to be drama-filled or traumatic. Sometimes change is gentle and beautiful. When butterflies appear in your life, it is a sign to lighten up, to

rejoice in the beauty and enchantment of nature, to laugh a little, and to experience the magick and the possibilities around you.

While you are out there enjoying the summer butterflies this August, take a careful look at the colors of the butterflies that you see most often. Lately I've been spotting the Pipevine Swallowtail, a large, gorgeous black and blue species. I am positive of its identification because it was so busy feeding on the tall purple garden phlox that I was able to dash inside the house, grab my Audubon Society field guide to butterflies, and follow that butterfly around the garden until I could match the photo to the butterfly. The butterfly didn't seem to mind. He was busy tasting the phlox blossoms.

Today while I was out on my early morning walk through the park's formal gardens, I saw a couple different butterflies: the yellow and black Tiger Swallowtail and also the classic Monarch, or maybe it was a Viceroy (I didn't get close enough to tell). I certainly spotted the orange and black wings quickly enough. However, the Viceroys are mimics of the Monarch, so you have to really look closely and carefully to tell them apart. The best way to distinguish the two types of orange and black butterflies is by noting that the Viceroy has a black horizontal stripe on its hind wings, while a Monarch does not. Also, the Viceroy is a bit smaller than a Monarch.

Just this afternoon, while I was watering in the back yard, I saw plenty of moths, painted lady butterflies, bumblebees, and some bright yellow butterflies. I suppose it was the air elementals' way of reminding me that they were around and about, watching the goings-on in the garden. Those bright yellow butterflies always make me think of the element of air and the elemental spirits. I also got to wondering what the butterfly's correct name was...

So I dropped the hose on the base of a hydrangea bush (that was dry and sulking in the heat) and scrambled inside quickly for my field guide again. I discovered that the yellow butterflies were Cloudless Sulfurs. As if in approval, one of the Cloudless Sulfur butterflies landed on the open pages of the book with its photo. It seemed to be admiring the picture and reading the accompanying text. I had to smile.

"Well, hello. Thanks for dropping in." I said to the butterfly. As I quietly complimented the book-reading butterfly, it skipped across the page to the text section and then fluttered off and headed over to the nearby Hidcote lavender that was pushing out a second round of fragrant blossoms.

While I was out there continuing the watering and quietly talking to the butterflies and bees, a thunderstorm popped up, but sadly it slid around us and off to the east. Lots of thunder and nice, cooling breezes from the south for a while—you could smell the rain in the air—but, sadly, not one bit of rain fell for me. I am sure that someone got some rain somewhere, but we did not get the rain in my neighborhood. It did cool off for a bit, from 97 degrees to 91, which was appreciated.

Damn, the gardens could really use a good free soaking of rain right now. I try to take the cycles and seasons of the year in stride, but it is sort of depressing watching the grass go dormant and brown until September's rains and cooler temperatures arrive. At least we don't have to cut the grass as often now. I'll have to content myself with all the butterflies enjoying the late summer flowers.

LATE SUMMER GARDENING

A PERFECT SUMMER day is when the
sun is shining, the breeze is blowing, the birds
are singing, and the lawn mower is broken.

James Dent

A week later and the extreme temperatures
have broken—we are back to the
low nineties and high eighties, and the hummingbirds are
back at the feeders. Sometimes
it feels like *The Wild Kingdom* out there
in the gardens; I never know what I'll find.
While I was working away in the perennial
beds recently, I looked up and found myself
face to face with a fearless male hummingbird. His red-toned head flashed in
the sunlight as I froze. I could not help
but smile as he hovered in midair and
watched me carefully, only about three feet away from my
face. Then, since I stayed still, he zipped over to the feeder for a snack.
I went back to my gardening and left him to his business. He flew
back over a few more times to check me out, each time getting closer to my

face—I could feel the bangs on my forehead ruffle from the air being displaced. Brave little bird. The hummingbirds who visit our gardens always make me smile, which is the gift of the hummingbird. The hummingbird is a symbol of energy, agility, and joy.

I spent two hours in the gardens yesterday. I ruthlessly pulled out some decade-old chrysanthemums that did not survive the summer heat wave, no matter how carefully I watered them. But they had a good run—well over ten years in the gardens. I will plant a few new and hardy varieties of chrysanthemums next month, in September.

Did yanking out old plants make me sad? Not at all. Sometimes unhealthy plants need to be removed from the garden. I'll amend the soil and get ready for the new plants next month. Besides pulling out dying mums, I also cut back the spent flower heads on the tall garden phlox, trimmed back the yarrow and the daylilies, and snipped off some broken, dried coneflower heads. They break sometimes from all the birds feeding on the dried-out cones.

It is that time of year when the goldfinches are out in force in the gardens. It's so enchanting to see those bright yellow birds weave through my yard and land on the thistleheads of the coneflowers for a snack. We have lots of coneflowers all over the gardens. The goldfinches know that our yard is a safe and plentiful place for a coneflower feast.

According to folklore, wherever goldfinches congregate is a place full of faerie activity. Either that, or they read the signs in my garden that say "Faerie Garden." Goldfinches are noisy and cheerful little birds, rarely silent, and they have an undulating flight pattern. When you watch them fly across the gardens, they seem to fly in an up-and-down pattern. While the males are singing away in their bright yellow summer plumage, the females are busy gathering food. At this time of the year, their preferred food source, the thistle from the coneflowers, is abundant, and their nesting season is in full swing.

For now, I keep watering the gardens every other day, while the containers and the pots get a drink twice a day. I prune back when necessary and keep doing the best I can. I ruthlessly cut back all of my hanging baskets a few weeks ago, in late July. They got a dose of fertilizer and are starting to push out new growth, so it was worth a few weeks of short hanging baskets.

I have been seeing pots of mums for sale at the local nurseries, but I am going to try to hold off purchasing any chrysanthemums until it gets cooler and we are closer to the autumn equinox. For now, the moon is waxing toward full, and the time of the Wort Moon has arrived.

FULL WORT MOON IN AUGUST

THE MOON IS at her full, and riding high,
Floods the calm fields with light.
The airs that hover in the summer sky
Are all asleep to-night.

William C. Bryant

One of the older names for the full moon in August was the Wort Moon. *Wort*, or *wyrt*, is an old Anglo-Saxon word that means "herb." During the hot and long days of summer, keep your herb gardens watered well and cared-for to survive the heat. At this full

Wort Moon, you can begin to harvest your tender herbs and enchant them for various spellwork. This is a time of the year that is dedicated to gathering magickal herbs and flowers for use later on. It is the first harvest, after all.

As you hang them up to dry and preserve, recite this cheerful Garden Witch's charm to sustain their magick. This charm originally appeared in a *Witches' Datebook* article I wrote several years ago.

> Under the full Wort Moon of yellow and gold
> May the magick within these drying herbs hold.
> I call on the earth, fire, water, and wind
> Let my Witch's herbal enchantment begin.
> To bring love, comfort, to protect and heal
> With these rhyming words, the spell will now seal.

The full moon is classically a time for enhanced psychic power. There is something about the summer months that always strikes me as a laid-back time for psychic activity. Maybe it's because we all revert back to childhood and feel like we should be on summer vacation. They aren't called the lazy days of summer for nothing, you know.

So psychic activity, to me, has always seemed quieter and easy during the hottest days of the year. Sometimes this is a good thing, while sometimes it can blind you to what is actually happening. It pays to stay tuned-in and to pay attention, no matter how lazy you might wish for the summer months to be.

Personal Lesson for Lughnasadh
CHANGE IS CONSTANT

> CHANGE IS THE constant, the signal
> for rebirth, the egg of the phoenix.
>
> *Christina Baldwin*

This year the coven would be gathering together at the Wort Moon in mid-August instead of at Lughnasadh, due to vacations and scheduling conflicts. We planned to gather in Fiona's gardens. It was the first time many of the coven members had seen her home. Built in the early 1920s, it was just a decade shy of being a century old and featured original stained glass and a fabulous new garden that the couple had been working on nonstop for almost two years.

The weeks leading up to this coven gathering had been filled with change. One of the core members decided to leave the group. After the announcement was made, it took a few days to sink in. This was a big surprise for the coven—one that saddened many of our members. This departure left us with a huge hole in the coven's foundation.

Prior to this August esbat gathering, during the dark moon in late July, myself and the remaining senior members of the coven had gathered together to discuss what to do in response to the latest developments with the group. Since one of the core coven members had left, it was quickly decided that a renaming and reorganization was the best course of action. While this was bittersweet, it was also necessary. The original coven name had been in place for almost a decade. Still, it felt right to rename the coven. After all, we would never be the same coven after experiencing all the hard lessons we had dealt with over the past few months.

So we sat down, opened a bottle of wine, and brainstormed. At one point later in the evening, everyone assumed their favorite thinking position: horizontal. I ended up flat on my back on the floor, staring up at the ceiling and fighting off the playful pounces of Ravyn's big black tomcat. If you were on the floor, Skeletor—who looks and is built like a mini panther—figures you want to rumble. So I tossed dog toys (no kidding, the cat is that big) to Skeletor while he happily chased them, and we all considered new coven names. Ember and Ravyn sprawled on either end of Ravyn's big sectional couch, cheering on the romping Skeletor and making suggestions to our list.

It took some time, as some of the names we first came up with sounded like retirement homes for Witches! I hesitate to list some of the other coven names we did come up with, as they are not fit for polite conversation. The giggling started and did not stop. I suppose some would raise their eyebrows at our lack of decorum, and to that I say *pfffft*. We had all been through the emotional ringer over the past weeks. The laughter was good—it was cleansing, and it raised positive energy.

Eventually the three of us conjured up a new coven name that not only fit but was a perfect symbol of our experiences so far as a group. As a matter of fact, once the title was suggested, we all sat bolt upright and stopped talking at the same time. Skeletor stopped still and looked at us all carefully. Then we just sat there and grinned at each other. Ravyn jumped up for her laptop to send an email to the other coven members announcing the new coven name. She also started work there and then on redesigning our coven's logo and Yahoo group page. So on that night, with a rowdy, witchy black cat, a bottle of wine, and a laughing trio of Witches, we figured it out—and a new coven was born.

In a weird bit of synchronicity, a random search on the Internet the next day had me stumbling across beautiful pendants that matched the new name of the coven. I quickly sent an email with a photo attachment to the group so they could take a look at the pendants, and everyone fell in love with them. The six of us each ordered our new coven pendants, and we all promised to bring them to the esbat in August so we could rededicate the coven and our new coven symbols.

Under a rising full moon on an August night, we carpooled to Fiona's charming house. Everyone was wearing their new coven pendants, ready to celebrate the esbat and the rebirth of our coven. It was a beautiful night; the ritual was sweet and intense. Standing under the moon and the stars in a summer garden with my coven sisters, I looked around and felt at home. We passed around Fiona's gorgeous crystal goblet filled with summer wine and toasted to each other and the magick of sisterhood.

It was a fresh start—a rebirth in the truest sense of the word. Best of all, a sense of fun and family was back, which made all of us realize just how much of a good thing this change actually was.

From the ashes of the old coven, a new coven was born—one full of promise, camaraderie, and friendship.

How I Spent My Summer Vacation...
A WITCH IN A TROUT STREAM

TIME IS BUT the stream I go a-fishing in.

Henry David Thoreau

A few days after the Wort Moon coven get-together, my husband and I took a mini vacation—no kids, just the two of us. As our youngest had just graduated from college, the "kids" were more than happy to have the house all to themselves. We only asked them to keep the house clean and the parties to a minimum.

We headed down to southern Missouri and a beautiful state park to get away from it all and so my husband could go fishing. He is an avid fly fisherman, and one of the draws of this particular state park is the trout fishing. So I talked him into renting a little cabin instead of camping in a tent…it was late August, and I did not relish the idea of camping in high ninety-degree temperatures. So we loaded up the car and took off for three days.

Yes, the two of us went fishing for three days. Okay, let me rephrase that. He fished—I hiked along the trails, waded in the spring-fed river, enjoyed the beauty of the natural surroundings, and tossed in a line and tried not to trip on the rocks or fall into the rapids. The river bed is rock-covered, and those rocks get slippery. I will also admit that I spent most of my time looking at the wildflowers growing along the stream and the hiking trails, as well as the trees and butterflies and so on.

On an average fishing day the hubs caught over thirty trout. If I was lucky, I caught six or seven. That's catch and release, by the way. The fun part is catching a rainbow trout and the fight they give you as you try to reel them in. Unless we are catching them for dinner, we release them immediately.

Oh, and forget any visions you may have of me prancing around in fancy fly fishing equipment and waders. I found out the hard way, when we were first married, that I trip constantly and fall down—a lot—when I wear waders. Maybe I'll be graceful in my next life.

The hiking trails along the water are rough, rocky, and uneven. It's not casual walking. You do have to climb over fallen trees occasionally and negotiate rocks, weeds, poison ivy, and mud. So instead of waders, I wear beat-up old tennis shoes for traction, which I don't mind getting wet, and an old pair of swimming shorts and a T-shirt or tank top, depending on how hot it is.

And to complete my fashionable ensemble, I strap a fanny pack around my waist. Inside the fanny pack is a stringer, extra flies, and a pair of pliers so I can quickly and easily remove the hook from the fish's mouth. My husband forgoes the fanny pack and adds a fly fishing vest to his swimming trunks, T-shirt, and old shoes. The only time I have ever seen my husband wear waders while he is fishing is when it is cold out.

The truth is, the fish don't give a damn what you are wearing. It's true—I've asked them. They always stare at you with big eyes like you are stupid for asking. Anyway, I've watched my husband quietly and modestly outfish people at that park for twenty-eight years now. It always makes me snicker to see folks in these fancy fly fishing ensembles that can cost hundreds of dollars, if not more, walk around with an attitude, yet they can't catch a fish to save their lives.

They certainly don't embrace the fun of it; it's all a competition to them. This is supposed to be relaxing and enjoyable. In the summertime waders get hot, plus they are bulky and uncomfortable. Besides, I'm on vacation. People are camping and relaxing… I'm not trying to impress anyone with my fashion sense. The trout stream is not a place for the fashionistas of the world.

Anyway, we were at the end of our first day of fishing, and twilight had just fallen; as luck would have it, the hubs and I were alone at that section of the stream. I was sitting on a rock ledge dumping the gravel out of my shoes and rinsing them out so the half-mile hike back up the road to the cabin would be more comfortable. My husband was casting just a few more times before we called it quits. Of course he caught two trout within moments of each other in the very place where I could not even get a bite. Typical.

I had just retied my shoes and was preparing to climb up the bank when a dragonfly buzzed past me. I turned to look, and the evening mist began to roll down over the river from the springs. In the park are the springs that create the head of the Current River. The water is crystal clear and icy cold. On summer nights a thick, white mist rolls down from the springs, and it's haunting and gorgeous. As I watched, the mist rolled downstream, and then dozens of dragonflies descended on the river in the area where we were both standing.

I waded back into the icy river and stood there, fishing pole forgotten upon the banks, while the dragonflies swarmed, buzzing, all around me. I had never seen so many all in one place before—some close enough that you could feel the air being displaced as they flew past your face. It was amazing. I lifted up my hands and stood there giggling, and that drew my husband's attention. He looked over and then waded out into the stream to join the dragonfly convention and me. We stood there side by side, quietly watching the dragonflies swarm around us and laughing occasionally as one flew up right in our faces as if to say, "What are you two looking at?"

Night began to fall in earnest, and as we silently stood out in the water, a pair of massive blue herons sailed down low over the stream, looking for a meal. Bats came out and flew drunkenly around, snacking on mosquitoes, and as we looked to the west we saw Venus appear in the twilight sky. I felt a weight slide off my shoulders that I had not even been aware I was carrying.

Sometimes nature reminds us that despite what we may perceive as dramatic, important events going on in our lives, there is a bigger picture out there. Between the reorganization of the coven, book projects, life in general, and upcoming tour dates, I was carting around a boatload of stress.

The dragonfly is a symbol of illusion. As we stood there in that icy stream, hand in hand, watching the stars blink to life in the twilight sky, I had to ask myself how much of what I thought was so damn important was real, and how much was an illusion? Okay, I might be going to Canada in a few months; I reminded myself that I would deal with the

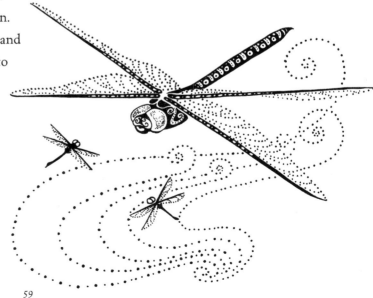

paperwork of applying for a passport once things were final. I had plenty of time. It did not have to be done today.

Yes, the coven had restructured itself, but it had stayed strong, and the six remaining members were more united than ever. We were all happy with the coven, and that was the important thing. It was a fresh start for all of us and, best of all, a sense of joy was back in the coven.

Yes, I did indeed have three book projects going at once: a tarot deck, my first novel, and the writing of this book was all happening at the same time. Plus I knew edits were only a few months away before *Practical Protection Magick* came out. September was literally a day away, and the fall tour schedule would be starting soon. But instead of getting anxious about it all, I thought maybe I should enjoy the fact that I had plenty to keep me busy—I could certainly never claim that I was bored.

Just as that thought popped in my head, a large blue dragonfly got right up in my face, almost hitting my nose. It was the strangest feeling of magickal confirmation. Those dragonflies reminded me that even though I was busy, and my life did get crazy from time to time, this was something I had been working toward for ten years. Maybe it was time to relax a bit—to just be and to let things evolve. To trust in all the hard work that had gotten me to this point in my career and to see what wonderful things flew into my life next.

Metaphysical lessons while standing in a trout stream at sunset? Stranger things have happened.

As I write this final section of the chapter, it is the last day of August, and I am typing away on my laptop in the cabin at the state park. This morning when I woke up, the temperatures were in the sixties; it was misty and cool until the sun cleared the trees.

Even the air smells fresher right now that the heat is subsiding. Yesterday as I hiked along the trout stream I noticed brushes of red along a few branches of dogwood trees. I pulled off my sunglasses to double check. Yes, there was definitely red showing through those leaves. The leaves on the black walnut trees in the woods and around the cabin were starting to turn yellow in a few places. When we go home in a few days I'll be watching the neighborhood trees to see if they are starting to show any hints of fall color.

As sun started to set on our second fishing day, I watched lots of leaves fall from the trees onto the trout stream to float away. Some of those leaves were lost to the extreme heat this summer, and some were just ready to fall. But all around me I could feel the change in the air. It was a bit chilly, and nuts were dropping from the trees and plopping loudly into the stream, which made me think of the story of the sacred salmon and the hazelnuts. Summer was winding down, and I could see the proof of that in front of me. I was content to just stand quietly and watch. For me, it's always humbling to see the Wheel of the Year turn.

As we hiked back to our cabin before it got too dark outside, the two of us decided that we'd take this trip at this time again next year, since we basically had the place to ourselves as we had gone to the park mid-week. It was a wonderful way to relax and recharge. After we returned to the cabin, my husband built a fire in the fire pit. We sat under the stars, blissfully alone, and roasted a few hot dogs and star gazed. At home we live too close to the city to see all of the stars that you can see way out in the country. It was gorgeous and awe inspiring.

So I relearned an important truth while on my summer vacation. Magickal lessons can happen anywhere. It's up to you to tune in and pay attention and to accept the lessons nature has for you. Watch the Wheel of the Year turn. Get out in nature, and experience its magick. Go spend some time outdoors, and see what you can learn this summer. Whether you decide to go camping or just take a picnic in a local park, just get out there, enjoy your nature religion, and see what you discover.

Reflections on Lughnasadh
THE FINAL DAYS OF SUMMER

WHEN SUMMER GATHERS up her
dreams of glory, and, like a dream, glides away.

Sarah Helen Whitman

During these last days of August and the first days of September, the days are a tad cooler and night falls noticeably soon each evening. Sure enough, when we returned home I noticed a few trees on my street that were changing colors just a bit. Summer is winding down, so enjoy the hot, sultry days while they last, for the cooler and shorter days and chilly nights of autumn are surely just around the corner.

The zodiac sign of Virgo begins in late August and rolls through the month of September. Virgo is an earth mother and the goddess of the earth. Some say that the symbol of Virgo is actually a representation of the goddess Isis, while others think that this is Demeter. Classically, Virgo the virgin is illustrated as a golden-haired maiden who is holding a five-petaled flower and a sheaf of wheat in her hand. Both of these symbols have links to the Goddess.

It is not surprising to know that the element associated with Virgo is earth, and the colors are earthy tones such as brown. Some say blue, perhaps to correspond with that gorgeous late-summer blue sky. Why not tap into the energy that is present during this sign's astrological influence?

It is believed that Virgos are a practical lot, and they are also organized and perfectionists—so let's use this opportunity to call for a little practicality and drive, and to get ready for the autumn harvests. This magick can help us begin new projects and to stay focused so we can complete our existing goals, all with a little help from the earth mother. So to close up this chapter, here is a spell that coordinates beautifully with the magickal energies that are naturally occurring at the end of August and the beginning of September.

Earth Mother Candle Spell for Late August

For this candle spell, you will need a seasonal and spicy-scented votive candle. (Look for votives that have a spicy herbal, cinnamon, or pumpkin scent.) Next, engrave a five-petaled flower on the side of the candle with a pin. When finished, slip the votive candle inside of a votive cup. Arrange a few stalks of dried wheat, autumn flowers, or other grains around the base of the candleholder. Ground and center yourself, and picture the earth mother in your mind. Now repeat the following spell verse three times:

Late August's candle magick falls under Virgo's domain
It has the power to make my goals succeed and sustain.
The earth mother's magick is practicality
I'll stay focused and determined, so mote it be.
Summer comes to a close and so autumn begins
During this time may I gather light and wisdom.

Close up the spell with these lines:

This spicy candle spell is spun from the heart
Worked for the good of all with a Witch's art.

Allow the votive candle to burn out in a safe place; it should take about eight hours. When the candle is spent, return the grains to nature as an offering. I wish you good luck on your new projects and goals this coming autumn!

CHAPTER 3

Autumn Equinox
Mabon

SEPTEMBER 20–23

THE MORROW WAS a bright September
morn; the earth was beautiful as if newborn;
there was a nameless splendor everywhere,
that wild exhilaration in the air...

Henry Wadsworth Longfellow

September is an interesting time of year. We begin with the intense heat of the summer but, as the month rolls onwards, there is a definite snap in the air. The air becomes crisp, and the sky is an incredible shade of blue. It is not unusual where I live to have the daytime temperatures hover in the eighties—and by the next morning, the temperatures are in the forties. The autumn rains come more often, and the grass starts to green back up in the suburban lawns. The late summer asters fade, and the chrysanthemums start to show their jewel-toned colors.

I think that sense of change is what makes the month so fascinating. The leaves are starting to turn, the garden is winding down, and nature is preparing for the coming winter. It may be hard to imagine on a bright and warm September afternoon, but the autumn is wafting closer with every day that passes.

A *Little History*
THE AUTUMN EQUINOX

AUTUMN—THE YEAR'S
LAST, loveliest smile.
William Cullen Bryant

The word *equinox* actually comes from the Latin word *aequinoctium*, which means "equal night." It's also the name of the month of September, which was the seventh month of the Roman calendar. This name is taken from the Latin word *septem*, which means "seven."

The classic seasonal mythology revolves around the goddess Demeter and her daughter, Persephone. Persephone was abducted by the god of the underworld, Hades, and taken to be his bride. Demeter searched the earth for her daughter, and as she mourned, all of nature declined and the earth became cold and barren. Eventually, when Persephone was reunited with her mother, Demeter's joy allowed life to return to the land. So Persephone becomes the bringer of the seasons. At the autumn equinox, when she returns to her husband, the earth grows cold, the nights are long, and no crops will grow. But when she returns to earth and to her mother, Demeter then allows her magick to return to nature. Life comes back to the land, and spring begins.

In Gaelic the month of September is identified as *An Sultuine*, the month of plenty. In Welsh it's called *Medi*, the month of reaping. The Anglo-Saxons called this month *Gerst Moanth*, the barley month. Barley was thought to be the first grain grown in Britain. Today there are many titles and names for this sabbat. Some traditions call it Mabon; others refer to it as Modron; other people call it Harvest Home. Nowadays, many of us simply call it the autumn equinox, or recently it's been labeled the Witch's Thanksgiving.

I personally have always referred to it as autumn equinox. When I was approached to write a book on this sabbat by Llewellyn, back in 2004, I stuck to my guns about the name, and they kept the title as it was written. Why was I so hard-nosed about that? Well, to be honest, there is no ancient Pagan festival of Mabon. Yes, *gasp*! How shocking! This whole riff we as a community went through in the 1970s and 1980s about the ancient Pagan tradition of Mabon is mostly made up. Here is where we need to be honest and not over-romanticize our history to death.

What was celebrated centuries ago were local harvest festivals. These Harvest Home celebrations were celebrated all over Europe at different times throughout the harvest season, depending on when the crops were ripe and ready to be gathered in.

I mean, think about it: would you leave your ripe crops standing in the fields and wait for a festival day, allowing the weather to ruin it or any animal or insect to come along and chomp on it? No! You would gather it in, calling on the aid of your friends and the community, and then you'd go assist your neighbors. Once all the crops in the area were safely in, the celebration truly began.

THE AUTUMN EQUINOX OFFICIALLY HERALDS THE FALL SEASON

EVERY LEAF SPEAKS bliss to me,

fluttering from the autumn tree.

Emily Brontë

The autumn equinox officially begins when the sun enters the astrological sign of Libra. As this date may vary from year to year, the sabbat's actual calendar date is not set. It may vary between the twentieth of September to the twenty-fourth. However, this day does mark the time of equal daylight and nighttime hours and the true beginning of the fall season. (Contrary to what the weatherman tells you on television, fall does not begin after Labor Day. It truly begins at the autumn equinox.) At this time of balance, meditate on bringing stability into your life and prosperity and abundance to your home this autumn.

Get outside and rejoice in the beginning of the changing leaves and the glorious colors, scents, and textures of the fall. Traditional harvest themes and natural items, such as local grains, fruits, and vegetables, will work nicely in your witchery and beautifully in your home's magickal decorations. Look around you; what do you see? Get outside and work in the yard. Fall is for planting! Plant some bulbs for next spring, and add some colorful pansies and mums now to keep the color going in your garden until late November.

Pick out a nice blooming shrub and add it to your landscape. Keep it watered so it will be established in its new home and ready to go come next spring.

Autumn Holidays
DECORATING THE MAGICKAL HOME

> "THAT PROVES YOU are unusual,"
> returned the Scarecrow; "and I am convinced
> the only people worthy of consideration
> in this world are the unusual ones."
>
> *Frank Baum*

At my house, our fall flag goes out the day after my birthday, which is smack in the middle of the month of September. I found a beautiful outdoor seasonal flag recently that looks remarkably like the cover of my book *Autumn Equinox*, and I had to buy it. It has a barn, fall leaves, a crow, and a scarecrow…it was like fate. (Well, that's what I tell myself when I rationalize my fall decorating obsession. Ahem.)

A week later, as we get closer to the actual equinox, the garland of silk fall leaves and orange, green, and purple lights go around the outside of the front door. The first available weekend before the fall sabbat, my husband and I take a trip to a local nursery, purchase some dried cornstalks, and haul those home in our old pickup truck. We used to be able to harvest our own cornstalks from the family farm but, sadly, the farm was sold a few years ago.

The cornstalks get tied to the front porch post on the day of the autumn equinox, and Six-Foot Stanley, the scarecrow, rules the front yard. The kids and families in our neighborhood seem to mark time by our scarecrow. He does have his own fan club;

every year, starting in September, some little urchin pounces on me in the grocery store and tugs on my pants to demand, "Hey lady, when are you putting up your scare-crow?"

My answer is always the same. "On the first day of fall."

"That's soon, right?" The child typically demands. So I tell them exactly which day Stanley will be making his appearance.

This is usually met with a giggle, a happy dance, and the child running off to their waiting parents as they shout over their shoulder, "See you on Halloween!" My husband and our own adult children find this hilarious.

Inside the house, the autumn decorations go out mid-September, and I have a great time sprucing up the mantle every year. (Yes, be warned: I am a trained floral designer...I can't help letting that side of me out to play every year at the autumn holidays.)

On the autumn mantle in the living room sits a small scarecrow I made myself when my husband and I were first married. His head is an orange Nerf ball—remember those?—and I made his overalls out of an old pair of jeans. This year, as I wrote this section, I was inspired to spruce up that mantle-sized scarecrow. He was, after all, over twenty-five years old. My mother had first taught me how to make these out of wire coat hangers, the Nerf ball head, and then scraps to make the clothes. So when another autumn sewing project was finished, I looked at the leftover scraps with an eye for sprucing up that scarecrow with better stuffing and a new shirt.

My husband and I recently had decided to go all-out and throw a big Halloween party at our house on October 30. Our adult children, my coven, and our friends were thrilled with the idea. So in late August I headed to the fabric store (coupon for 30% off Halloween fabrics in hand) with the idea of sewing up some Halloween café-style curtains for all the kitchen windows.

Since we had the idea to do a "Go Gothic or Go Home" theme, I had envisioned finding black-and-white fabric with skulls or creepy skeletons, black-and-white spider webs, or maybe a vintage-inspired pattern for Halloween curtains.

What I ended up with was actually a better idea. All the skeleton stuff was a little cutesy. Most of the Halloween fabric had neon green and neon orange in it, or the pattern ran up and down, and I wanted it to run horizontally. My kitchen windows are five feet wide but only about three feet tall. If I found fabric with a horizontal pattern, I could take advantage of that and wouldn't have so many seams to piece together, so the pattern on the fabric would be pleasing to the eye.

So as I stood there surrounded by bolts of neon-colored (and somewhat annoying) Halloween fabric, I realized that my initial bright idea was not quite as brilliant as I had first imagined, because my kitchen walls are a medium-sage green. That, and I have a lot of reproduction vintage Halloween décor, and I did not want the curtains to clash.

Feeling deflated, I put all the Halloween material back and decided that maybe I should look at an autumn pattern instead. That way, I could get longer use out of the "holiday" curtains. If I found material with some green in it, I could hang the new curtains up on the first day of fall and leave them in place until Thanksgiving.

So I hunted around and found some gorgeous seasonal fabric of tumbling, natural-looking oak leaves on a black background. The leaves were orange and green, with metallic gold skeletal leaves scattered throughout. I knew that this green would be pretty against my sage-painted walls, and the black background and deep orange-red of the leaves would complement my vintage-looking pieces.

Once I had the new curtains sewn and hung up, I was very pleased with the result. They looked stylish and elegant, not cutesy, which relieved me. Even my husband liked them, and he thought I was nuts when I had announced I was going to make new curtains for the fall months, simply because I sew about as well as he repairs cars. Translation: Unless it's a simple project, there is an unbelievable amount of cursing, swearing, and things that can go wrong. Craft projects, straight seams, pillows, and simple repairs or alterations, I can handle—anything else and it gets really risky. As I cleaned up the fabric scraps, I realized the mantle scarecrow could indeed get a make-over this year.

So our old scarecrow was taken apart. I bound the basic wire coat-hanger frame back together with floral wire (originally I had used masking tape to keep the frame together). I pulled out all the newspaper stuffing in his arms and legs and instead used quilt batting for new, improved stuffing.

When that mantle scarecrow was originally made, we had just bought the house and had our first baby, so I had used what I could find around the house to put the scarecrow together—scraps from the quilt I had made for our firstborn son and some newspaper to stuff the scarecrow with. Hey, it held together for twenty-six years before needing a makeover!

Now he's all gussied up in a new black, green, and orange shirt that matches the kitchen curtains, and he sits tall thanks to that newly wired-together frame and the batting for stuffing. Around him are two small white artificial pumpkins, a tiny ceramic jack-o'-lantern that lights up, and a treasure I found several years ago: a clever, very real-looking pumpkin that has the illuminated announcement of "The Witch Is In!" carved into its front.

Tucked under, behind, and around these items are silk fall leaves in greens, browns, and oranges. Also tucked into this arrangement is a fallen deer antler, and my celestial candlestick holders display off-white tapers with orange bittersweet-looking candle rings around the tapers' base.

I carefully save and store these items every year and reuse them for my decorations. I use those huge orange and black plastic storage bins, and they keep the decorations neat and in good shape for the yearly autumn arrangements. It is practical and affordable to reuse these items. It took me time to build up the floral displays, but I watch for sales and use coupons whenever I purchase decorative items. Actually, I get three holidays out of the basic fall mantle arrangement: autumn equinox, Samhain, and Thanksgiving.

This basic mantle arrangement stays in place until October 1; at that time, I switch out the off-white taper candles for black, add a few more black accent pieces—like midnight-colored eucalyptus and a small black-feathered raven—and I goth up the mantle for Samhain. The small white artificial pumpkins get turned around to display the messages that are written on them in large black script: one says "Magick," while the other says "Spells." The switchover takes about five minutes flat, because I am merely building off of the base of the mantle's floral arrangement that is already in place.

But is that all? Nope. After Samhain is over, on November 1 I pull out the black foliage and replace the black tapers for those off-white ones. I remove the light-up pumpkins and the raven. I add bronze, gold, and burnt-orange glittery foliage and sparkly pinecones to the base of autumn leaves and the white pumpkins and scarecrow. The white pumpkins get turned around to hide their messages again. Next, I tuck in a strand of white lights and miniature glass ornaments also in those metallic bronze, brown, and gold tones, and then my mantle arrangement morphs again—this time into an elegant, festive, and sparkly fall display that stays in place until the day after Thanksgiving.

I admit it…I have a sickness. There is a reason my friends accuse me of being a cross between Martha Stewart and Samantha Stephens.

For your own home, try creating your own autumn display on the mantle or a shelf. Consider arranging a garland of autumn leaves over the doorway. You can also wrap a string of orange or sparkly white lights into a fall garland and drape it over the mantle or a sturdy shelf. Be creative—see what you can conjure up! Oh, and here is a tip: the best autumn and Halloween floral pieces and decorating items hit the stores in late July, August, and early September, so keep your eyes open and start plotting.

Tuck in some cute miniature pumpkins and gourds grouped together on that shelf or mantle this fall. Pumpkins are quintessentially an autumn icon. The pumpkin is a lunar fruit and is associated with the element of water. And yes, you should incorporate them into your autumn equinox sabbat celebrations. Nothing says harvest time like the pumpkin.

For more texture to your nature-theme decorations, you could go foraging through the woods and add some fallen pine cones and brilliant leaves to your harvest garlands to dress things up a bit. Pine cones symbolize fertility, and they are a symbol of the God; plus their natural shapes are stunning. How about the grapevine? Decorate a grapevine wreath for the fall months, weave a ribbon pentagram in there, and dedicate it to Dionysus.

If autumn leaves are not available to you in your climate, then take a trip to the local arts and craft store and pick up some silk leaves in brilliant colors or, better yet, preserved oak leaves. Yes, they are dyed in brilliant fall colors, but they are still oak leaves. You can reuse them for years, and best of all, the oak tree (and its leaves) brings the magickal qualities of protection, prosperity, and wisdom into your home; ditto for the acorn. Look around your neighborhood and see if there are any acorns under the oak trees. Acorns, being the fruit of the oak, share in those magickal attributes.

Tie a rustling bundle of cornstalks to your own front porch to celebrate the earth's blessings at harvest-tide. Pick up some decorative and colorful ears of ornamental corn. Those can be hung up quickly and with a minimum of fuss. Then you'll have a natural harvest decoration to enjoy throughout all of the fall months.

HARVEST MOON MAGICK

THE MOON LOOKS upon many night
flowers; the night flowers see but one moon.

Jean Ingelow

Traditionally the Harvest Moon occurs at the full moon closest to the autumn equinox. Typically this occurs in September; however, every couple of years it will fall in October. Some calendars classically list the September full moon as the Harvest Moon whether that month's full moon is closest to the equinox or not.

The best way to tell when the true Harvest Moon will occur is to find the date of the equinox (when the sun enters Libra) on the calendar, then count the days to the full moon in September. Now go back to the date of the autumn equinox and count forward the number of days until October's full moon. Whichever full moon has the lower number of days from the equinox—*that's* the Harvest Moon. Also, you should know that getting the official Harvest Moon date mixed up happens. It happened to me last year. So if it happened to you, too, don't worry—the sky will not fall in and the world will keep on spinning.

The full Harvest Moon usually looks larger than other full moons due to the angle of the earth and because of refraction, a bending of the light. In the simplest of terms, the cooler fall air curves the light near the horizon and makes that Harvest Moon appear bigger. The fabulous color associated with the Harvest Moon comes from the quality of the air in that lower atmosphere. When you look at the moon close to the horizon, you are seeing it through a lot of dust, dirt, and pollen from the harvested crops. This gives us that gorgeous reddish-orange color that the Harvest Moon is famous for. Depending on where you live, that color may be blood red to yellow-orange.

The Harvest Moon has an amazing effect on folks; even nonmagickal folks tend to be awed by it. The point is that this is a powerful day for you to work magick on, so use it! The traditional magicks associated with the Harvest Moon include abundance, prosperity, and completion. The night of the Harvest Moon would be a perfect occasion to celebrate the season of the harvest and to take a moment and reflect on what you are thankful for, such as freedom, friends, home, and family.

Full Harvest Moon Spell for Blessings

Set up a pretty altar full of seasonal accessories such as apples, grapes, acorns, miniature pumpkins, and colorful fall leaves. Think of how enchanting white pumpkins would be for this ritual. If you were having a coven get-together in the fall on a full moon, you could do an entire white pumpkin theme. After arranging your altar, place two taper or pillar candles in holders. You will need one white and one orange candle. The orange candle will represent the harvest season, and its color does increase your energy level. The white candle symbolizes the full Harvest Moon and all of her magick.

Once you have things arranged to your liking, take a few moments to ground and center yourself. When you are ready, repeat this harvest moon blessing:

> Beneath the light of the Harvest Moon so bright
>
> I am thankful for many blessings tonight.
>
> I celebrate the bounty of the good green earth
>
> Lord and Lady, bless my home with health, peace, and mirth.
>
> By the light of the full Harvest Moon this spell is spun
>
> Bringing autumn blessings to all and harm to no one.

Allow the candles to burn out in a safe place until they go out on their own. Keep your altar setup out and enjoy it throughout the fall. If you need to change out the fruits and vegetables, then do so, and have fun updating the altar and keeping it looking beautiful during the season.

Pagan Pride Day
Or How to Go to a Pagan Festival and Still Enjoy Yourself

PRIDE IS THE recognition of the fact
that you are your own highest value and,
like all of man's values, it has to be earned.

Ayn Rand

One of the fun things about the month of September are the Pagan Pride Days (PPDs) that pop up all over the United States. Typically these are held in the month of September and sometimes early October. Even though autumn may be beginning, the weather could still be hot, so you need to keep that in mind as an attendee.

Over the years I have been fortunate to speak at various PPDs in Kansas, Missouri, Tennessee, and Georgia. I have seen elegant, fun opening rituals that impressed me and casual "get your Pagans in a circle" kind of opening rituals. (You have to say *Get your Pagans in a circle* with a John Wayne swagger, Pilgrim.) With this casual opening ceremony, everyone got together, introduced themselves, and said welcome. I thought it was great. I saw a coven of women do the closing ritual at the Nashville Pagan Pride Day one year, and it was simply amazing; everyone attending it got goosebumps.

I have enjoyed shopping at the vendors, sitting in on the free lectures and classes, and the camaraderie of meeting Pagans from all over the country. It's always fun and always different every time. To ensure that you have a good time at your PPD, here are a few only slightly snarky rules to help you enjoy yourself and keep your sense of humor intact.

Rule Number One: Follow the Festival Rules and Be Polite

Do not bring alcohol or any illegal substances as per the event rules. Do not take photos of the people at the PPD. If you want to snap a few pictures of you and your friends, that's one thing, but do not take anybody else's pictures without their permission. Not sure what the rules of the day are? Ask.

Be polite and wait your turn, whether that is for the bathroom, to pay for your purchases at the vendors' row, or just to work your way through the crowd. Also, mind your manners. If you are sitting in on a lecture, do *not* argue with the presenter or monopolize the discussion. That's rude and unfair to the other attendees. If you would like to speak to the lecturer, do so later, after they are done, but use your manners. Don't pick a fight, and don't play the "I'm smarter than you are" game.

Rule Number Two: You Are Responsible for Your Children and/or Pets

If you are bringing your kids along, do not turn them loose to run amok. Yes, some PPDs do have children's activities. But you can't just dump them there and leave. Do not expect anybody else to supervise or discipline your children; you are the parent, that is your job. You are responsible for them and any mess they make. Know your children's whereabouts at all times. Pagans tend to be a protective bunch, but PPDs are public events, and anybody can walk in. So just like if you were out in a crowded mall with your little ones, be aware, be smart, and be safe.

The same rule goes for pets. If you are bringing your dog to the park, bring a bag to pick up any mess they may leave behind. Be considerate and do not assume everyone adores dogs. Some folks may be allergic to or afraid of dogs. Also, make sure your pet can handle a large crowd and lots of people who will want to pet them. Not everyone understands about asking before touching someone else's pets.

If it is hot, bring drinks and water for the kids and pets. Small children get very hot down low to the ground, whether they are in a stroller or holding your hand, especially surrounded by all those people. Make sure that both the kids and pets get a break in the shade and stay hydrated.

Rule Number Three: Meeting Authors

Here is the deal: authors are just people who have a lot to say. We have so much to say that we write it down and turn that into books. I have met all kinds of authors: Pagan authors, fiction authors, romance writers, young adult fiction writers, mystery writers, suspense writers, and a few incredibly famous, world-renowned, and successful "my books were turned into popular television series" authors. No matter what they write, they are basically all the same. And they are regular people.

Yes, it can be scary to meet your favorite author. You want to say hello and get your book signed, and maybe get your picture taken with them, but you don't want to sound foolish or embarrass yourself. I know, because I've been on the other side as the fan.

I had the chance recently to be a guest speaker at a romance writer's convention, where I lectured to the romance novelists about Witchcraft so they could use the real information about the Craft and write better fictional characters. It was a great opportunity, and I enjoyed myself thoroughly.

I was excited and nervous about this, because one of the perks was doing a book signing at a bookstore with the best-selling female romance novelist in America. The other cool thing was that the keynote speaker for the event was another woman whose books had become a popular cable television series in its third season.

I met the keynote speaker for the conference on our first night at the hotel. All of the speakers came in a day early. We hung out in one of the romance writer's rooms drinking bad wine, and I ended up doing tarot readings for a few of them. It ended up that the keynote speaker I was so nervous to meet was a wonderful Southern lady. She is quietly funny, warm, and very down to earth. We hit it off right away and still keep in touch.

So on the day of the big book signing, when the other best-selling author walked in, all the other writers (including the keynote speaker) went silent. *Damn.* This tiny woman in four-inch heels was a powerhouse, and I was shocked that no one even said hello to her. It was her store that the book signing event was held in, after all.

We had a few moments before they started to let people in to the event, so being a typical Midwestern woman, I figured it was only polite to go over and introduce myself.

I stood up, my heart in my throat, walked around my signing table, and approached the woman whose best-selling books I had been enjoying for over twenty years. I stuck out my hand, introduced myself, and said thank you for having me in her store for the book signing.

A communal gasp sounded from all the other writers in the room. *Oh, shit.*

The woman looked up at me—she's diminutive—and she seemed slightly surprised. She shook my hand and said welcome, nice to meet you, and blessed be, which had *me* sputtering in surprise. Then she turned her back, went over to her table, and sat down with her publicist. I turned around and went back to my signing table and tried not to pass out, while the other romance authors looked at me in horror. Apparently I had just committed a major faux pas.

I got through the book signing, and I sold a ton of books. It was a thrill every time someone came by with an armload of my nonfiction books mixed in with these other very successful romance author's books. Both the owner and the manager of the bookstore kept me well stocked and were happy to keep bringing me more books to sign. After almost four hours, I was staggering. Over three hundred people came to that event.

During the event I would look up from time to time to see that powerhouse of a woman looking over at me carefully—which, I will admit, scared the crap out of me. We were directly across the room from each other, and as I chatted people up, posed for pictures with fans, and signed books all afternoon, I would look up to see both her and her publicist watching me. As the event wound down, I asked the author's husband, who is the owner of the bookstore, if I could get a few copies of his wife's latest book to have her sign for me.

Her husband was wonderful and told me to go get in line now, and he'd be right back with the books. So I fished my camera out of my purse and got in line as the last of the eventgoers left, hoping that maybe I could get a picture taken of myself with my favorite author.

As I silently waited, the author's publicist looked up at me and asked if I had had a good time. I smiled, and we chatted. Then she asked me if I had any of my garden books left. I said yes. And she asked me for one, and would I mind signing it?

So I turned around and happily walked back over to get a copy of *Garden Witch's Herbal* and handed it to her. As I walked back, the owner of the shop jokingly called over to me to stay in line like he had told me, and he brought me three copies of his wife's latest book. He handed me the books, commented on how happy he was at how many books I had sold, and dashed off to handle some store details.

So I waited as the publicist handed the author those three books, and she personalized them. When her publicist told her that the last book was for Ellen, the author's head snapped up, and she focused on me.

"Oh, Ellen…the Witch." And she grinned. Then she stopped and said in a completely different tone, "Do you have any of your gardening books left?"

At that point, her publicist picked up her copy of *Garden Witch's Herbal*, waved it at her, and teased that she had one *and* that hers was signed. My mouth hit the floor. I tried to act casual, like I stood and chatted up best-selling fiction writers who have millions of books in print every day.

I smiled and looked over to see two copies left. I offered to get her a copy and took a step back toward my table. She jumped up and announced that she'd go get it herself. I just gaped at her. She was pinned in behind her table with boxes of books stacked all around her. There was no way she was getting gracefully over those boxes in four-inch heels. I heard myself ask if she was going to leap the table or something, and in fact she did just that.

Before you could blink, she leaped up and nimbly cleared those stacked boxes, dashed over, grabbed a copy of my book, and let out a triumphant *aha*! Then she grinned, shoved the book at me, and asked me to sign it for her.

I don't think my hands have ever shaken so hard. One of the romance writers grabbed my camera and snapped a picture of the two of us.

So yeah, I know what it's like to meet an author whose work you have admired. It's scary and a little overwhelming. But if you act like a normal, sane person and if you are polite, you will have a pleasant meeting. Truthfully, meeting the readers is the best part of being an author. It's what makes all those hours banging away at the keys of your computer worthwhile.

Rule Number Four: Dress Weather Appropriate

Is it hot outside? Are you going to need bug spray and sunscreen? Can you wear sandals, or are walking shoes a better choice on uneven grass and terrain? We don't need to have a "what not to wear" intervention here, but for Goddess's sake, use some common sense.

I have met folks at PPDs dressed in street clothes, Pagan or Witch-themed T-shirts, and jeans. I've seen tie-dye, sarongs, ritual robes, or folks wearing cheap black witchy costumes and pointy hats from Walmart. I have admired stylishly attired women and girls in floaty sundresses with matching faerie wings, seen guys in kilts, and observed individuals dressed in serious faerie garb with an attitude that could choke a horse.

Once upon a time, one wanna-be faerie scoffed at me for showing up to "his" Pride Day in a nice tank top and shorts. It was 104 degrees that day, and the heat was intense. The sneering gentleman in question was in layers of velvet and leather, complete with plastic pointy ears, and he was sweating profusely.

Tragically, his "ears" kept sliding while he haughtily lectured me. When one of his ears slipped off and hit the ground, I bent over and silently handed him his fallen ear while he was still in mid-rant. He snatched the fallen ear out of my hand…and then I lost it. I started to giggle.

Was that a smooth move on my part? Ah, no. You had to be there. I smile just thinking about it. The "faerie" was not amused and threatened me with dire magickal repercussions for not taking him seriously. Apparently he was Grand High Pooh-Bah or something. I tried to stop laughing. Really, I did.

He continued to threaten me while he tried to put his ear back on, and that only made me smile even bigger at him. Eventually I was able to catch my breath. I patted his arm and told him thanks, that he had just made my day. I walked away with a smile and tried to rein myself in.

But he did not see the humor in it, and I, of course, couldn't even look at him for the rest of the day without my eyes watering and trying to hold back the giggles—which only made him angrier. At one point in the afternoon, his whole coterie wafted by my author table, all wearing huge, heavy costume wings, with bells a-jingling, and en masse looked down at me with derision at my practical attire. I have never tried so hard in my entire life to keep a straight face. I dressed as nicely as possible with the extreme heat, and honestly, that guy and his merry band looked like poster children for heat stroke.

While some of the outfits were amazing, being downwind of these folks was less than pleasant. How they walked around in the extreme heat like that without passing out, I'll never know. I heard later through the Pagan grapevine that the Grand High Pooh-Bah ended up going to the hospital that night…not for elfin ear loss but for heat exhaustion.

Moral of the snarky story? Dress weather appropriate, stay cool, and keep a good sense of humor at your PPD. Take your family, your magickal friends, circle or coven mates and make a day out of it. Be friendly and as polite as possible, stay open to learning something new, enjoy the people-watching, have fun shopping, and, most importantly, just enjoy yourself.

Ellen's Garden of Witchery Journal
SEPTEMBER PROJECTS

I CANNOT ENDURE to waste anything
as precious as autumn sunshine by
staying in the house. So I spend almost
all the daylight hours in the open air.

Nathaniel Hawthorne

Recently my husband decided that September was as good a time as ever to do some major yard work and to go ahead and add the last panels to our wooden privacy fence. Over the past year we had slowly been expanding it. The year before we had added two new eight-foot-long panels down the side of the yard. During late spring, we had added even more panels and expanded the fence down to the bottom of the yard and started across the back. I came home one sunny morning from an early jog, thinking I'd shower and then work on this book, only to discover my husband, full of yard-work plans, cheerfully waiting for me.

So instead of hitting the showers after my workout, I instead changed into my grubbiest clothes and helped my husband dig post holes, mix and shovel concrete, and get posts set into place. Who says romance is dead?

Actually, for me, that kind of work is fun. I like working in the yard. So on day two of the project, the crosspieces of the fence will go in place, and then we will begin the nailing of the wooden slats. That will be the quick part of the project, as he uses an air gun to nail the boards in place. Once that is finished, we need to give the garden a good cleanup. Fall is officially upon us, and I need to deadhead the hosta bloom stalks and tear out a few expired tomato plants.

Gardening is all about the cycles of nature. There is a time to plant, a time to gather, a time to build a privacy fence, and a time to tidy up the garden. We still had a good two months to enjoy the gardens and the various late-season flowers that would bloom through out the autumn, but for now it just needed a little attention and a bit of sprucing up.

Also, I wanted to put up our scarecrow in the front yard. Since my husband was home on the day of the equinox, Six-Foot Stanley went up right on schedule. As we attached him to the support pole in the front gardens and I fussed with straightening out his clothes and stuffing, a schoolbus came to a halt at the stop sign in front of our house. I heard a bunch of middle-school kids start to yell and cheer, and then we heard "Hi Stanley!" shouted out the schoolbus windows. (I told you, all the kids in the neighborhood know Stanley.)

So after Stanley was all straightened out, the garland of lights was placed around the door and the timers were all set, I planted four new mums in the garden. These new mums were just starting to show some color, and they went in where I had to remove the old plants that did not survive the summer heat. I planted two new bronze and two yellow chrysanthemums. So I dug and amended the soil with composted manure and planted away. The rest of the front yard's chrysanthemums looked pretty good and were setting blooms right on schedule. Also, out of the six inexpensive little pots of mums I had planted the year before in the back gardens, two of them had survived and were now massive—as in shrub size.

I wondered when they bloomed if they would be orange, yellow, or red. To my delight, I discovered a day later that both were a deep red; my favorite! Now, as September winds down, they are starting to bloom a tiny bit, and the color is gorgeous. They will be stunning all through the month of October.

Personal Lesson for the Autumn Equinox
MESSAGES AND APPRECIATION

EVERYONE MUST TAKE the time
to sit and watch the leaves turn.

Elizabeth Lawrence

The week after the autumn equinox, while I was out for my morning walk, I noticed that many of the trees in my neighborhood were showing their autumn colors, which I have always thought to be a very magickal thing. My neighbor's pair of dogwoods were really starting to go from dusky green tinged with red to bright red, which made me smile, and it also made me nod to myself as if to agree with the tree's timing. The enchanting and bewitching season of fall was upon us.

From a scientific perspective, there is a good reason why leaves turn colors in the autumn. As we know, at the autumn equinox itself, night and day hours are equal. Then, as we move into the autumn, the night hours increase right up until the winter solstice. Now, in September, even though the temperatures are mild, the waning of the daylight hours makes the production of chlorophyll in deciduous tree leaves slow down and eventually stop altogether.

As the green color—the chlorophyll—fades, the colors underneath the green of the leaves begins to peek through. Those colors are always there; the green simply masks it all summer long. Also, if we are lucky and have cool nights and lots of bright, sunshine-filled days in the early fall, we will have brilliant color in the leaves. The more sun, the brighter the fall colors. This is why the old timers always said that a rainy fall washed the color out of the trees. Lots of rain equals lots of clouds, which means not as much sun. It really is all up to the sunshine and the cooler temperatures to give us a brighter, more spectacular show of autumn foliage.

So while on my morning walk, I contemplated the changes in the coven so far this year. We had gathered together the weekend prior to celebrate the equinox, and the ritual was lovely. Things seemed to be settling down, and the coven was moving forward. Talk was focused on the upcoming Witches' ball, the gothic Halloween party my husband and I were throwing, and our plans for celebrating Samhain together as a coven. I was really enjoying the group and our magick again.

As the weather had turned a bit cooler, I decided to head up to the local high school track one morning to jog a couple of laps just before the sun came up. In the autumn I have to go early, otherwise the high school marching band is up on the football field practicing. So I got there with time to spare and had the track all to myself, which is just the way I like it.

I hit it and listened to my iPod and watched the sky brighten as the sun began to rise. As I was finishing up, I noticed that all of the birds that typically fly around the area were scattering. When I started on my final lap, I saw the crows fly off with loud, harsh calls, which made me wonder what would make them vacate the field. Perhaps a hawk? Were the band kids coming onto the track? When I turned the corner to the backside of the track, I caught movement out of the corner of my eye. A large bird seemed to be flying alongside me as I jogged. I turned my head to get a better look at the bird.

He sailed along about shoulder height and three feet over to my right. He flew ahead and sat on the metal fence along the backside of the track, just a few feet away, to watch my progress. It was a peregrine falcon. I was able to get a good look as I jogged past the bird. While smaller than a red-tailed hawk, the peregrine is still a good-sized raptor.

The falcon is one of my totems, and it's always a kick for me to see one, especially that close. I had seen this species of bird in my back yard and around the neighborhood before. A few years ago, a peregrine had landed on an elm tree branch in the yard and sat there and watched over my coven during a dusk garden ritual. While we worked our magick, the bird sat on that branch and ate a mouse. Since we stayed quiet and did not run around or shout, the falcon stayed for a long time. The falcon visit was quite the hit with the coven ladies.

As I jogged up even with the bird, I called out a quiet good morning and kept jogging right past him. Then, to my surprise, he launched himself off the fence, followed me, and then quickly passed me again.

Perhaps he thought that this crazy middle-aged lady would keel over out there jogging before the sun came up, so he figured a meal was imminent. But he kept flying along with me and would swoop in close to my lane and then fly ahead and watch my progress. It almost seemed like he was playing.

Delighted and inspired, I decided to add another lap and see if the falcon would keep accompanying me as I jogged. He did. It was the strangest feeling, having that bird fly along just out of arm's reach, then shoot ahead and land on the fence or the player's bench at the edge of the football field and wait for me again until I caught up to him. Around the track we went, and I was just about to finish my extra lap when suddenly the falcon wheeled right and took off, straight up and over, like a bullet, to the neighboring line of large trees.

I had a split second to wonder why he had left when another jogger passed me on the track. The young man called over, "What kind of bird was that?"

I called back, "A falcon—wasn't he awesome?"

He turned to jog backwards as he passed me so he could still talk, and he asked with a good-natured laugh, "Really, that was a falcon? He was big! What would make him follow you around like that?"

"Magick!" I grinned back at him.

93

In response the young jogger smiled at me, then gave me a friendly salute and turned and took off for his workout at a very fast pace. As for me, I slowed down to a walk. Now that my laps were finished, I wanted to cool down and head for home. I turned to walk home from the track, and watched the sun rise over the tree line and said a quiet thank you to the God and Goddess for the day, for my blessings and for the special visit with the falcon.

The peregrine is not a rare bird. If you have ever seen a blue-gray "hawk" that was good sized but not as big as a red-tailed hawk, you probably have seen a falcon. The peregrine is thought to be one of the most widespread birds of prey. Today, science has classified hawks and falcons into separate families, and these birds are an entirely different genus.

The peregrine feeds almost exclusively on smaller birds such as songbirds, doves, and pigeons. (Which would explain why all the songbirds took off before I noticed the falcon.) But they will occasionally snack on small mammals or rodents. It also prefers to hunt at sunrise and at dusk, and it prefers open space for its hunting—so that open practice field and the football field were ideal.

Also, the falcon is a bird with some fascinating magickal lore. The Egyptian god Horus was a falcon-headed god. The Norse goddess Freya owned a falcon-feather cloak that enabled her to shapeshift into a flying falcon. These all-seeing deities were magickal and powerful. In some magickal traditions both the hawk and the falcon are symbols of the dawn, swiftness, the all-seeing eye, divine messages, and fresh starts. How very appropriate!

Reflections on the Autumn Equinox ## THE SEASON OF THE WITCH

THE SCARLET OF maples can shake
me like a cry of bugles going by. And
my lonely spirit thrills to see frosty
asters like smoke upon the hills.
William Bliss Carman

The autumn equinox is the beginning to our most bewitching time of year, so let the magick of this wonderful fall season inspire you! Tip up your face to the golden autumn sunshine and be motivated by the energies and the sense of balance that is so prevalent at this time of the calendar year. Find a local Pagan Pride Day to attend. Be thankful for our freedom of religion. Go all out and celebrate the harvest. Decorate your home lavishly, plant fall-blooming flowers in the garden, bake some bread, or take the family apple picking.

Put up a scarecrow in your front yard, hang up a charming autumn flag, and tie some rustling cornstalks to your porch posts. Go to a local high school football game and cheer on your home team. Have a fall feast and roast a turkey, bake an apple or a pumpkin pie, and have fun celebrating this colorful and enchanting season. Create your own magickal traditions for the autumn with friends and family. Those memories will last a lifetime.

Celebrate the bounty of the earth and watch carefully for the lessons that nature has for you as she puts on her final colorful show of the year. Be thankful for your health, your home, and your loved ones. May you walk your path wisely this autumn, listening as the leaves rustle in the breeze and fall softly from the trees, with an appreciation and reverence for the natural magick that is always around you.

CHAPTER 4

Samhain

Halloween

OCTOBER 31

THE SWEET CALM sunshine of October now
warms the low spot; upon its grassy mould
the purple oak-leaf falls; the birchen bough
drops its bright spoil like arrow-heads of gold.

William Cullen Bryant

Ah, October! Such a gorgeous month. I went out of town to the southern United States to do a Pagan Pride Day in early October, was gone for two days, and came home to discover that the pretty autumn colors I had started to admire in the trees before I left for the author event were now in full show and had changed over to vibrant and strong hues.

Trees were now in their glory, with gorgeous shades of yellow, gold, red, and orange. The locusts in the neighborhood went from green to gold in a day. The burning bushes were a neon red this year; the sweet gums were bright and beautiful; and there was a sprinkling of fallen, crunchy leaves on the ground. My chrysanthemums in the gardens were rolling into full bloom while the other perennials' foliage had turned golden yellow and were starting to die back. The spicy, musky scent of autumn rolled over my town, and I could feel the veil between the worlds getting thinner.

A few days later when I went out for my bi-weekly jog, I quietly let myself out the back door at six AM. To my delight, I stepped out into full inky-colored darkness. I walked up to the track in that chilly air, looked overhead at the constellation Orion, and enjoyed the pre-dawn, the quiet, and my laps around the track. It was wonderful and creepy and rejuvenating all at the same time. By the time I walked back home, the eastern sky was brighter, but I had still beat the sunrise. There is a lot of night in October, and honestly I think I like it that way.

A Little History
A Fire Festival

JUST BEFORE THE death of flowers, and
before they are buried in the snow, there comes
a festival season when nature is all aglow.

Author Unknown

The names of this sabbat are many, one of the most witchy being the Celtic/Druidic Samhain (which translates *sam*, "summer," and *fuin*, "end"). This is pronounced *sow-when* and it is the Celtic New Year. To the ancient people, Beltane was the first day of summer and Samhain was the first day of winter—literally the "summer's end."

We also have Hallowmas, November Eve, and finally Halloween. To the Victorians this was Nut-Crack Night, Snap-Apple Night, or All Hallows' Evening, which turned into All Hallows' Eve, and then finally the contraction Hallowe'en.

Also, it is interesting to note that there is no god named Samhain, contrary to popular belief. Samhain was an agricultural observance. In the old days, this was the time to bring in the last of the crops, store them away for winter, and gather in the herds. The smoke of the community bonfires was thought to purify both people and livestock. According to tradition, herds of cattle were driven between two bonfires on Samhain so that the thick smoke would kill off any insects on their hides. At this time the livestock was culled to eliminate the weak and to ensure that there would be enough food to sustain the people for six months.

This sabbat was traditionally a holiday of bonfires, abundance, and community feasting. This was the final harvest and gathering in before the harshness of the winter months. Samhain was a time to add a layer of fat to the people and their livestock before winter set in. It was both a festival and a gathering together for celebration, safety, and protection.

Samhain is considered a greater sabbat along with Imbolc, Beltane, and Lughnasadh. Samhain at its core has always been a fire festival. Today you may use petition magick and write down on a slip of paper an old habit that you wish to release, and then offer it to the flames of a Samhain bonfire. The original purpose of this holiday's bonfire was to destroy anything negative left over from the previous year, so this act will give your petition magick a nice punch of power.

On the hilltops at sunset, Samhain bonfires were lit in honor of the Old Gods—and they still are today, now we just use chimineas or fire pits. Haven't you noticed that in recent years people love to drag their outdoor fire pits to the front of the house and sit outside in the front yard or driveway to greet the trick-or-treaters on Halloween night by firelight? What was old is now new again.

Don't forget all of the candles that are lit this night in addition to those flickering lights inside of pumpkins. Those candles illuminating the home and the carved jack-o'-lanterns on Samhain/Halloween night are a type of fire magick as well.

Death and Transformation
DEATH TAKES A HOLIDAY

> OCTOBER IS NATURE'S funeral month.
> Nature glories in death more than life. The
> month of departure is more beautiful than the
> month of coming—October than May. Every
> green thing loves to die in bright colors.
>
> *Henry Ward Beecher*

In our traditions, death is not to be feared; it is all part of the cycle. We are born, we live, we die, and we are reborn. Consider some of the most popular themes of this time of year, such as ghosts and graves. There is also the skeleton and, of course, the skull. There are some traditional celebrations that take this to a whole new level. For example, in Mexico and the southwestern United States, the second day after Halloween is a huge event. This is a day to honor the beloved dead, and skeletons, cheerfully decorated and fun, are the main theme. Customs include building private altars to honor the deceased in your family; decorating with sugar skulls, fresh marigolds, and the favorite foods and beverages of the departed; and then visiting the graves of your relatives with these items as gifts.

This is, of course, *El Dia de los Muertos* (the Day of the Dead), November 2. This holiday has Aztec roots. The Mexican holiday uses skulls and skeletons in a humorous light, decorated and dressed—and doing the same activities they would have done in life. The skeleton is considered to be very attached to the person's spirit it once belonged to. Marigolds are a large part of this holiday celebration. They are bright and cheerful flowers that balance out the atmosphere and are traditionally added to the ancestor altars or strung into garlands that are hung up to decorate for the holiday.

If you are busy with your children and grandchildren on Samhain night and entertaining the neighborhood trick-or-treaters, you could always celebrate with your magickal friends on this day instead. Keep in mind that Samhain begins at sunset on October 31 and ends at sunset on November 1. You do have options. In the past, my coven has celebrated Samhain on November 1 or 2 depending on our schedules. There are many similarities between the Celtic Samhain and the honoring of the dead and this Hispanic festival called the Day of the Dead. It is something to consider.

Samhain occurs within the astrological sign of Scorpio—a sign associated with death and transformation. This, again, is nothing to fear, because this then leads to change, renewal, and the regeneration of life. This is the time of the year when the veil is thin—the doorways between our human world and the spirit world are wide open. Spirits do walk, and anything is possible. At Samhain the earth "gives up" its dead; basically the lines between what is physical and what is spirit get blurred. It's wonderfully creepy, ancient, and fun.

Because of the veil being thin and spirits wandering, ghosts and graves are woven into the culture and celebration of this sabbat. According to Druidic traditions, prayers, food, and offerings of burning candles to the dead and to the Good People (the fae, or Sidhe) were left on doorsteps and on altars at Samhain. These offerings were also left at places thought to be Sidhe mounds, as the mounds were open and the Sidhe were out and wandering. They could be disguised as masked revelers or as ordinary people traveling about. In the old days it was best to leave them an offering to be sure you did not offend the fae or your beloved dead who may come by and check on you.

Masks, Guisers, and Trick-or-Treaters

At twelve o'clock you must be ready
And hold your pumpkin good and steady.
For by its rays of candlelight
On Halloween all things are bright!

Victorian Halloween Postcard

According to tradition, the Druids and Pagans also wore masks at Samhain to disguise themselves from any roaming Sidhe, or trouble-making spirits. The Druids and Witches were free to wander about on Samhain without attracting the attention of the fae or the dead because they were cloaked and in disguise. This eventually turned into the tradition of Halloween "guisers," a Scottish custom.

Guisers would go from house to house partying, singing, and getting coins, nuts, fruits, or baked treats. This eventually led to kids dressing up in old clothes or costumes and masks and going to the neighbors for a treat or looking for mischief to get into. In fact, the majority of our Halloween traditions come from the Scottish and Irish immigrants who came to America and Canada in the 1800s. However, it wasn't until the early twentieth century that the commercialization of Halloween began. Today, vintage Halloween cards and party items are still the most sought-after and expensive types of all holiday collectibles. This vintage artwork is full of bewitching images and clever old spells and charms.

It was in the 1930s when the phrase "trick or treat" was first used in a ladies' magazine, describing ideas for the celebration. It quickly caught on—the idea being if you gave kids candy they would not trick you or target your property for mischief. Community Halloween events followed, and the trend from mischief—such as stealing gates (a popular pastime in rural communities), soaping windows, or the unfortunate habit of throwing rocks or destruction of property—turned to going out and snagging candy from your neighbors instead of trashing the neighborhood.

By the 1960s the baby boomers turned Halloween into a widely popular event for children. Mass-produced costumes replaced the homemade ones, and prepackaged candy replaced the simple homemade treats of the past. I still remember standing in line, waiting to get into houses, when I was a kid in the late 1960s. Back in the day, my sister and brother and I would go inside people's homes and choose between homemade popcorn balls, cookies, or caramel apples. Once we snagged our loot, we would go back out to our father, who was standing on the curb, flashlight in hand, waiting for us. Now when I hand out candy to my neighborhood trick-or-treaters, it's all storebought and "fun-sized" candy bars. I only hand out homemade items to family and a few friends.

Today Halloween is the second-largest retail sales–producing holiday in the United States, and it's not just the kids who love it. Adults are crazy about celebrating this bewitching holiday, too. It gets bigger and bigger every year. Halloween magazines—which I admit to collecting—and even Halloween-themed home decorating and cooking shows are the norm these days. It's a lavish, over the top, witchy, and wild October festival! From gothic decorations to Halloween tableware, outdoor lights to elaborate yard displays, and costumes to candy, Halloween/Samhain is here to stay.

Colorful Signs of the Season

A WOODLAND IN full color is
awesome as a forest fire, in magnitude at
least, but a single tree is like a dancing
tongue of flame to warm the heart.

Hal Borland

Ah, it's that wonderful time of year when Witches are suddenly in vogue. A vast array of bewitching-themed items can be found in every store across the land, typically starting in August. By the time October arrives, houses and shops are decorated with orange lights, fall leaves, blooming mums, colorful gourds, cornstalks, pumpkins, and scarecrows. Oh, and ghosts and pointy hat–wearing Witches, of course. In all the excitement of decorating and preparing for the sabbat, don't forget the hidden meanings. Let's take a look at the magickal symbolism behind these holiday colors and the familiar items of the Halloween season. It is important not to forget what they truly mean to us today.

The classic colors of the holiday are orange and black. As Witches, what do these colors mean to us? We have orange to symbolize the sun as it sets, the magick of the Samhain bonfire flames, brilliant fall foliage, and the color of pumpkins. Orange is a color that magickally brings energy and vibrancy to any spell. It is also linked to communication and restoring energy and bringing abundance. What better color than pumpkin orange, at this time of year, to work magick with and for communicating with the spirits of those who have passed on before?

Now, the color black symbolizes the Crone, midnight, bindings, banishings, and protection magick. This is a power color and a popular one with all magick users. On a practical note, being dressed in an ebony cape or cloak allowed practitioners in the old days to blend into the night and not be seen. This came in handy for traveling about, whether they were gathering components for a spell or traveling to a coven meeting.

The color black actually absorbs energy (which makes it popular for protection work) and it is all colors combined. Black is a potent shade to incorporate into your sabbat spells and charms. There is something mysterious and magickal about the midnight hue. From a dark night sky to the deepest, richest soils to the classic cast-iron cauldron, the color black is a powerful tool.

Cauldron Magick

Hence the cauldron
became an instrument of magic,
especially of women's magic.

Doreen Valiente

The classic Witches' cauldron is a tool that often takes some time to acquire. You may search for years until you find just the right one. Typically black, the cauldron should be made of cast iron and fireproof.

The cauldron is considered to be a symbol of the Goddess, the womb, and the sacred hearthfire. Magickal cauldrons are a part of many myths and legends. The cauldron is the forerunner of the Grail, according to some scholars. At Halloween I try not to wince when I see stacks of plastic ones all over the place in stores. I do own a plastic cauldron, but I only use it for handing out candy on Halloween night to the trick-or-treaters. Somehow a Witch answering the door holding a huge black cauldron full of candy seemed very appropriate to me.

For ritual use I have a large cast-iron cauldron with a handle that I found rusted and forgotten in the corner of an antique store. I got it for a song, and with a little steel wool and some rustproof black spray paint, it was as good as new.

If you want to find an affordable cast-iron cauldron without a big search, go to a hunting and camping superstore and check out the cast-iron cookware. Seriously! I send my students to the Bass Pro Shop all the time. Then they call me all giddy because they scored a nice iron heavy-duty cauldron for a much more affordable price than out of a New Age catalog. Really, go check out the camping cookware. They have classic heavy-duty iron cauldrons with the handle and three feet—the whole shebang. You will find many sizes and affordable options, and best of all they are fireproof and often come with a lid.

The cauldron has links to many deities: the Dagda, Cerridwen, Hecate, and the classic wise old Crone. The cauldron's three stabilizing feet not only keep it from tipping over, they are also a reminder of the Lady's triple aspect. The cauldron also symbolizes regeneration and the four elements. There is earth for the metal of the cauldron, fire for the blaze that is lit under it, water that is brewed inside of the cauldron, and the steam (air) that rises from the brew. Finally, we should remember that the cauldron also represents the transformational magick of the Witch.

An Elemental Cauldron-Blessing Ritual

Here is a simple but powerful elemental blessing for your own cauldron. Have a representation of each of the four elements there: a tablespoon of salt, a small dish of water, a lit candle, and a smoldering stick of incense. First pass the cauldron through the smoke, then let the candle flame touch the base of the cauldron. Next, sprinkle a bit of water inside the cauldron, and lastly do the same with the salt. Then hold the cauldron up and out, using both hands, and repeat the verse:

While the flames underneath dance with fire's warm mirth
The metal of the cauldron represents the earth.
Water boils inside, in steam air does rise
Four bound in one, the elements reprise.
I consecrate this now by fire, earth, air, and water
Goddess, bless me now, and smile down on your sons and daughters.

Clean up your supplies. Snuff out the candle and incense, and relax. Your cauldron is consecrated and ready to go. If you like, you can do this on a new moon for fresh starts and beginnings or a full moon for an extra punch of power.

A Touch of Nature's Magick at Samhain

The tint of autumn, a mighty
flower garden blossoming under the
spell of the enchanter, frost.

John Greenleaf Whittier

In all of the rush and excitement of the Samhain holiday, it is easy to forget that often the most practical and magickal of items are to be found very affordably, courtesy of good old Mother Nature.

Check out those falling leaves and the flowers from the garden. Take a new look at your pumpkins, gourds, and apples. There is magick there! Have you thought about going outside and seeing what you can incorporate from nature into your sabbat celebrations and magick? During the nineteenth century, Halloween was a family theme harvest supper. And many of those symbols survive in our modern celebrations today—apples, nuts, caramel apples, and don't forget those pumpkins. Much of our Samhain/Halloween folklore comes from fruits, flowers, and such, so why not run with this idea and see what you can conjure up for your Halloween festivities and Samhain rituals?

The Jack-o'-Lantern

May jack-o'-lanterns burning
bright of soft and golden hue
pierce through the future's veil
and show what fate now holds for you.
Victorian Halloween Postcard

Samhain/Halloween just wouldn't be the same without the supernatural flicker of jack-o'-lanterns. There is something about those carved and glowing pumpkin faces that put us in a festive mood. The jack-o'-lantern was a Celtic custom, and the ancient people originally used a hollowed-out turnip or cabbage to make their lanterns. These lanterns were a handy way to light their path home after the community bonfires on Samhain night. An ember was dropped inside the hollowed-out cabbage or turnip, and the vegetable was thick enough to illuminate and not burn. This night marked a time when the veil between our world and the world of the spirits was thin, so faces were carved in the turnip lanterns to frighten away angry ghosts or spirits that were thought to be wandering about, looking for trouble.

Years later, when Irish, Scottish, and English immigrants arrived in the New World, the pumpkin made an ideal choice to replace the turnip. It was in season, readily available, and a gorgeous harvest color. Plus this fruit was large, inexpensive, and easy to carve. The magickal correspondences for the pumpkin are as follows: it is considered to be a lunar fruit, and it is linked to the element of water. Also, you can use the seeds in spells to promote invisibility. Interested? See my book *Garden Witch's Herbal* for a pumpkin seed spell.

For the past few years, fresh pumpkins have become more and more expensive. There was a serious problem with the pumpkin crops a few years ago in the American Midwest, and between floods one year and drought the next, the pumpkins became more and more pricey. (Not to mention the price increase and scarcity of canned pumpkin.) There was a pumpkin shortage, and the phrase "pumpkin apocalypse" caught on at the local grocery stores. This year when canned pumpkin came in, I stocked up in early October, as we were warned that there may not be any canned pumpkin available for baking come late November and to buy the canned pumpkin while they had it (which I, and many of my friends and family, did).

So between the scarce cooking pumpkin and the pricier Halloween pumpkins for jack-o'-lanterns, many folks went ahead and picked up artificial foam pumpkins for carving. The good side to these foam pumpkins is that they are still carvable and they last for years. Just pop a battery-operated light inside and you're good to go, and they're more fire-safe. The bad side is that they can be even more expensive than the real thing. So just like the artificial holiday evergreen tree, the choice is yours. The foam pumpkins are fun to have and to reuse annually, but I still go ahead and carve up several real pumpkins every year.

This Samhain season, why not use the jack-o'-lantern as it was originally intended: to scare away evil and to frighten off negativity? Those flickering faces can do more than just serve as a beacon for the neighborhood trick-or-treaters. The jack-o'-lantern can also be put to good practical magick use in your Samhain/Halloween celebrations.

Jack-o'-Lantern Spell

First, prep your pumpkins by scooping and cleaning them out. Then carve your jack-o'-lantern into any expression or bewitching pattern that you desire. Afterwards, arrange the pumpkins in a place of prominence. Once you have the fresh pumpkins in place, then add a few tealights in the bottoms of the pumpkins.

PLEASE NOTE: *never* use a live flame inside of a foam pumpkin—it is a fire hazard. Only use candles with a flame inside of a fresh, real pumpkin.

When dusk falls, begin to light all the candles in your pumpkins. Repeat this Halloween jack-o'-lantern charm as you go along lighting the carved pumpkins at sundown on Halloween night:

See this pumpkin all glowing gold?

Protection for my home it holds.

Frighten off evil and turn back negativity

This spell is cast by the magick of All Hallows' Eve.

When the last of your jack-o'-lanterns are lit, close up the spell with these lines:

The wheel year spins on and I celebrate this time.

I seal up this Samhain spell with a simple rhyme.

Apples
THE MAGICKAL FRUIT OF SAMHAIN

SURELY THE APPLE is
the noblest of fruits.

Henry David Thoreau

Many folks think of the apple as the fruit that goes with the autumn equinox/Mabon only, but to be honest it has many more magickal ties to the sabbat of Samhain. Apples have a vast amount of magickal folklore in many religions and traditions. The apple has been unfairly called the forbidden fruit; on a more positive note, they have also been called the fruit of the gods and the fruit of the underworld. It is interesting to note that in the Druidic tradition, apples were used as an offering to the dead. The practice speaks of burying fresh apples on Samhain so the souls of the deceased can feast on them while they are waiting to be reborn.

Apples are associated with many goddesses, and here are a few you may be familiar with: Aphrodite and Venus, and Ishtar, Astarte, Gaia, Hera, Cerridwen, the Norse goddesses Freya and Idunn/Idunna, and, of course, Pomona, our Roman goddess of the apple tree, the orchard, and the apple harvest.

Apples and Witchcraft lore also have a long and colorful history. Crosswise-sliced fresh apples make great natural pentacles on an altar no matter what time of year it is. In herb magick, the apple tree and its fruit are considered to be feminine and are associated with the element of water and the planet Venus. The apple fruit is used for love, passion, friendship, wisdom, and healing magicks. In the language of flowers, a cluster of apple blossoms signifies attraction, while the apple blossom itself promotes fertility. The fruit has a slightly different meaning in the language of flowers. Here, the apple fruit represents wealth and fecundity, which, when you think about it, shouldn't come as much of a surprise.

The foliage and twigs of an apple tree may also be worked into spells to promote good health, long life, and knowledge. Also, a wand made out of an apple branch and covered in nine silver bells is thought to be especially potent. You may have heard of this before, as an apple wand decorated in such a way is called a silver bough.

Apples are thought to be the container of life and a symbol of immortality in many magickal traditions. There is the Celtic Isle of Apples, or Avalon, that was ruled by Morgan le Fay. Also, there was the Greek gardens of Hesperides, where a sacred apple tree grew that bestowed—you guessed it—immortality. This particular apple tree was a wedding gift to the goddess Hera from Gaia herself, when Hera married Zeus. The tree was attended in the garden by nine handmaidens of Aphrodite, who were called the Hesperides. Legend says the nine maidens joined hands around the sacred apple tree and sang as the sun set and the evening star rose—which is the planet Venus. And, of course, we have Idunn's or Idunna's golden apples that kept the Norse gods both vital and immortal. The apple, no matter what magickal culture venerated it, was thought to hold the essence of the soul.

The Enchanting Apple
A VICTORIAN HALLOWEEN TRADITION

YOU WOULDN'T BELIEVE
on All Hallows Eve
what lots of fun we can make
with apples to bob, and nuts on the hob,
and a ring-and-thimble cake.

Carolyn Wells

The apple was an integral part of Victorian Halloween celebrations on October 31, a date the Victorians called Snap-Apple Night. It is interesting to note that some contemporary folklorists have now linked the festival of Pomona—who they describe as a goddess of "fruits and seeds"—to the modern celebration of our Halloween. Considering what we know of the apple and its magickal lore, I can only say, "Well, it's about time!"

The Roman goddess Pomona was actually the keeper of the apple orchards, and she traveled the land with her pruning knife, tending to and caring for all the apple trees. Pomona was an independent soul, but she eventually found love with a very determined young man named Vertumnus. All he had to do was use a little magick, and he so impressed the goddess with his enchantment that she fell for him and professed her love right there in the apple orchard.

Today, working with apples in your Halloween/Samhain spells and charms makes good magickal sense, as apples are both a fruit of love and a fruit of wisdom. Inside the apple is the star of knowledge, and slicing an apple horizontally will reveal the Witches' star hidden within. So the old bobbing for apples game may have actually been bobbing for wisdom…

Considering the folkloric significance of this fruit, it's not surprising that in the old days, young women believed that on Halloween night, they could divine the name of their future husband by reading apple parings. Try this Halloween/Samhain night spell to go along with your love-apple divination.

A Halloween Apple Spell
for Love Divination

To perform the Victorian apple peel trick, you must pare an apple in an unbroken chain and then flip the apple peel over your shoulder into a previously placed pot or cauldron of water. The peel will unfurl in the water, taking the shape of the first letter of the first name of your true love.

Chant this as you toss the apple peel:

Apple peel, apple peel, let's you and I play a game
Take the shape of the first letter of my true love's name.
By the mystery of love and the magick of Halloween
With the help of Pomona, now make your symbol clear
to me.

Now take a look and see what letter appears. Good luck!

A *Samhain Apple Muffin Recipe*

Apples are at their best-tasting and in season come September and October, and the varieties are endless. They make a traditional, enchanting, and delicious addition to your Samhain festivities, so go ahead and conjure up a little kitchen magick. Bake an apple pie or apple crisp, or whip up some hearty apple bread or healthy apple muffins and share it with your loved ones this autumn.

In keeping with our apple theme, here is a tasty lowfat apple-oatmeal muffin recipe that my family and covenmates all love. These are wonderful, very moist, and—unless you tell them—no one will ever know these tasty muffins are lowfat and (dare we say it?) healthy!

2 cups apple, peeled and shredded
(I like Granny Smith apples for this)
1½ cups all-purpose flour
1 cup quick oats
⅔ cup firmly packed brown sugar
1½ teaspoons baking powder
½ teaspoon baking soda
½ teaspoon salt
½ teaspoon cinnamon
A pinch of nutmeg
¼ cup fat-free milk
2 tablespoons canola oil

1 teaspoon vanilla extract

1 cup plain fat-free yogurt

2 egg whites

Peel and remove cores from apples. Then, using a handheld grater or a food processor, grate the apples; set aside. In large mixing bowl, combine flour, oats, brown sugar, baking powder, baking soda, salt, and spices. Stir.

In a separate medium-sized bowl, combine milk, oil, vanilla, yogurt, and egg whites, stirring together with a whisk until well blended. Add wet ingredients to the flour bowl and stir until moistened. Blot shredded apples on a paper towel to remove excess moisture, then add apple to the mix and stir.

Spray a muffin tin with nonstick cooking spray or use paper liners. Spoon batter into muffin tin. Bake at 400 degrees for 20 minutes. Yields 12–15 muffins. Store these in an airtight container. They also freeze well.

• • • •

Ellen's Garden of Witchery Journal
October Garden Magick

BITTERSWEET OCTOBER. THE mellow,
messy, leaf-kicking, perfect pause between the
opposing miseries of summer and winter.

Carol Bishop Hipps

On a surprisingly warm morning in mid-October I looked over my front gardens and considered. Our scarecrow, Stanley, was up; the orange lights were on the house; and I had indeed planted a few more mums in late September to fill in the old chrysanthemums that did not make it through the hot summer months.

My ornamental grass was turning a gorgeous shade of gold, the fairy roses were still blooming away in bright red, but the wave petunias were pretty well finished for the year. I knew the local greenhouse and nursery still had plenty of pretty mums for sale, as I had just happened to stroll through their stock on my morning walk. So I decided to see if I could catch a good sale and plump up the front flower gardens for the fall. Besides, I wanted to put in a few more chrysanthemums that day and work in the gardens while the weather was still warm. So I got cleaned up from my morning workout and headed off to get a haircut, run a few errands, and then hit the nursery.

I found some pretty yellow mums, four small pots for ten dollars total, and then stumbled across a bronze-orange monster-sized mum just starting to open its blooms. Because I have lots of pink and purple shades in the perennial garden all spring and summer, I tend to avoid purple flowers in the autumn. I usually go for the deep reds, the bronze, and the bright yellow or orange. And with so many varieties and flower forms to choose from in the chrysanthemum, everybody can find something they like.

But this year, I still ended up with a couple more sale containers of dusky purple button mums too. They really did look cute when I tucked them in a bare spot in the front gardens. That purple just popped against the green and yellow autumn perennial foliage.

Here's a tip: when you buy chrysanthemums for the autumn garden, purchase the plants with lots of green buds that are only just starting to show their colors. That way, when you plant it, the mum has a few days to settle in to its new home, and then it will begin to slowly open its blooms over the next few weeks.

If you buy your mums when they are already fully in bloom, those flowers are actually at the end of their bloom cycle. They will only look good for a week or so before they start to fade, because the plant has to decide: does it keep blooming, or should it put its energy into staying alive in the new home? Since its bloom cycle is almost over anyway, it puts energy into staying alive—which translates to droopy, dying flowers right after planting.

Also, when you take the mum out of the pot, if the roots are tightly compacted around the dirt, loosen them up with your fingers so the roots will spread out in the garden soil. If it is really tight, you may need to make a few snips into the root ball to loosen up those roots. If you do not do that, the roots will never spread out, and the mum will probably not survive the winter months. Water the mums well when you plant them, and keep on watering them every couple of days to ensure a longer bloom period and a plant that can look vibrant well into the month of November.

Samhain Flower Magick with the Chrysanthemum

Men say that in this midnight hour
The disembodied have power.
To wander as it liketh them
By wizard oak and fairy stream.
William Motherwell

Don't you just love the chrysanthemum? These hardy and reliable seasonal blossoms are big, bold, and spicy. They add glorious color and fragrance to many a yard or container at this time of year. Chrysanthemums are probably one of the most unsung flowers when it comes to magick, because they are so common. The chrysanthemum (*Dendranthema* hybrids) is affectionately known today as "mum."

The name of this flower comes from the Greek words *chrysos*, meaning "gold," and *anthos*, meaning "flower." In ancient times Greeks would wear garlands of chrysanthemums to keep away those dreaded evil spirits.

For the modern, practical Witch, the mum is a fabulous, protective fall flower that wards the home and keeps away wandering ghosts. Since these flowers are available in a wide range of jewel-toned colors, you can also match the color of the mum to specialize your Samhain spellwork. These flowers do pack quite a protective punch, and since they are readily available in the fall months, why not work with the seasonal magick already inherent within them?

The Magick of Chrysanthemum Colors

RED—"I love you"

BURGUNDY—"passion"

WHITE—"truth"

YELLOW—"happiness and wisdom"

GOLD—"for protection" (just like the Greeks once did)

ORANGE—"energy and bounty"

BRONZE COLORS—"a happy hearth and home"

PURPLE—"power and protection"

PINK—"friendship and affection"

A Samhain Night Flower Fascination
to Ward Off Ghosts

Here is a chrysanthemum charm for you to perform on Samhain/Halloween. Choose whichever color of flower you think would best match your magickal intention, and add a few blossoms to a vase or just bless the mums that are already growing in the yard. (If you take a look at the wording of this spell, you will see that you may either say Halloween or Samhain—it's up to you, and either way will work out fine.)

> A *flower fascination I spin on this Halloween/Samhain night*
> *Keep spooks and specters far away; repel bad luck from my sight.*
> *Hear my words and let the magick flow both hither and yon*
> *This spell will last and ward my home until the break of dawn.*

Close the flower fascination with:

> By *the magick of Halloween/Samhain, as I will it, so must it be.*

Personal Lesson for Samhain
PLAN AHEAD AND ENJOY THE CELEBRATIONS

OCTOBER GAVE A party; the leaves by
the hundreds came…the chestnuts, oaks,
and maples, and leaves of every name.

George Cooper

Halloween stress. These two words are well known to Witches in the month of October. For some folks, holiday stress and anxiety kicks up around the December holidays. For Witches it kicks in around mid-October, and if you don't keep it in check, it will ruin your Samhain celebration and your Halloween festivities.

Yes, this is our time of year, and it is a blast for us to celebrate it lavishly. However, it's also very easy to get wrapped up in stress…and then, before you know it, you can't even enjoy yourself because you have so much to do. I heard from other Witches all over the country this past year about how overwhelmed they were with their own celebration plans. Between the local masquerade balls, coven Samhain celebrations, and family Halloween plans, many of them felt jumpy, worried, stressed out, and anxious.

My theory is that this happens for a couple of reasons. The first reason is the most obvious: the veil is thin during this time of year. As Witches, we do work to develop both a magickal and a psychic sensitivity, so why are you so surprised that suddenly you feel everything? Everything linked to magick gets turned up to full volume the closer we get to Samhain—including your own intuition and your sensitivity to the emotions of other people.

Reason number two: we get more public attention during October than at any other time of the year, especially if you are a public Witch. Suddenly everyone wants to talk to you or wants you to give them a tarot reading or to have you check out their "haunted" houses. Even the neighbors and your acquaintances get a bit more Wicca-curious. Not all of the attention is positive. Whether it's some goofball of a politician or a comedian, comments can be made, and it can affect your family and/or your job, and sometimes that just gets old.

I recommend drinking more water, getting regular exercise, and eating healthier to help combat the Halloween stress. Healthy habits really help in minimizing stress. Feeling overwhelmed? Go lace up your walking shoes and take a walk. Enjoy the pretty leaves and the cooler weather. You will feel so much better after you get some exercise. All of those endorphins are doing their thing and naturally relieving your stress.

Psychic protection techniques will really help you now. Whatever your preferred psychic protection technique is—a protection spell, a balancing meditation, working with a power stone, charging an amulet, or just enchanting and then drinking chamomile tea—all of these stress-busting suggestions are tools. Use them.

Your best bet is to take all of this in stride, work on a psychic cleansing for yourself, and to put on a cheerful face. Try to laugh and deal with it the best you can. If the stress gets to be too much and it's taking over your life, then talk to a friend or a counselor. I am a firm believer in therapy. You can combine therapy with magick.

Also, I strongly suggest either simplifying your life in October or planning everything well in advance. If you are planning on attending a Witches' ball, start shopping for your formal clothes early. (It's the best way to catch a sale.) Right around August, stores start pushing homecoming and formal dresses. They also run sales on suits, dress shirts, and ties. So think ahead and save some money while you are getting all fancy for the ball.

For example, this year I got a formal black and ivory tea-length dress for the local Witches' ball on sale for $45—it was originally $165. It was marked to half-price for homecoming season, and then I got an additional 30 percent off because I opened up a charge account to the trendy mall store where I rarely shop. I paid off the bill as soon as I got it, then cut up the card. Score! I love a good sale.

On the other hand, consider starting your costume creations and designs in July and August, not October. Give yourself plenty of time to work on your own (and your family's) costumes months in advance. Besides, costume and Halloween fabric and patterns always go on sale in the summer months anyway, just like the best decorations are snapped up in August as soon as they hit the stores. Plan ahead. Then make a schedule for all of the activities you have planned for Samhain and Halloween, and stick to it.

As mentioned previously, my husband and I had decided to throw a big gothic Halloween party. We decided to do this the day between the local Witches' ball, which is always the last Friday of October, and the actual day of Halloween. It was just the way the calendar worked out. The Witches' ball was on Friday the twenty-ninth, and our party would be on Saturday the thirtieth. Then our family celebration of Halloween, which fell on a Sunday this particular year, would be on the thirty-first.

Our adult children and our friends were thrilled; my coven was delighted. Then the pressure hit. If a well-known Witch throws a Halloween party, then it better be a damn good one—which is why my husband and I started our costume and party plans in July.

I made a romantic steampunk outfit for myself. I ordered a Victorian ecru-colored lacy blouse and tailored it to be form-fitting. I used my own long, black swishy skirt and added lots of gears to a wide leather belt with old trinkets dangling from it. A friend shipped me a clockwork-decorated hat she had made for me to borrow.

My husband decided to be an elegant Victorian vampire. We even found him a coachman's hat and red coffin-shaped glasses to wear. Our adult kids did more modern, trendy vampires, from *True Blood*–inspired characters to the Joker.

Our usual indoor Samhain/Halloween decorations were tweaked a bit. A few weeks prior to our party we had added a bit more of a gothic flair to them, and my husband added additional orange outdoor lights to the back gardens for the party. We set up the fire pit in the back gardens and arranged all the Adirondack chairs around them. My sons stacked firewood for the pit, and my oldest son would tend the fire during the party.

My husband even ordered huge black lights to replace the big fluorescent lighting in the garage, where we planned to dance. The garage is his domain, and holy cats, he took decorating it seriously. Now everything in the garage, including the fake spider webs and spiders, glowed in the dark. We even switched out the indoor lighting to lower-watt bulbs to make it look creepier inside the house.

I composed a weird poem invitation that had gothic costume suggestions, printed it on Halloween paper, and mailed the invites out to our guests. Our friends went crazy plotting out what they would wear: steampunk, vampires, pirates, gypsies, Witches, dark angels, a corpse bride and groom, Harry Dresden, even a Day of the Dead elegantly gothic señorita.

We planned a basic menu. I would make mulled apple cider and keep it warm in a big slow cooker. I purchased a bottle of blackberry wine and found a bottle of vampire wine—no kidding, it comes from Transylvania.

I planned to bake creepy black and red cupcakes and decorate them with sugar skulls and little picks that said "Pick Your Poison." I also would set up a big black and orange candyscape in old apothecary-style jars and set out gothic-patterned cellophane bags so the guests could each take some candy home—you know, trick-or-treating for the grownups.

We also asked all of the guests to each bring a "horror d'oeuvre" to share. (Which makes it easier on the hosts, and it lets everyone get into the spirit of things.) People love to help with a big party—so let them.

My coven sister Ravyn would come over a few hours beforehand and help us get everything ready, while another coven sister, Ember, and her husband would bring the music and be in charge of that. I made up a schedule and planned everything out as well as I could. We decorated the entire house a little bit at a time the weeks before Samhain, and it was over the top. So, party preparations under control, we got ready for the craziness of the final days of October to begin.

Reflections on Samhain
EMBRACING THE DARKNESS

SHADOWS OF A thousand years
rise again unseen,
Voices whisper in the trees,
"Tonight is Halloween!"
Dexter Kozen

This year as my husband and I added the last phase of outdoor decorations (all of the tombstones and spot lighting) to the front gardens, it ended up that the local school-buses cruised by as they took the kids home from school. There were bunches of kids hanging out the bus windows, calling out compliments to us.

We both turned and waved to the kids, which got us a cheer. I called back "See you on Halloween night!" and the bus crowd went wild. A bit later, my husband was wiring in the spotlighting for the tombstones. We were calling back and forth to each other as he checked the lights to make sure the spotlight came on when the landscape lights did. As we finished up the lighting, a couple of gangly middle-school-aged boys walked past the house.

You know that age? Early teens, still wanting to go out on Halloween night but wanting to be cool. So I smiled cheerfully at the boys and said "Hey, guys." The boys were interested but trying desperately not to look like they cared what an old married couple were doing out in their front yard.

A week before Halloween. With tombstones. And electrical wiring.

They stopped and looked over at the house. "Your yard is always so awesome," one of them quickly announced in a voice that cracked. He looked over at his friend to see what his friend's reaction would be.

I hid a smile and said, "Thanks, we'll see you guys on Halloween."

"Are you gonna have the good candy again?" the other boy asked me, also in a squeaky voice.

"Don't I always?" I answered with a grin.

"Sweet," was the reply from both boys.

As they walked off I heard one of the boys say, "That's the Witch lady." The other one looked over his shoulder at me and said, "Yeah, she's cool."

Ah, the highest of compliments. I had to smile.

As I write this, it is the afternoon of October 31. Samhain has rolled around again. Our gothic Halloween party was last night, and we all had a blast. Our party guests wandered from the living room to the kitchen, then out to the black-lit garage, and finally outside in the back gardens under the stars and around the fire, and back again.

The weather was perfect, the food was great, and the mood was fun and festive. The night flew by. People were asking as they left if we would do it again next year, and I imagine we will. As we hauled all the carved party pumpkins to the front yard to arrange a big display for tonight's neighborhood trick-or-treaters, my husband was commenting that he already had ideas for next year's costumes. He wants to build a coffin for folks to have their pictures taken in at the next party.

I am tired but happily so, and mostly I am content to be at home. I am looking forward to a quiet night tonight with just the family and, of course, being entertained by all the neighborhood kids out trick-or-treating. I do not travel on the thirty-first of October. This is a family day, and I would not have it any other way. Plus, the kids in the neighborhood love coming to our house on Halloween, and I would never let them down. Once the neighborhood urchins are all done with the trick-or-treating, I'll light a few candles in memory of my grandparents and hold a quiet and solitary Samhain ritual to pay my respects. I do this every year. It's private and personal—and, to me, relaxing.

So my final advice is to remember to smile and take pleasure in the magick and the meaning behind those classic Halloween symbols, from ghosts, skeletons, and tombstones to cauldrons and chrysanthemums to apples and jack-o'-lanterns. Go ahead, bedeck your home lavishly, work your seasonal spells, and enjoy all those classic decorations and representations of the Samhain season…and be aware of what they truly symbolize. For us, it is a powerful time of year.

The true mystery of Samhain is the turning of the Wheel of the Year to the darkest nights and the cold months of the coming winter. Celebrate the final gathering-in and honor the memory of your ancestors and beloved dead. Open up to your inner wisdom during this time of the year and embrace the dark.

Witches don't cringe at things that go bump in the night. We hold on tight and enjoy the thrill! This year, don't let the craziness of the season get you down. Plan ahead, minimize your stress, and enjoy. Happy Samhain!

CHAPTER 5

Yule

Winter Solstice

DECEMBER 20–23

BREW ME A cup for a winter's night.
For the wind howls loud and the furies fight;
Spice it with love and stir it with care,
And I'll toast our bright eyes,
my sweetheart fair.

Minna Thomas Antrim

As the dark and cold days of December came upon me, I was happy to be back at home and finished with traveling for the year. I had attended a Yule festival in Montreal earlier in the month and was the keynote speaker, and it was a blast. I had the chance to catch up with some author friends of mine and to meet a few other Pagan authors whose work I have enjoyed. I had never traveled outside of the country before, and Montreal is very French and feels European. For me, this was a big adventure.

To my delight, I found the people of Montreal to be warm, friendly, and amazingly bilingual. I think one of my fondest memories of Montreal was walking back to the hotel with all the other authors from the festival after dinner, in the snow, and finding a little bakery that was filled with Yule log cakes—or *Buche de Noel*, as they call them.

Picture a couple of middle-aged Witches squealing in delight and rushing in to check out the bakery cases, then dragging the other authors and the hosts of the event in with them. There were cases of these gorgeous mini cakes in different flavors, and I could not resist picking up a mini Yule log cake and having it boxed up so I could take it back to my hotel. Nobody left that bakery empty-handed.

When the weekend festival was over and I returned home, we decorated the trees (yes, we have more than one), put the white icicle lights up on the house, and finished up our holiday shopping. There were presents to be wrapped, cookies to be baked, and gatherings of family and the coven to look forward to. The days flew by. I think there is something about the month of December that just makes it go faster, almost as if the calendar year is in a hurry to complete itself, and so the passage of time is somehow rushed ahead.

This year there was no gradual changeover to the colder days of winter. It seemed to go from fall to winter in a finger snap. A snowfall in early December, followed by bitter cold and then a layer of ice, curtailed me from my regular walks outside. So I spent a lot of time bunkering in at home, happily writing away. I also took some time to look back over the past year, come to a few conclusions, and basically came to terms with the changes in my life.

Yule is a perfect time to focus on our goals to remove blocks and other spiritual and emotional clutter that may be keeping us from moving forward as we would wish. This way, we can embrace the rebirth of the sun and celebrate light returning with an open mind and a light heart.

A Little History
HERE COMES THE SUN

> AT REST, HOWEVER, in the
> middle of everything is the sun.
>
> *Nicolaus Copernicus*

The winter solstice, also called the December Solstice, occurs exactly when the earth's axis is titled the farthest away from the sun. In the Northern Hemisphere the sun's daily journey in the sky is at its lowest point. Also, the sun's noontime elevation appears to be the same for several days before and after the solstice, which explains the origin of the word *solstice*, meaning "sun stands still."

In the Northern Hemisphere this festival occurs on the shortest day or longest night of the year, in the sense that the length of time elapsed between sunrise and sunset on this day is a minimum for the year. This marks the beginning of an astronomical winter. For Witches and Pagans it is a time to celebrate the rebirth of the sun. The winter solstice's date moves around year to year, anywhere between December 21 and 22. Sometimes the winter solstice will fall on December 20 and 23, but that is more rare.

Like the other sabbats that occur on a solstice or equinox, the winter solstice, or Yule, is generally celebrated at the time when the sun enters the zodiac sign of Capricorn. Following the date of the December or winter solstice, the daytime hours begin to grow longer and the nighttime hours shorter.

The pre-Christian holiday of Yule was the premier holiday in Scandinavia and Northern Europe. The Yule season, or tide, was a time for feasting, drinking, gift-giving, and gatherings while the people celebrated the light returning to the land. However, during these dark and cold days, folks were also aware and a bit afraid of the forces of the dark.

The popular name for the sabbat at the winter solstice is Yule, which comes from the Norse *Jol*, representing the winter solstice celebration. It is also linked to the Saxon word *hweol*, meaning "wheel," similar to a German word meaning "the turning of the wheel" or "the rising of the sun wheel." The ancient Romans celebrated the winter solstice between December 17 and 24 each year in a weeklong festival called Saturnalia.

SATURNALIA

O WINTER! RULER of the inverted
year…I crown thee king of intimate delights,
fireside enjoyments, home-born happiness…

William Cowper

For the Romans, a weeklong winter solstice celebration was one of their biggest parties of the year. The poet Catullus described Saturnalia as "the best of days." This was a designated holy day in the Roman calendar, and what started out as a one-day celebration eventually grew into a weeklong party, no matter how many times the old Roman government tried to rein it in. Originally the celebration was held on December 19, but when the calendar was changed by Julius Caesar, the weeklong Saturnalia celebration was moved to December 17–23.

Saturn was the god of the Golden Age. During his festival school was out, masters and slaves might trade places for a day, the Lord of Misrule reigned supreme, togas were discarded in favor of more relaxed clothing, and the feast of fools added to a bawdy and wild atmosphere.

We know that holly and ivy were used at this celebration to honor Saturn, who was originally a god of agriculture. His wife's name is Ops, and she was a goddess of riches and opulence. The Romans gave one another evergreen holly wreaths, hung them on their doors at the holiday, carried swags of it in processions, and decked images of Saturn with the greenery. Ivy was also worn to ward off drunkenness and as a nod to Bacchus, the god of the vine. It is also rumored at Saturnalia the ancient Roman priests cut down pine trees and took them into the temples, where they were decorated.

The Romans celebrated the return of the sun with drinking, resolutions, and gift giving. It's interesting that today the resolutions and the drinking have been moved to our New Year's celebrations and not the solstice. Back in the day, popular gifts in Rome were candles (to symbolize the returning of the sun) and clay figurines (for fertility). During this weeklong festival, garlands and wreaths were displayed, feasts were held, gifts were exchanged, friends were visited, and masked revelries and parties were the theme—think Mardi Gras, Carnival, and New Year's all rolled into one. You know that had to be fun.

Now let's take a look at some of our richest traditions and folklore from the Norse Pagans. The Germanic, Scandinavian, and Northern European people added depth, legend, and traditions to our winter holiday celebrations as we know them today.

Santa:
SHAMAN OR SHAPESHIFTER?

> HE WAS DRESSED all in fur, from his head
> to his foot, and his clothes were all tarnished
> with ashes and soot...His droll little mouth
> was drawn up like a bow, and the beard
> on his chin was as white as the snow...
>
> *Clement C. Moore*

The Norse god Odin, or Wodan, was rumored to visit the earth during the month of December in disguise and was thought to visit his people. He would slip in quietly and join groups around their firesides and listen in to see if they were content. Sounds a bit like another popular December figure, doesn't he? Where do you suppose Santa came from, anyway? It's only been the last seventy years or so that Santa morphed from a bearded, fur-covered wizard to the jolly and plump red-and-white Coca-Cola version of a jolly old elf.

Some will point out the tale of a bishop born in Turkey named Nicolas during the third century as the forerunner of Santa. Nicolas became known for his anonymous gifts to the poor. He was rumored to have snuck into houses at night to leave food and money. Some legends speak of how he donated gold for the dowries of a family with three daughters, so they could all be wed. Eventually he was made a saint, and Saint Nicolas was given his own celebratory day on December 6.

It is illuminating to note that in the northern country of Lapland, shamans used reindeer to pull sleighs for travel. Traditionally shamans wore bells to announce their presence and to frighten away evil. As to where the colors of red and white came from, some have suggested this is a nod to the hallucinogenic properties of the fly agaric mushroom. This fungus, while intensely poisonous, was once used by shamans in Lapland for vision questing and was even fed to the reindeer. This is not recommended today, as the fly agaric is illegal to possess. I suppose if those shamans of old had enough of those mushrooms, they would feel like they were flying—that is, if they did not accidentally expire from the poison.

We could also speculate the color of red is linked to the element of fire and the return of warmth and light, and the color white for the midwinter snows. Some accounts suggest that the Druids may have worn robes of white and red when gathering mistletoe for the winter solstice.

In Holland we find another Yuletide character called Sinterklaas. He also possessed a white beard, wore a magickal red cloak, and rode the wild December skies on a white horse. Sinterklaas was believed to have flown over the rooftops of the home, bringing gifts to the children who were kind. In Holland, children left their shoes by the chimney, filled with straw and treats for Sinterklaas's horse. He returned the favor by tucking little presents and sweets into their shoes or boots.

However, I think taking a deeper look at Odin, or Wodin, is worth the time. There are certainly a lot of similarities between Odin the shapeshifter and the shaman-like qualities of Santa Claus. For example, Odin has a long white beard and is a master of disguises. He loves to play tricks and is considered to be both a shapeshifter and a sha- man. One of Odin's more illuminating names is actually Julnik; another is Yuli.

Odin ruled over the month of December, which was called Jule. This period of time was referred to as *Jultid*, or Yuletide. Odin is pictured as an older man with a flowing white beard and an eye patch or a hat pulled low over his missing eye. He was typically covered in fur, as befitted his cold northern climate, and he also possessed a shape-shifting cloak. Odin rode through the winter skies dressed in warm furs on an eight-legged horse named Sleipnir. This magickal horse had runes engraved on its teeth.

Odin is a patron of shamans, occultists, and the keepers of secret knowledge. He is married to the goddess Frigga. Frigga stayed happily at home while her husband took to the skies for his wild rides. Frigga is the mother of Balder and is associated with spinning, the keeping of hearth and home, wisdom, fertility, and children and their protection. If you have ever lost a child, as Frigga lost Balder, it was believed that Frigga has claimed you for one of her own. The Yule log is also associated with Frigga, which makes sense. The Yule log was burned in the hearth, and keeping a home and raising the children is an honorable task, and one to be revered.

So Odin wandered among his people, and people felt energized and happy in Odin's presence, whether they actually knew he was there or not. Sounds like a precursor to the spirit of the season, does it not?

THE WILD HUNT AT YULETIDE

THERE'S A WHISPER on the night-wind,
There's a star agleam to guide us,
And the Wild is calling, calling…let us go.

Robert William Service

During the Wild Hunt ancestral spirits are thought to come back to earth. The deity who ruled over this is Odin, who is actually the leader of the Wild Hunt. The Wild Hunt was traditionally a procession of spirits and heroes. In European traditions, during the twelve days of Yuletide (those last days of the calendar year), these spirits traveled in a procession to visit families and loved ones.

This may explain why, in Scandinavian lore, it is believed that the spirits of children were along for the wild ride on the night of the winter solstice for the purpose of coming back to earth to visit their parents. These children who had passed over were thought to be under the care of Frigga, so I suppose she turned them loose to travel with Odin so they could visit their loved ones.

I personally was surprised to discover that the Wild Hunt has more ties to Yule than any of the other sabbats we celebrate today. The Wild Hunt was traditionally a procession of spirits and heroes. After Christianity took over, in an effort to demonize the hunt, it began to be called the Parade of the Damned. It's sad to me that they attempted to turn what was originally a joyous, mysterious, and powerful thing into something frightening. The Wild Hunt is also called Asgard's Chase, Spirit's Ride, and Holla's Troop.

According to legend, if you were caught by the Wild Hunt, you had to keep going with them until they were finished. This was a type of spirit possession, and one where you were truly "along for the ride." The only way to protect yourself from being swooped up and carried along on those wild winter nights was to consume the herb parsley. The folkloric treatment for the madness that follows having seen the hunt was also to eat fresh parsley.

On wild and windy nights the hunt is out. The procession of spirits led by Odin on his eight-legged horse is indicated by winter storms, howling winds, thunder, and lightning. Another of his cohorts along for the ride was the goddess Freya, a patroness of seers, a shapeshifter, and an all-purpose deity. Other deities along on the wild ride include Hulda (other variations are Holle and Holda). This is a northern German Mother goddess. Holland may have gotten its name from her: Holle's land. Hulda/Holle/Holda was known as the Queen of Witches, and it was thought that Odin's congregation of spirits traveled together with Hulda's host of Witches.

In German fairy tales, Hulda is known as Mother Holly, or Mother Holle. She travels about in a long, snow-white hooded cloak. Hulda is a Snow Queen and is associated with Epiphany and fertility. It is thought that when she fluffed up her feather bed, the feathers fell to earth as snow. Hulda is thought to be surrounded by unborn babies. She is their guardian and releases them to be born into the world of men. It is not surprising to learn that she is a deity of fertility and birth.

From the Southern Alps we have Berchta. Offerings of dumplings and pickled herring were left to Berchta and put out on rooftops so she could "grab and go" as she flew by on the Wild Hunt. These wild, white ladies visited the home at Yuletide and were believed to be goddesses that could bridge the gap between the living and the dead.

LUCY AND ST. LUCIA

SINCE SHE ENJOYS her long night's festival.
Let me prepare towards her, and let me call
This hour her vigil, and her eve, since this
Both the year's and the day's deep midnight is.

John Donne

St. Lucy's Day is celebrated on December 13 and is a celebration of the reborn sun. St. Lucia, or Lucy, is the bringer of light. This Scandinavian festival kicks off the start of the Yule season and the annual struggle between darkness and light. Lucy is called a faerie queen, a white lady, and a saint, and some European countries even identify her as a Witch.

Originally the observance of the shortest day of the year, the winter solstice, was celebrated on December 13. Then those seven days were added to our modern calendar, so the rebirth of the sun occurs now around the twentieth of the month. Today Lucy's Day is sometimes referred to as "Little Yule." Lucy herself is pictured as a blond young woman with long hair. She is wearing a white robe belted with a red sash and has a woven crown or wreath of evergreen lingonberry foliage on her head. The wreath in her hair is studded with nine lit white candles. Variations on her name include Lucia, Lussi, and Luca.

In Sweden she is a Queen of Lights, a bringer of gifts, and is immensely popular. According to legend, Lussi, or Lucy, appeared at a time of great famine. She stepped across frozen lakes and brought food to the people who were starving. It is traditional in Sweden for a girl from the family—some sources say the oldest daughter and some say the youngest—will dress up as Lucy. The daughter acting the part of Lucy will serve her family coffee and saffron sweet rolls called *lussekatter* on the morning of December 13. Other foods associated with Lucy's day include gingersnaps, sweets, and saffron buns with raisins.

Lucy is one of many visiting white ladies who materialize all over Europe at the close of the calendar year. In England Lucy is associated with the faeries, in Germany she is associated with the elves, and in Hungary she is associated with Witchcraft. Her name, Lucy, may come from the Latin word *lux*, meaning "light." In a weird synchronistic moment, I realized that I was researching and writing about this Yuletide being on her actual festival day, December 13, which inspired me to create a candle spell for her that you'll find shortly.

My acquisitions editor, Elysia, shared with me stories about Lucy's festival day from Hungary, where Lucy is known as Luca. Hungary has some great folklore surrounding Lucy's Day. On the thirteenth of December you are to build a stool with either nine or thirteen different woods. You are to work on the stool a little at a time for thirteen days, finishing up the project at midnight on the twenty-fourth. Then you are supposed to bring the stool to church with you, and after the service you are to stand on it, allowing you to be able to see the Witches. (What Witches are supposed to be doing at a midnight Christmas Eve service, no one knows.)

However, now that you have spotted them, you are supposed to throw poppy seeds on the way home to protect yourself from those tricky Witches. Apparently the poppy seeds are irresistible to them, and they will stop and pick them up—allowing those stool-toting, poppy-seed-throwing folks to make good their escape.

Lussi, or Lucy, also has links to the Wild Hunt and to Witchcraft in Norway, where she overcomes the darkness. As a member of the Wild Hunt, Lucy/Lussi is out and about, traveling over the land with Odin, Freya, Bertcha, Holda, and various other spirits and nature spirits. I find it very interesting that in Norway, the darkest days of the year were called *Lussinatten*.

From Lucy's Day, December 13, until December 24, it was believed that spirits, gnomes, and trolls all wandered the earth. If Lussi caught you out working when you were not supposed to be, she would punish you. It was believed that animals could speak during this time, and traditionally they were given extra food. Outdoor bonfires and candles all devoted to Lussi were popular parts of the local celebrations. People played music and tossed incense into the bonfire flames as they celebrated the sun changing its course and the light returning to the land.

A Candle Spell for Lucy and Little Yule

If you'd like to call on Lucy this year, here is a candle spell for her. Work this on "Little Yule," December 13, Lucy's festival day. This candle may be lit and relit whenever you'd like during the Yuletide season. The magick will hold as long as you burn the candle. By using a tall pillar candle or a seven-day jar candle, you can burn this spell candle off and on throughout the darkest days of the year, the *Lussinatten*.

Gather together the following:

- One large white pillar candle or a white jar candle
- A candleholder or a simple saucer to hold the candle
- A sprig or two of seasonal greenery such as holly or pine to set around the outside of the base of the candle (optional)
- Lighter or matches
- A safe, flat surface to set up on

    Option: You could add saffron to the candle if you have any. It is an expensive cooking herb, so don't go crazy—just add a few strands. If it is unavailable or out of your budget, then do as I do and use a vanilla-scented pillar candle.

Once you have your candle set up, light the pillar and repeat the spell verse:

Lucy, I call on you to bring light into my life

Illuminate my path and brighten up these dark nights.

Bring prosperity to my family and Yuletide cheer

Surround us with your loving warmth as I call you near.

With hope and love, this Yuletide candle spell is spun

For the good of all and bringing harm to no one.

Let the candle burn as long as you would like; just keep an eye on it. You may pinch it out and relight it as you'd like during the season. Just repeat the charm when you relight it, and you are good to go!

DECKING THE HALLS

PERHAPS THE BEST Yuletide
decoration is being wreathed in smiles.

Anonymous

I just adore the Yuletide season. This is probably because my Martha Stewart side gets to come out and play. Okay, okay, I admit that side of me doesn't so much play as run amuck if it has any reason to put up seasonal decorations...

Besides being a trained floral designer, I used to design and decorate holiday trees for a chain of arts and craft stores. One memorable year I had a seasonal job that required me to decorate about one hundred trees (approximately ten trees each at ten different stores), all with different decorating themes and colors, all over the St. Louis area and even into southern Illinois. You should have seen my silver and white ice and crystal tree. I also did a very popular Victorian Santa tree, a sugar plum fairy tree, woodland/bird trees, a Saturnalia tree in royal blue, purple, and gold, all with masks and lots of glitz and glam, and my personal favorite: a celestial-themed tree—they were all awesome, and people went insane over them.

I think that started my obsession and affection for themed winter holiday decorations, and as a Witch I want to make sure that my Yuletide décor at home reflects the enchanting meanings behind the familiar Pagan symbols. Every year I get tons of letters from people complaining that they'd love to decorate their home for Yuletide and put up a tree for their kids, but since they are Witches or Pagans, they don't feel like they should…which is ridiculous.

Did you know that up until the 1950s, decorated trees and greenery were not allowed in most Christian churches? Wanna know why? *Because they were considered too Pagan!* "Deck the Halls," one of the most popular carols of all times, contains not one Christian theme in it. From "the blazing Yule before us" to "troll the ancient Yuletide carol," this old carol is thought to be Welsh in origin and has been around since at least the sixteenth century. Come on, people, get in the spirit of the holiday season!

Look, don't make me show up at your house with a box of Yuletide decorations and floral designing tools (ask my coven sisters—I have been known to descend on a unsuspecting Witch's home who refuses to get into the spirit of the season)… Oh, and a tight budget does not stop me either, because nature is one of the best sources for winter holiday décor. Evergreen branches and pine cones, bright green ivy, holly branches with red berries, rose hips, and dried hydrangea flowers… Pop some popcorn the old-fashioned way and string it up on your trees! Fresh cranberries can also be strung up. Add gilded oak leaves, acorns, magnolia branches, and red twig dogwood… Look around carefully at nature; there are many gorgeous and festive things you can use.

If you don't have any pine or holly in your own yard, try asking a neighbor if you could take a few branches for your holiday decorations. It doesn't hurt to ask. I actually have a standing agreement with a local church that I can take some of the holly branches from their very large and overgrown holly bushes for my own floral projects every Yuletide season. Since I know how to correctly prune the branches and not damage the shrubs, I cut extra and share it with the altar guild ladies of the church, and then they work it into the church's decorations.

No more excuses: Yuletide was and is a Pagan holiday; I say we take it back and show everyone how it's done! If you really want to decorate lavishly for the Yuletide season, go for it. Just be creative and incorporate the sacred plants and our magickal symbols of the season into your decorations and celebrations.

Ellen's Garden of Witchery Journal
THE PLANTS OF YULETIDE

> IT IS ONLY when the cold season comes
> that we know the pine and cypress
> to be evergreens.
>
> *Chinese Proverb*

I have always found it interesting on many levels that the first day of winter, the coldest and most harsh of seasons, actually begins at the time when our daylight hours begin to increase again. After the dark days of late autumn, the light will slowly begin to return to the land. Even though it is winter, the sun will rise a bit earlier and set a bit later each day until Midsummer. Perhaps this is nature's way of reminding us to keep the faith during the coldest part of the year and to not give up hope that the earth will renew itself and that life will return to the land.

While this sounds a little dramatic in modern times, in the old days seeing signs of greenery in the forest and surrounding landscape during the bleakest time of the agricultural year was both a blessing and a promise. And for those of us who follow the Old Path, it still is.

I believe that this is one of the reasons why herbs and evergreen plants are such an integral part of the winter solstice lore and traditions. Since my garden is quiet and sleeping away under a blanket of snow at the moment, I want to discuss those classic plants associated with Yuletide: the evergreen, holly, ivy, and mistletoe.

Evergreen

The evergreen tree is one of the most beloved symbols of the winter holiday season. Draped in dazzling lights and colorful ornaments, the green branches of the evergreen were used to symbolize that life would indeed return to the land. Pine, spruce, and fir trees were considered the seat of the gods; they were the guardians of the forests. The Scandinavians called the spruce tree the "tree of life." In herbal magicks the spruce is also a protective tree.

The balsam fir is a popular winter holiday tree for decorating due to its symmetry and long-lasting fragrance. According to herbal folklore, a fresh branch of fir laid across your bed prevented nightmares, while a branch displayed above the barn door would keep your grain safe from would-be thieves.

The pine tree became a symbol of immortality and rebirth. The fragrance of pine needles was considered to be the "forest's incense." Interestingly enough, burning pine needles is a way to banish negativity and manipulative magick. Placing pine boughs above your doorway keeps negativity and illness from entering, while it encourages prosperity to build within the household. Also, the scent of fresh pine in your home will help to cleanse the atmosphere of the entire home. At the winter solstice the Druids once burned branches of pine to help lure the sun back to earth, and this may be one of the earlier forms of the Yule log.

Bringing evergreen branches and boughs into the home during the darkest days of the year was an act of sympathetic magick. It was often believed that bringing the evergreen branches of pine, spruce, and fir into the home was a way to worship the spirits that guarded the forests. As the pine aligns itself to prosperity magick, adorning your home with this fragrant greenery will add a little of nature's own seasonal magick into your home. Nothing smells like fresh pine, and according to aromatherapy the scent encourages protection, healing, purification, and wealth. Pine has the astrological association of Mars and is aligned to the element of air. In the language of flowers pine symbolizes endurance, friendship, and spiritual energy.

Holly

The holly (*Ilex*) became popular in midwinter festivities thanks to the many magickal cultures and traditions throughout time. As one of the few plants that remains luxuriant and green all year long, the holly—along with pine and ivy—became important symbols for the winter solstice. The holly plant is sacred to the Roman god Saturn, a god of time and agriculture. The Romans first decorated with holly wreaths and greenery to celebrate Saturnalia, a weeklong feast and the big blowout for the Roman year. Gifts were exchanged and wreaths made of holly were prominently displayed everywhere during this ancient midwinter festival.

The holly also has links to Druidic lore because of the plant remaining green throughout the bleakest days of the winter months, and it has ties to faerie lore as well. It was thought that the faeries who lived in the holly bush came inside in the winter months to take a break from the cold temperatures and harsh conditions, so those displayed holly branches made prime hiding spots for the winter faeries. Another interesting bit of Yuletide folklore states that if you place a sprig of fresh holly on your bedpost, this was thought to encourage sweet holiday dreams.

The prickly holly leaves offer protective energy to both people and animals. This herb is associated with the season of midwinter, as you would expect. Besides being linked to the Green Knight and the Holly King, it is also sacred to the Teutonic goddess Holle, or Holda, as the red berries represented drops of her blood.

According to plant folklore, if a holly bush is grown on your property, it will guard you from lightning strikes and is generally considered a protective plant. Also on a practical and earth-friendly note, those red berries are attractive to songbirds, and it adds four-season interest to your outdoor landscape. This year, bring some of nature's magick into your home and add some fresh sprigs and branches of holly to your indoor decorations. Remember to keep the prickly leaves and berries well away from young children, and enjoy the natural enchantment of Yuletide. You can always pick up fresh branches of holly from the local florist in mid-December for your decorations if you do not have a bush growing on your property.

Finally, the holly shrub has the planetary correspondence of Mars and/or Saturn and is aligned to the element of fire. In the language of flowers, holly foliage symbolizes foresight, good will, and a happy home, while the red berries represent Yuletide joy and protection.

Ivy

The ivy is a Pagan symbol of eternal life. The botanical name for the common ivy is *Hedera helix*. This plant is sacred to Bacchus and Dionysus. For this very reason ivy was banned from Christian celebrations, as it was believed that when it was displayed, unrestrained drinking and feasting might take place. (Just like in the old days when Saturnalia was celebrated and those lusty deities were so popular.) The ivy was thought to have the power to ward off drunkenness.

Ivy is the feminine herbal counterpart to holly because of its embracing nature, while the thorny holly plant was considered masculine. Occasionally you will still see references to the Holly King and the Ivy Queen. Today the evergreen ivy has become one of our more popular evergreens for midwinter celebrations. It has the planetary associations of Saturn and the elemental correspondence of water. According to the language of flowers, the ivy promotes protection, fidelity, and fertility. If you'd like to add the magick of ivy to your home at Yuletide, pick up a trailing ivy plant and place it in your home for the Yuletide festivities. According to herbal lore, anywhere ivy grows it repels negativity and bad luck. Oh, and yes: both variegated and solid green ivy may be used successfully in your herbal decorations and midwinter charms.

Mistletoe

The European mistletoe (*Viscum album*) was called the Golden Bough by Aeneas. It also had the folk names of the kissing bunch, kissing bush, or "all-heal" by the Druids. The plant folklore surrounding the mistletoe comes from not only the Druids but the Greeks, the Norse, and the Anglo-Saxons.

Mistletoe is the common name for a group of hemiparasitic plants, meaning a plant that is parasitic and also photosynthetic. The hemiparasites may obtain water, minerals, and other nutrients from their host plant as well as the air surrounding them. While it was once considered a cure for all poisons, *Viscum album* is considered to be a toxic plant. To be on the safe side, keep all varieties of mistletoe foliage and berries well out of the reach of children and pets this holiday season.

The North American variety of the mistletoe has the botanical name of *Phoradendron flavescens* and is grown commercially for holiday decorations. Mistletoe is a striking soft-green parasitic plant that grows on deciduous trees such as apple, ash, hawthorn, birch, and occasionally oak trees. The plant forms pendent bushes 2 to 5 feet in diameter. Mistletoe has been found growing on almost any deciduous tree, preferring those with soft bark. Finding mistletoe growing on an oak tree is rare, which is why the Celts and Druids prized it so. Mistletoe is still used today for fertility; the white berries were thought to resemble drops of semen, hence its links to fertility magick.

The mistletoe was thought to have been gathered in great ceremony by the Druids, and it was then divided up and distributed to all present as a symbol of harmony and fertility.

Some say the tradition of kissing under the mistletoe came from the Norse legend of Balder. The Norse god Balder was the best loved of all the gods. His mother was Frigga, goddess of love and beauty. She loved her son so much that she wanted to make sure no harm would come to him, so she went through the world securing promises from everything that sprang from the four elements—fire, water, air, and earth—that they would not harm her beloved Balder.

Leave it to Loki, the trickster god, to find the loophole: mistletoe. He made an arrow from its wood. To make the prank even nastier, he took the arrow to Hoeder, Balder's brother, who was blind. Guiding Hoeder's hand, Loki directed the arrow at Balder's heart, and Balder fell dead. Frigga's tears for her son then became the mistletoe's white berries. In the version of the story with a happy ending, Balder is restored to life, and Frigga is so grateful that she reverses the reputation of the offending plant, making it a symbol of love and promising to bestow a kiss upon anyone who passes under it.

Amusingly, in old English customs, mistletoe was thought to keep you safe from Witchcraft. You were supposed to wear a wreath of it around your neck for that! In

Scandinavian countries this plant was considered to be so sacred that if enemies happened to meet under it in the woods, they were supposed to lay down their weapons and declare a truce for the day.

This may have encouraged the custom of hanging mistletoe over doorways. As you entered, it was understood that you were abiding by a pledge of peace and friendship, which was sealed with a kiss (or more likely an embrace). Not unlike holly, the mistletoe also extended an invitation to the nature spirits to come inside from the cold on those long winter nights and bring with them some good luck for the family whose home displayed the mistletoe.

Mistletoe has a vast array of magickal folklore attached to its golden boughs. Mistletoe is a parasitic plant and is aligned to the element of air. It is considered to have masculine energies and has the planetary association of the sun. Mistletoe is the state floral emblem of Oklahoma. In the language of flowers, mistletoe states that "I overcome difficult situations."

Herbal Charm for Yuletide

Try this simple Yuletide charm as you hang up and arrange your Yuletide greenery in your abode this year. Deck your halls and mantles as you like; then, as you finish, repeat this charm with intention. This charm incorporates the four featured Yuletide plants of this chapter: pine, holly, ivy, and mistletoe.

When a Witch decks the halls with boughs of holly
Expect that the Yuletide feast will be jolly.
Green ivy for good luck and fertility
Add pine boughs and branches for prosperity.
The Druid's golden bough we called mistletoe
Encourages kisses and make cheeks to glow.
Now add a touch of magick and a pinch of glee
Welcome renewal in Yuletide's season of peace.

Close up the charm with these lines:

By the bright magick of a midwinter sun
As I will, so mote it be, and let it harm none.

GINGERBREAD AT YULETIDE

AND I HAD but one penny in the world,
thou should'st have it to buy gingerbread.

William Shakespeare

This is an old-fashioned recipe and one I use every year. You can ice these cookies if you like, but my family and friends prefer them plain.

These are a fabulous cookie with a cup of coffee, warm cider, or hot tea. (My father eats these with applesauce. I gave him a big bag of these cookies with a jar of applesauce for his birthday this past November; he was thrilled.) At my house, my adult children get quite annoyed if I do not bake these cookies at the winter holidays. Now that two of my sons are out of the nest and share a fancy apartment, they actually volunteer to come over and "help" me bake so they can get their share of these cookies. They have become a Yuletide tradition.

Recently I began bringing these cookies to my sister's home for Thanksgiving for the kids to snack on. However, while waiting for the turkey, the adults devoured them as well. My twelve-year-old niece, Livvy, quietly announced that she'd like for me to teach her how to make gingerbread cookies. Her father (my brother) wholeheartedly agreed. (He loves these too.) So I'll have my niece over to my house this year while she is on winter break, a few days before the winter solstice, and show her how it's done.

At the moment, ginger is a very popular cooking spice. You can't turn on a cooking show without someone extolling the uses and values of fresh ginger. Fresh ginger root

is easily found in the produce section of most grocery stores. Also, you may wish to try crystallized ginger. Those smaller pieces would be ideal for baking and for magickal work.

You may find it interesting to note that ginger (*Zingiber officinale*) has the planetary association of Mars. It is aligned with the element of fire and may be worked into spells for love, prosperity, and success. You can sprinkle ground ginger over documents, papers, and contracts for success. Work with the whole ginger root for protection magick. A small piece of the root or some crystallized ginger easily could be added to protective sachets or charm bags.

Finally, ginger may be eaten to boost personal power before you start your spell-casting; the ginger is thought to "fire you up." By raising your energy, you can then channel that into your magickal workings. If you want to try that, then I suggest eating the crystallized ginger if you are looking for a boost, or just bake up some gingerbread cookies on a cold winter's afternoon. I have to say, there is something magickal about a warm gingerbread cookie. Here is the recipe that I use. (NOTE: Blackstrap molasses gives these cookies a darker color and a deeper flavor, though you can use regular molasses too.)

Gingerbread People Cookies

1½ cups dark blackstrap molasses (12-ounce bottle)

1 cup packed brown sugar

⅔ cup cold water

⅓ cup vegetable shortening (such as Crisco; do not use butter)

7 cups all-purpose flour (yes, 7 cups of flour)

2 teaspoons baking soda

1 teaspoon salt

1 teaspoon ground allspice

2 teaspoons ground ginger

1 teaspoon ground cloves

1 teaspoon ground cinnamon

Assorted cookie cutters: gingerbread men, stars, trees, bells, wreaths, crescent moons, snowmen…

Mix molasses, brown sugar, water, and shortening in a large bowl. Mix in remaining ingredients by hand. Cover and refrigerate at least 2 hours.

Heat oven to 350 degrees. Roll dough ¼-inch thick on a floured board. (This is important! The dough has to be thick, not thin, or your cookies will not stay soft.) Cut out the holiday shapes with floured cookie cutters. Place about 2 inches apart on a lightly greased cookie sheet or a sheet sprayed with nonstick cooking spray. You may also use parchment paper for a quicker cleanup.

Bake 10–12 minutes or until no indentation remains when touched. Cool. These cookies also freeze well.

• • • •

Personal Lesson for Yuletide
THE WITCH MEETS SANTA

IT'S ALWAYS GOOD for us to pause
And think a while of Santa Claus
That jolly symbol we revere
When we approach the changing year.

Marshall M. Morgan

On a cold and dark mid-December evening, my husband and I decided to go take in our town's historic district's holiday celebrations. So we bundled up and went down to enjoy the old-fashioned atmosphere. This is a huge event, and the shops are open on Main Street for two special nights during the week in the holiday season. It is a lot of fun and very festive. The cobblestone roads are lit with white holiday lights, lots of fresh evergreen garlands, and candles for the festivities. Santas from many other lands and other costumed holiday characters are out and about roaming the streets, carrying lanterns, chatting up the tourists, and telling their tales.

We no sooner got out of the car than a freezing drizzle began. The weatherman had said it was supposed to hold off until later that evening. Apparently he was wrong. Again. Resigned, I pulled up my hood and tied my scarf tighter around my neck.

We had no sooner started walking down the sidewalk when a cry of "Good Yule!" made us both turn around. There stood Santa Lucia, or St. Lucy. We both automatically called back "Good Yule!" and the woman portraying Lucy jolted, smiled, and waved at us. Apparently most folks do not answer her back in kind. Anyway, her costume was spot-on: white robe, red sash, a wreath of evergreen in her long blond hair. She had battery-operated flickering candles in her crown for safety, and they looked great. She was immediately pounced on by several small children wanting the cards that each of the characters pass out. (It's kind of a "thing"—you are supposed to collect all the different holiday character cards each year.)

I had to smile at the synchronicity. It just warmed my witchy heart to hear somebody cry out *Good Yule*. I had only just finished writing the Lucy section in this chapter a few days before, and now the first character we saw was Lucy. During the week all the holiday characters are rotating. There are thirty of them, so there is no way to know who will be out during the week. On the weekends all of the Santas and characters are out, but on a weeknight—well, you never know which ones you will see. Cheered despite the cold and the miserable freezing drizzle, my husband and I walked along the sidewalk arm in arm and did a little window shopping.

My husband remarked that with the weather coming in, any smart Santa would be holed up in the local winery, staying warm and dry. I could only agree. So we strolled along and were delighted to notice that the Santas we did see were out and about, jovially working the crowds, posing for pictures with children and adults, and passing out those cards, freezing rain or no.

A bit later, we were just about to duck into one of our favorite shops when a booming male cry of "Good Yule to you!" was called from behind us. Emphasis on the *ooh* in "you." It sounded like the Muppets' Swedish Chef saying "yoooooou."

We turned around to discover the Scandinavian Santa Julenisse, complete with his goat, Yuley. He climbed up the steps to join us on the shop's covered front porch, and he winked at the costumed carolers who were staying dry and singing away under that covered porch.

I started to chuckle as my husband shot me an incredulous look, and then he started to grin. I mean, really—we've been married for almost thirty years, you'd think he'd be used to these little coincidences by now. Apparently my chuckling and my husband's grinning was all it took for the actor to launch into his accented monologue about his native costume, who he was, where he came from, and his sidekick, the stuffed animal goat Yuley.

He informed my husband and I that if we were good this year, then he would knock on our door on the night of the twenty-fourth and hand us our presents himself. If we were naughty…well, then he would knock, run, and hide in the bushes, and then he and Yuley the goat would laugh at us. Julenisse was funny, friendly, and cheered the both of us immensely.

He handed us both a card and departed, saying "Good Yule." And then he explained that in *his* country people say "Good Yule."

I replied back, "We say it around here too, sir. Good Yule!" On cue, the Victorian carolers asked us if we would like to hear a song; I requested "Deck the Halls," and they launched into a four-part harmony without missing a beat. My husband only shook his head, laughed, and opened the shop door for me. Who says there is no magick in the season anymore?

Reflections on Yuletide
THE REAL REASON FOR THE SEASON

BLESSED IS THE season which engages
the whole world in a conspiracy of love.

Hamilton Wright Mabie

The sun and all its magick rules the Wheel of the Year, especially now. Sometimes in December it can be tough for a Witch to be bombarded with all the manger scenes and baby Jesus stuff. Instead of sulking or copping an attitude, focus on the Pagan elements that are still all over our popular culture's celebration of the season.

Go ahead and cheerfully say "Good Yule" or "Happy solstice" in response to a "Merry Christmas," or just say "Happy holidays." First off, it is more polite and certainly thoughtful to say *happy holidays* to the public at this time of year. And if you say it with a smile, you will get a smile in return.

Go ahead and send out holiday cards. What's stopping you? There are beautiful cards featuring nature themes, snowmen, and Santa Claus, and also there are Pagan greeting cards you can buy individually. This year I found a cute Santa in a wheelbarrow with a mini tree and a bird perched on the toe of his boot. It was gardenish, natural, and festive, all at the same time.

Personally I go for the cards that are blank inside and then write my own message. Or you can make your own cards. Head over to yon local craft supply store and have at it. My friend Ember makes her own cards every year, and they are stunning. I save the ones she makes every year and scrapbook it with my coven photos from our Yule celebration.

Feeling bombarded by all the holiday music? Maybe you need to listen with a whole new set of ears, my witchy friend. There are plenty of popular holiday songs that are less Christian and more celebratory. How about "Winter Wonderland," "Let It Snow," and every Pagan's favorite, "Deck the Halls"? You could live on the edge and sing other carols and holiday songs, just substitute the word *solstice* for *Christmas*. It works out great.

I personally take a fiendish delight in singing the "Carol of the Bells" and switching out the word *solstice* for *Christmas*…I sang that song my senior year in high school. I was a member of the a cappella choir—you know, the choirs that sing without musical accompaniment? I love that song. Like most altos, I can still do piggyback harmony…

but I digress. I mean, think about it: solstice and Christmas have the same amount of syllables, so it works out lyrically. The possibilities are endless. "It's beginning to look a lot like solstice everywhere I go" or "I'm dreaming of a white solstice."

This works as well with the more modern songs that we grew up with. How about that old song that was sung by Burl Ives, from the animated *Rudolph, the Red-Nosed Reindeer*? "Have a holly jolly solstice. It's the best time of the year!"

Improvise, adapt, and enjoy yourself and the winter holiday season. This is the time to celebrate the rebirth of the sun. The light half of the year begins, and our daylight hours get longer and stronger every day. The winter solstice truly is the reason for the season.

CHAPTER 6

Imbolc
Candlemas
FEBRUARY 1

LET US LOVE winter, for it
is the spring of genius.

Pietro Aretino

At this time of year your magickal focus turns inward. This is a wonderful opportunity to quietly center your personal powers and turn your attention to yourself. It's time to take stock and to work on personal development and your intuitive gifts. Yes, you can actually strengthen your own psychic talents. This is done in a solitary fashion, with good old-fashioned experimentation and practice. You need to be alone to do this type of work. Sometimes, whether you are a member of a coven or not, a Witch has to do some solitary work and put some effort and emphasis on personal development, your own psychic abilities, and soul searching. There is no better time for this, in my opinion, than around Imbolc.

The winter holidays are behind us, our routines have returned to normal, and now that January has ended and February begun, we settle in and brace ourselves for the final months of winter. At the coldest time of the year, when connecting outdoors with nature would be uncomfortable or risky due to extreme cold for many of us, your best option is to bunker inside your warm, comfortable home. Allow the cold, ice, and snow to wrap around and separate you just a bit from the rest of the world. It's like a natural barrier to intrusion and interruptions.

Don't think of the snow and cold as a prelude to cabin fever, think of it as a time of introspection and personal journeying. Now, should you live in a more mild climate and it is not cold and snowy outdoors, then lucky you. However, the Wheel of the Year's energy is still in play, and the energy is still focused internally. Test yourself in simple ways with your psychic talents at this time of year. This may be as simple as working more with your favorite divinatory tool such as the tarot or runes, or perhaps this would be a good time to practice working with a pendulum. Use this quiet and introspective season to buff up your skills and see what you learn.

Incorporate all of these skills into your magick. Dare to take a good, hard look at your shadow side. Shadow work is considered to be a deeply personal type of magickal reflection and study. We each need to look inside and face our shadows and see what we are so afraid of. Take a look at what you try to keep hidden and ask yourself what you can do to heal, change, or embrace about yourself.

I have seen this intellectualized to death, with elaborate rituals and so forth. Try sitting down, putting on some music that you like to meditate to, and then focusing on yourself; see where that leads you. Use your divinatory tool and ask what it is you most need to know, then apply that information to your life and make some positive changes. This is shadow work—looking at the darkest, scariest aspects of the self, facing them, learning to work with them, and then to moving forward wiser for the experience.

What you are doing is calling out the shadow side of yourself and bringing it into the light, which is a perfect activity for this season. Imbolc brings us the gifts of intuition, inspiration, and light during the darkest days of the year. We only need to be brave enough to go in search of them.

A Little History
A Festival of Candlelight and Inner Light

> Just as a candle cannot burn without fire,
> men cannot live without a spiritual life.
>
> *Buddha*

Imbolc is considered one of the four greater sabbats, which are the sabbat dates from the Celtic calendar that do not change over the years. Like many Celtic holidays, this sabbat begins at sundown on February 1 and goes until sundown on February 2. This is the festival day of the Celtic triple goddess Brigid. As I researched this particular sabbat I had to dig deep for good information, but I found it quietly shining out at me in very unexpected places.

While looking through old folklore books about the winter holidays, I was fascinated to discover little tidbits of history about an old February celebration the Christians called Candlemas, or Imbolc, as it is typically called in Witch and Pagan circles today.

You may also see it simply referred to as Brigid, which takes its name from the goddess whose festival day this is. Honestly, calling this sabbat Candlemas has fallen a wee bit out of favor, as many modern magickal practitioners find it a bit too Christian of a title for the sabbat.

Seems this early February holiday had more than a little controversy surrounding it (even for the Christians). *Well, well,* I thought. *Dissention even among the Christian ranks? Really?* Now I was intrigued.

Here is what we know: in the old days, the holiday was also known as "the processions with candles." In the Middle Ages the church blessed candles for the whole year on the date of February 2; thus the name Candle-mass began. It was actually a mass, or ceremony, for the candles.

Here is where I perked up. *Okay, so let me get this straight… a ceremony or ritual was performed to make the candles sacred and to remove any negativity from them so they would be filled with a holy purpose?* Well, hello. Candle anointing and blessing, anyone? That's very basic Craft practice.

It also seems that for a time the practice of candle burning to mark the holiday of February 2 fell out of favor. (Because it was just a bit too—wait for it—Pagan.) According to one source, the actual blessing that was invoked on the candles was so "in whatsoever place they shall be lighted or put, the devil may depart or tremble and fly away, with all his ministers from habitation, and not presume to disturb it" (Crippen, *Christmas and Christmas Folklore*, 172).

Back in 1548, the Church of England discontinued the practice of "candle-bearing" on this day. However, it did not stop some of the local clergy, who marked the day by the use of an "exceptionally large" number of lit candles and tapers.

Then, almost a hundred years later, in 1628, a Puritan observed that a certain local bishop had renewed the custom of setting up candles in honor of our lady. I am making a wild assumption here that when the book said "Our Lady" that the author was actually referring to Mary—you know, that gal who is called a Divine Mother?

To paraphrase Shakespeare, *a mother goddess by any other name*…. I mean, honestly; take a good look at all the statues and versions of the Virgin Mary. Many of them show her standing on a slim sickle of a moon. Both antique and modern representations of Mary are usually of a woman surrounded by starry skies or with an ocean or floral backdrop and standing on a crescent moon. I double-checked—I even braved a Catholic supply shop to look at the more popular prayer cards…the things I do for my readers.

Yeah, there I was, all discreet with a tucked pentagram under my sweater and perusing through various plastic statues of Mary and laminated prayer cards. It was kind of fun being all undercover and everything. Every time I found another picture of Mary with the moon—that same crescent moon that is a symbol for our Maiden aspect of the Goddess—I made a mark on my (invisible and imaginary) Goddess scoreboard.

And don't even get me started on all the iconic Aztec images that are associated with the picture of the obviously pregnant Lady of Guadalupe, also known as the Empress of the Americas. She is dark, wears a turquoise robe, is wreathed in the flames of the sun, and stands on a black crescent moon. Even the pattern of her rose-colored dress has Aztec designs in it.

Ever wonder why all those natives converted to Catholicism so quickly way back in the day? Because this vision and manifestation of the Divine Mother was seen in Mexico on Tepeyac Hill, where a temple to an Aztec goddess once stood. The Lady of Guadalupe is an icon filled with familiar Aztec imagery; that's why she was embraced by the indigenous people so quickly. Guadalupe was one of their own.

But back to our Puritan Candlemas tale from the 1600s…supposedly it took the bishop all of an afternoon climbing up ladders and so forth to make the daring candle display for Our Lady in the cathedral church. It was remarked upon that the number of candles lit were a staggering two hundred and twenty. In addition, there were sixteen torches burning. How scandalous!

Still, it's hard to keep a good festival of light down. Furthermore, it was noted in 1790 in *Gentlemen's Magazine* that a contributor had written how a few years prior, while attending a service on the Sunday before Candlemas, one collegiate church was lit up "from an immense number of candles." Well, well. Isn't that interesting?

CANDLEMAS AND IMBOLC

IF CANDLEMAS DAY be fair and clear,
there'll be two winters in the year.

Old Scottish Proverb

In the Witch's Wheel of the Year, Candlemas, or Imbolc, is one of the four cross-quarter days. It is the halfway point between winter and spring. On this day, weather divination was performed to see if the winter would end early or if it would hang on until the bitter end, well into April. In the old days and in Europe, it was a hedgehog who was the divinatory animal in question. If he came out of his burrow and it was sunny, then he would see his shadow. This was thought to frighten the hedgehog, and he was supposed to go back in his den and sleep the rest of the winter away—six more long weeks.

In the United States we don't have hedgehogs. What we have is a groundhog, and his special day of February 2, also known as Groundhog's Day. This is the halfway point between the winter solstice and the spring equinox. There are all sorts of weather omens to tell people when spring will truly begin. It was sunny this year on Imbolc, and true to form, winter held on for every bit of those six following weeks!

This was a day for weather omens and magick. Another old favorite gardener's proverb was "When the forsythias bloom, expect two more snows." (That certainly held true here this year too.)

In early February it can be hard to picture that spring is only weeks away, as ice coats everything and snow and winds howl outside. But go take a look at the buds on the trees—they *are* getting bigger. Each week that passes brings us that much closer to spring.

While researching the sabbat of Imbolc, this winter I spent weeks in the library going through research material, only to find next to nothing. I managed to resist the urge to growl in frustration while perusing the stacks, as the librarians do tend to frown upon that sort of behavior.

These would be the same librarians that send you the death ray glare if you start laughing too loudly in the research section of the public library. A Witch can only take so much over-romanticized Christianity while researching a Pagan holiday, for Goddess's sake! We won't mention what happens when you drop your head to the table in frustration and then sit there, head down on top of the reference books, and mutter to yourself.

For example, did you know that the historians of old found it *peculiar* that the church's festival matched up to the day of the festival of *Bride*? This supposedly long-forgotten deity is known by many names, including Brid (which is pronounced *Breed*) and Brigantes, Brighid, or Bridget.

Let me just be the first to say, "Well, duh!" *Of course* it matched up. The Christians tried to adapt this festival and make it into their own to convert the people to the new religion, just like they did with Yule and Christmas. One folklorist from the 1920s commented that there was even a "quaint Irish custom" held on February 1, the night before Candlemas, where the women of the house would set a basket containing a sheaf of oats on the hearth before retiring for bed in the evening.

As they placed the basket on the hearth, they were to have said, "Brid is come; Brid is welcome!" If in the morning there should appear shapes of symbols in the ashes of the fire, it was an omen of prosperity for the coming year. This is actually an old Pagan custom to welcome the hearth goddess Brigid into the home for the year. Variations on this "custom" are still being practiced by magickal folks today.

Also, I found it hilarious that the 1920s-era folklorist in question was scandalized that there had continued a practice in some British counties of a school-sponsored "Candlemas bleeze," or bonfire. Apparently, whichever young boy and girl brought the most furze (evergreen shrub) wood for the bonfire were crowned King and Queen of Candlemas. They were crowned, enthroned, and saluted.

Afterwards, the whole school threw a party with biscuits (cookies) and whisky punch, and spent the rest of the day playing games and generally making merry. Yes, that is correct. Whisky punch. At. School.

Damn, you know that had to be a popular celebration. The account of the Candlemas revelries ends amusingly with the author's prudish opinion that the "best thing about this custom was its discontinuance" (Crippen, *Christmas and Christmas Folklore*).

THE GODDESS BRIGID

THE STORY OF the sun goddess who brings light back to the world is ancient, but it's also a story for our time that offers hope for renewal.

Bando Tamasaburo

Brigid is a very popular goddess with Witches and Pagans today; she is a Celtic triple goddess of smith-craft, the hearth fire, and the flame of inspiration for bards and poets. Brigid is described as a titian-haired maiden wreathed in flames or surrounded by a bright light. Brigid was born at dawn, and the light was so bright when she came into the world that the cottage looked as if it were on fire. If you are looking for a solar deity to lead you out of the dark days of winter or for healing, illumination, or inspiration, she's the perfect deity to call upon.

Many Witches get so wrapped up in the idea of Brigid with the smith's anvil and forge and of her sitting quietly by the hearth flame that they sometimes forget there is more to this deity than first appears. This is a deity with staying power. She was a goddess who walked the lands and brought light and life everywhere she went.

You may recall that the people loved her so much that even after Christianity took over, they refused to give her up—so the church homogenized her into a midwife to Mary. Saint Brigit then became the patron saint of the family and the hearth. Even so, that's not too far off the original mark. Prayers were offered to Brigid the goddess, as she was a patroness of childbirth, and also to Brigit the saint, again for the safe delivery of a child. Brigid does have many links to healers and midwives, who were often one and the same.

This goddess is also connected to sacred springs and wells of healing. According to Celtic folklore, the goddess Brigid was the daughter of the Dagda and a woman of the Tuatha de Danann, so she came from a god and a woman of the fae. This was no meek maiden sitting quietly by the fire. As a goddess presiding over healings and births, she held an awesome amount of power. Brigid became the wife of Bres and was mother to a son named Ruadan.

This goddess was honored across Ireland, Wales, France, and Spain. She was called the Triple Brigits or the Three Mothers. She also had the title of "Fiery Arrow." Her sanctuary was in Kildare, Ireland, where a sacred fire was kept lit continuously for nine centuries. It was said that nine priestesses attended her sacred flame at first, then after a time this duty was passed to nuns from the convent at Kildare. The fiery Brigid, it seems, will always find a way to bring illumination and inspiration, no matter what guise she is in.

An Imbolc Spell to Celebrate the Goddess Brigid

Here is an Imbolc night spell that calls for illumination. As you would expect, this spell calls upon the goddess Brigid; it is her festival day, after all. Work this magick after sundown on February 1. Ask her to bring illumination, healing, and inspiration into your life. She is sure to show you the way.

Gather these supplies:

- 9 plain tealight candles (these burn for approximately 4 hours)
- 9 glass holders for the candles
- A representation of Brigid (such as a picture—check the Internet and do an image search)
- A lighter or matches
- A safe, flat surface or altar to set up on

Set the tealight candles in their holders and arrange them in a circle. Place the picture of the goddess flat on the work surface, in the center of the candleholders. Begin with the candle at the top of the circle and light them all, going one by one and in a clockwise manner.

Once they are all flickering away, repeat the verse:

These nine candles do illuminate this Imbolc night
May Brigid bring inspiration and joy to my life.
Just as those nine priestesses once tended your flame
Triple Brigid, bless me now as I call your name.

Bride, Brigit, and Brid—all of these sacred names and more

Please bring warmth, enlightenment, and healing to my door.

By light and magick, this spell is spun

For the good of all, with harm to none.

Close the spell up with:

Brigid is come!

Brigid is welcome!

Allow the candles to burn out in a safe place until they go out on their own. Save the picture of Brigid for future workings or add it into your book of shadows. Happy Imbolc!

If you care to jazz up this spell a bit, you could add more corresponding items to your altar. White and red flowers are lovely; carnations would be good, as they have a spicy scent and are associated with the element of fire. Plus, they are affordable.

Some classic magickal correspondences for Brigid include milk, freshly baked bread, the four-spoked Brigid's cross, and the colors of red and white for fire and ice— the fire of the hearth flames and the ice and snow outside covering the land.

I prefer to use the colors of purple and white for Imbolc because it makes me think of the purple crocus and hellebores popping out of the white snow. At this time of year, this is a visualization that keeps my hopes up while I wait for winter to end so I can finally get back to working in the gardens.

Herbal Magick at Imbolc

Nature gives to every time and
season some beauties of its own.

Charles Dickens

Depending on where you live, it may be hard to wrap your mind around herbal magicks in the coldest and darkest days of winter. But honestly, herb magick may be worked at any time of the year, even for those of us in the northern climates or just the four classic seasons. Sometimes I think we need to work even more with plants and herbs during the darkest times, as this will cheer us up and help us to stay connected to the natural world.

Plants associated with the goddess Brigid include some of the earliest blooming spring flowers, those hellebores and crocus. The hellebore (*Helleborus*) is a plant that has had a steady rise in popularity for the home gardener over the past few years. The hellebore is a popular plant for the cottage garden due to its reputation of magick and Witchcraft and its very early blossoming time. Many varieties are evergreen or frost resistant. These shade-loving perennials are both decorative and deer resistant; also, many of the varieties are considered to be poisonous—which is why deer leave them alone.

Hellebores are considered classic Witch garden plants. They bloom in late winter or early spring and are often in shades of purple, deep burgundy, and green. The flowers may come in a single or double-flowering varieties, and they are quietly beautiful. The

common name is green or black hellebore. The botanical term is *Helleborus niger*. Its folk name is Lenten rose or Christmas rose.

Hellebores are excellent plants to work with for protection magick in the Imbolc season. Keep in mind, however, that they are not to be consumed. Hellebores and digitalis have similar effects. The hellebore plant is sacred to the goddess Hecate, as are most poisonous plants. This plant is associated with the planet Saturn and has conflicting magickal information when it comes to an elemental assignment. Some sources say its elemental correspondence is water, while others say fire. (How appropriate for an herbal Imbolc tie-in, as Brigid is also associated with fire and water!)

Hellebore Herbal Spell for Protection and Hex-Breaking

According to herbal folklore, hellebore banished evil and could counteract baneful magicks. It can be grown in the home garden to allow its natural magick to filter out for protection. This flowering plant is also used to break hexes and curses; you may use the fresh flowers or a leaf for this purpose. However, please be careful with this perennial. I would place a leaf or a single flower in a charm bag. Be sure to wash your hands well after touching this plant. Remember, it is toxic.

Another safer option is to work with the plant where it grows in the garden. This is a similar practice to what I suggested in my book *Garden Witch's Herbal* in the wildflowers and witchery chapter. As it is illegal to cut or dig up wildflowers, I suggested that readers leave the plants alone in the wild and work with them wherever they happen to find them. Apply that same idea of working with the hellebore plant in the garden while leaving it undisturbed.

Hunker down next to the plant and hold your hands out above it (a couple inches above the blooming plant is perfect). Now ask the plant to lend its energies to yours. When you feel the energy of the plant begin to tingle against your palms, then repeat this herbal protection charm:

> *Hellebore, hear my plea on this winter's night*
> *Protect me well and cause my enemies fright.*
> *May your natural magick now protect and defend me*
> *As I break any hex or spell that was cast against me.*
> *By the powers of the earth, this spell is spun*
> *As I will, so must it be, an' let it harm none.*

Quietly thank the plant in your own words for lending its energies to yours. Stand up and leave the plant as you found it. Go about your day assured that your herb magick will work and work well.

An Imbolc Recipe to Warm Your Heart

Winter is the time for comfort,
for good food and warmth. For the touch
of a friendly hand and for talk beside
the fire: it is the time for home.

Edith Sitwell

Yes, we are making the jump from toxic plants to a seasonal Imbolc recipe. Made you wake up and pay attention, didn't it? There is something about baked goods on a blustery winter day…they just make you feel more cozy.

If you are in the mood to bake, consider the following recipe. This is a family favorite for blueberry scones. Scones are an easy quick bread to make; this recipe is for a lowfat version. Now, don't turn up your nose because I said "lowfat." You can enjoy these delicious pastries in moderation and not have to worry so much about the calories!

Blueberries are available year-round and are a very magickal fruit. They are also very good for you, as blueberries have the highest antioxidant capacity of all fresh fruit. Plus, fresh blueberries are rumored to keep you fit, healthy, and, best of all, they are natural mood-lifters. Also, according to old folklore, blueberries are supposed to help protect you from psychic attack and negativity. That's a win-win in my book!

Blueberry Scones for Imbolc

2½ cups all-purpose flour

¼ cup sugar

2 teaspoons baking powder

⅛ teaspoon nutmeg

2 tablespoons chilled butter

½ cup fresh blueberries (picked over and rinsed)

1 teaspoon grated lemon zest

⅔ cup plus 2 teaspoons skim milk

1 beaten egg

1 egg white

Spray a baking sheet with nonstick cooking spray or line with parchment paper; set aside. In a mixing bowl, stir together flour, sugar, baking powder, and nutmeg. With a pastry blender, cut in the butter until the mixture resembles coarse crumbs. Fold in blueberries and lemon zest, then make a well in the center of the dry mixture.

In a separate bowl, mix together ⅔ cup milk, egg, and egg white. Add milk mixture all at once to dry mixture. Using a fork, stir until just moistened.

Turn dough out onto a lightly floured surface. Quickly and gently, knead the dough by folding and pressing dough for 10 or 12 strokes, or until smooth. (Don't overknead the scones—it makes them tough. Handle them gently for best results.)

Pat out kneaded dough into a 9-inch circle, then cut into 10 wedges (think pizza slices). Transfer wedges with a spatula to the prepared baking sheet. Brush tops of the scones with the 2 tablespoons of milk.

Bake in a 450-degree oven about 12 minutes, or until the scones are a light golden brown.

Serve warm with lowfat butter or light cream cheese. These make a wonderful treat to share for your Imbolc gatherings!

• • • •

The Value of a Coven Sister

"Help one another" is part
of the religion of sisterhood.

Louisa May Alcott

A week before Imbolc I received a call and a request for magickal help from my friend Noir. Noir and I go way back—she had once been a student of mine, and we had known each other for years. Noir was now living about four hours away from my hometown, but we still saw each other a few times a year and chatted on the phone often. Noir was happily married, and she and her husband have an adorable little boy.

Noir had a close friend who had been struggling to conceive for years, and her friend had decided to try fertility treatments one more time. The young woman in question and I had spoken the previous year, and she had asked me if I ever saw her with children—emphasis on the word *saw*. I had done a clairvoyant reading for the young woman, and during that reading I had a vision of her with a mini van, cheerfully hauling a bunch of kids to soccer practice. But what I saw were children of many different races piling out of the van, so, to me, this symbolized that motherhood was going to be in her life—but probably through adoption.

We talked about that, and she told me that her husband wasn't ready to go through the trial of adoption. They really wanted to try conceiving a baby of their own, even if that meant the expense and stress of fertility treatments.

The young woman seemed a little down after our reading, but as she was a close friend of one of my friends, I quietly told her if she ever decided to try fertility treatments, I would happily work magick for her to help increase her chances of a successful pregnancy.

Well, several months after the reading, the young woman was gearing up for her next round of fertility treatments. She had asked Noir to contact me and to request my help on a magickal level. When Noir asked me about working the magick for her friend, I was happy to agree. Not only because I liked the young woman but because the timing was excellent—Imbolc was only a week away.

Imbolc is all about life springing out of the darkness. It's a time of fertility and a time of hope and new life. Plus my coven was meeting together in a few days, and I knew they would be happy to send along some magick to a woman who needed a little extra help with her fertility treatments. I sent out an email to the coven. They were happy to help, and they all agreed that the timing was excellent, so we added some magickal work for her into the plans for the Imbolc celebration.

A few days later, the coven met for our Imbolc celebration. We met at Ember's house, and what a lovely time we had. The weather behaved itself (no snow or ice that night), so everyone had an easy drive. Since we gathered together later in the evening, we ate a late dinner. Each of us always brings a dish to share. Fiona brought an awesome salad, Ember made yummy vegetable soup, I brought a bottle of wine and some fruit, cheese, and crackers, Ruby brought spiced wine, and Ravyn, bless her, made a wickedly good cheesecake with berries and brought along a bottle of blackberry dessert wine, which was very suitable for the sabbat.

Herbal folklore has it that blackberries are associated with the goddess Brigid. It's interesting to note that in herbal magick, the berries and leaves of the blackberry (*Rubus fructicosus*) are used for both healing and prosperity spells. Since Brigid is often called on for healing, this makes perfect sense to me.

Fresh blackberries may be pricey during the winter months, but they are fun to indulge in for your sabbat celebration. You could always pick up a bottle of blackberry wine like my coven sister did. Yum! One of my favorite local Missouri wineries makes a fantastic semi-sweet blackberry wine that is wonderful paired with chocolate. This would be a very appropriate and delicious libation for your Imbolc celebrations.

So we shared dinner together, had a couple glasses of wine, and caught up with each other. One of our members had to work at the last moment and was unable to attend, but five out of six were there, and Yule seemed very far away as we sat and visited and enjoyed each other's company.

We celebrated with a ritual for transformation and moving from the inner contemplation to an outward manifestation. It was a simple but lovely ritual, and the five of us gathered around the altar, each lighting white candles while we honored the goddess Brigid and spoke about the things we wished to have manifest during the year—success, prosperity, good health, happiness, and so forth. We also sent energy to the young woman who was starting fertility treatments. That particular part of the ritual was interesting. A big jolt in the energy was felt, and everyone stood there and grinned at each other.

Our coven rituals are always written by whoever is hosting the gathering, and we take turns throughout the year. That way everybody shares in the responsibility, and with each of us taking turns, it gives us a nice balance and some variety to the rituals themselves. Typically we choose the dates for our coven gatherings for the coming year at the Yule gathering. We all sit down with our calendars for the coming year and figure out who's taking what day, where and when we will gather together to celebrate the sabbats, and then we also try to work in a nice balance of full and dark moon gatherings as well. It makes for less stress and more fun when everyone takes a turn writing and leading a ritual.

After the ritual was finished, we sat and visited and laughed until the early morning hours. We have such a great time when we all get together. Maybe it's just one of those witchy things, but I feel closer to and have a stronger bond with my coven sisters than I do to any of my relatives (not counting my husband and children, of course). To me, family is not so much about bloodlines. It's about love and the people who you let into your heart—those individuals are your family. Fiona brought this up that night, and I think that this particular old saying is very true: "One genuine friend is more valuable than a thousand relatives."

When I link hands with the women in my coven and we raise energy together, the sheer force astounds me every single time. So, to me, the real value of a coven sister is that not only are they my dearest witchy friends, they are also the family of my heart.

Postscript: A year later, the woman we did magick for is five months into a healthy pregnancy, and another coven member—who had been told she could not conceive—just had her first baby.

Ellen's Garden of Witchery Journal
Greenhouse Therapy

No winter lasts forever,
no spring skips its turn.

Hal Borland

It's easy to get down in the dumps by the end of winter. You think you are doing so great and then, before you know it, you have the wintertime blues. There is a condition that happens to folks who do not get enough sunlight in the winter months. It's called seasonal affective disorder (SAD). There are treatments for this, and one of them is light therapy.

I know: I battle with this every year, especially in late winter. The popular theory on this is because I am part plant. I mope when it's cold and gloomy out and I can't get outside to take my walks or work in the gardens. The winter holidays keep me busy, and it does not kick in until mid-February. That's when I start watching for gardening magazines and scowling out through the windows and complaining about the snow, ice, and cold, wishing for spring.

The best cure I have ever found? Well, if it's not too cold, then I bundle up and take a brisk walk outside. Or if it's snowing, then I cowboy up, dig out the cars, and then shovel the snow off the sidewalk and driveway—anything to move and to get outdoors.

Should I really feel blue and it's very nasty and bitter cold, then I go to the local nursery greenhouses and walk around inside of them for a half hour and simply enjoy the green. Oh, that yummy warmth inside—the rich, earthy smell of the potting soil, the moisture and the humidity, and that blast of green—it all really helps me. After all, green is the color of hope and of life.

So on nasty, frigid days, if I'm really missing the light and the warmth and the color green and my gardens, I quietly walk around inside of a local greenhouse. It cheers me up the minute I hit the doorway. I walk around and soak up the warmth and vibrations of all those plants that are rushing to grow. I close my eyes, breathe deep, and pull in that garden smell. I let the bright green color of the foliage fill me up with power and cheer. And it works like a charm!

Now, before someone accuses me of vamping the plants, relax. I'm soaking up atmosphere—the scents, the sounds, the colors—not the life force of the plants themselves. Sheesh. Write about psi-vamps once and everyone starts pointing fingers.

Anyway, you can safely soak up the smells, the light, and the sounds in a lush greenhouse. Try it for yourself. The worst that could happen is you'll end up scooping out the best new varieties of plants for your garden or taking home a couple of houseplants. Besides, I'm sure the greenhouse staff would be devastated to sell you something during their slow season.

If you want to give something back to the greenhouse, then buy some plants from them while you are there or in the spring—that's what I always do. As the greenhouses have cheered me up during the winter, I repay them by supporting the greenhouse with my business and by also planting the flowers, herbs, and shrubs and caring for them for the rest of the plant's life cycle. It works for me. Try it for yourself the next time you are down in the dumps with the wintertime blues.

Greenhouse Charm

Here is a little greenhouse charm that you can say to yourself while you get a dose of plant magick and greenery. Just shut your eyes, soak up the warmth and those delicious, earthy smells, and repeat the charm quietly.

> *All around me now, new plant life does happily grow*
> *My spirits are lifted despite the cold and the snow.*
> *Green is the magickal color of life and hope*
> *Refresh me and remove any reason to mope!*
> *By the powers of the moon, stars, and shining sun*
> *As I will, so shall it be, an' let it harm none.*

Feel free to walk around and indulge yourself for a while in the greenhouse. See if you can find a simple houseplant to take home and care for. Once you return home, sit back, relax, and enjoy the rest of your day.

Personal Lesson for Imbolc
RELAX, REST, AND RECHARGE

> IN THE DEPTH of winter, I finally learned
> that within me there lay an invincible summer.
>
> *Albert Camus*

The winter season of 2010–2011 was especially brutal. Here in the Midwest we saw more snow by January than we had in the past two years combined. After being hammered in late January with a foot of snow, then blizzard conditions including ice, sleet, and even more snow, a friend invited me to come on a winter vacation, all expenses paid. I snatched at the chance the way a drowning person grabs a life preserver. Going to the beach in early February? Warmth, palm trees, the beach, a warm ocean, and the smell of sunscreen…let me think about that. Oh, *hell* yeah.

Then we were inundated with severe nonstop winter storms the week before my trip, and I really started to worry. When the weather forecast called for another round of ice and snow on my scheduled departure day, I bumped up my flight to leave twenty-four hours earlier, paid the difference, and booked a hotel room for myself for one night at the resort where we were staying. That way I knew I would be there when the rest of the gang arrived and not stuck at home in an airport because of winter storms. I will admit that my nerves were shot watching the weather forecast. I did not even sleep a wink the night before my trip. But I did manage to dodge the storm and was able to bug out a day early and leave for my vacation. To. The. Beach.

I suppose some people might be nervous about flying alone and getting a room all by their onesies. As I travel alone all of the time, it was no big deal to me. Actually, I was thinking adventure! As my plane descended into Fort Lauderdale, the white, puffy clouds cleared, and all I saw was blue skies and miles of ocean. Once I landed at my destination I was greeted with 80-degree temperatures. I tucked my winter coat away in my suitcase, peeled out of my sweater, and could not stop smiling. I stood at the terminal and waited for my hotel shuttle in a T-shirt and jeans and was actually sweating.

I enjoyed the thirty-minute shuttle ride to the hotel. The driver took the back way to avoid traffic, and as we cruised through the lovely neighborhoods that lined the waterways, I admired little cottages and grand houses all done in stucco and painted bright, tropical colors. There were tile roofs and amazing tropical gardens everywhere I looked.

I gasped at the sailboats parked behind the houses in the canal and lost my mind over the blooming bougainvillea hedges that soared to twenty feet in height. I fell in love with the palm trees and tropical flowers and tried not to go into culture shock at the difference between leaving the deep snow, gloomy skies, and frigid temperatures at home and then arriving in a tropical, colorful paradise.

I arrived at the hotel, checked in, dumped my luggage in my room, and changed into a swimsuit and cover-up in record speed. I packed a beach bag and was on the beach, standing in the ocean, in less than fifteen minutes.

Once I hit the beach I just stood there and grinned like a fool. There I was, standing under a warm, sunny sky with the ocean lapping around my ankles. In February. I pulled a celestial-patterned sarong out of my bag, spread it out on the sand, and sat on the beach in silence for about an hour. It was glorious.

All of the pressure I had been carting around slid off my shoulders. I was able to breathe again and felt about five pounds lighter. After a while I could not just sit there motionless, so I took myself off for a long walk on the beach before coming back to the resort and taking a twilight dip in the pool (another treat). Then I headed back to my room to clean up and wander into the hotel's restaurant for a sandwich.

That night the Super Bowl was on, and after dinner I strolled into the bar at the hotel and ordered a margarita. I sat at the bar and chatted with other folks, all of whom had also fled south and away from the snow. I indulged in a plate of fresh fruit. After a while the game and the crowd noise was a little much for me, so I headed up to my room and crashed.

I got up before sunrise the next day armed with a flashlight and my tote bag and headed down to the beach, where I sat in the pitch dark and waited for the sun to rise over the ocean. It was well worth the wait. The ocean sounds different in the dark, and as I sat and watched the stars blink out one by one, I was amazed at having the beach all to myself. Then the sky brightened, and the sun broke through the clouds that were low on the eastern horizon. It was incredible.

For the next five days in a row I was up before dawn, sitting on the beach and waiting for the sun to rise over the Atlantic Ocean. Each day's sunrise was different, and as soon as the sky brightened I would take photos and then go on long, long walks, searching for seashells and beach glass. Some days it was warm and sunny, others it was cloudy and a bit chilly. Each day brought its own treasures and lessons.

At the halfway point of my morning walk I would find a nice spot in the sand, spread out my celestial sarong like a blanket, and sit with my journal and pen and write. I did not work on any book projects…I wrote for myself. I sipped from my bottle of water, ate a granola bar, and pondered the mysteries of life, such as they were to be found on a quiet beach at sunrise.

I usually walked from six AM until nine AM—three glorious hours all to myself. Just me, the ocean, the shells, and the seagulls.

Somehow, while hunting for shells and beach glass, I found myself again. I got out of the crazy schedule of deadlines and demands that my life had become, and I remembered who I was. What Ellen wants and why Ellen started to write in the first place. The only writing I did while on vacation was in my journal, and that was a pleasure.

I think it was my third day in Florida when the tide was low, the Portuguese man-of-wars had been swept out to sea, and I hit the mother lode of gorgeous little shells. I was so thrilled each time the waves tossed one up that I was up to my knees in the surf and my jacket pockets were bulging. When I hit the halfway point of my three-hour walk I sat down, transferred my shells to my tote bag, got out my journal, and started to write.

I was amazed at how light I felt sitting there, and I wondered what other lessons the gods had in store for me that day. A seagull landed nearby and inched his way to my side. He eyed my granola bar and ambled over closer and closer.

I looked over at him and said, "I'm on to you, buddy."

He ruffled his feathers, cocked his head to the side, then walked right up and stopped about three inches from my knee and then stayed there quietly.

So for about a half hour the seagull and I shared that little section of beach, and I thought deep thoughts and wrote in my journal. Finally I gave in and shared a tiny bit of my granola bar with that gull. He dropped a feather and I picked it up and tucked it into my journal. Then he followed me all the way back to the hotel.

For me, Florida brought many surprises—some personal lessons and, most importantly, some spiritual healing. I will always be grateful for my time there.

Reflections on the Season of Imbolc
FEBRUARY THAW

> SURELY AS COMETH the Winter, I know
> There are Spring violets under the snow.
>
> *Robert H. Newell*

As I write this, the snows and ice have melted; in the past week the temperatures have hovered near the 50-degree mark. Makes me wonder if I brought some of the warmth of Florida back home with me. Spring is still weeks away, but the feet of snow we had is melting, and the days are warmer. I know we will have another round of snow again, but it's nice to see some change in the temperature.

While I watch the snow and ice melt, this seems to be an excellent time to do a little psychic cleansing. Why not work with the energies already present? There is no better way to close up the winter season and get ready for the fresh opportunities of the coming spring.

A Winter to Spring Psychic Protection Spell

This psychic protection spell requires some visualization on your part. To begin, I recommend working this spell in daylight hours. Bundle up as needed and stand outside in nature, with your feet securely on the ground. Tip your face up to the February sun…know that its strengthening rays are slowly bringing life back. Spring is coming, and winter will lose its grip on the land.

During this in-between time as winter fades and a new season of growth awaits is your best opportunity to clear out any old negativity, psychic goop, or unhappiness that you may be carrying around. It's also an excellent time of the year to strengthen your personal psychic protection. So let's get started!

As you repeat this spell verse, imagine that sunlight swirls around you in a colorful stream; it's your call as to whether the energy streams clockwise or counterclockwise, so go with whatever seems correct to you. The light you are visualizing can be any color or a rainbow of colors, so feel that sunlight and get the circle of energy spinning around.

Hold your hands up and feel that energy circle and spin around you. Then repeat the following spell verse:

> As the winter season fades and the spring begins
> This psychic protection magick around me spins.
> Light and warmth increase across the land
> And strengthens this magick from where I stand.
> As the snow and ice of Imbolc will surely melt away
> I am refreshed and ready for whatever comes my way.
> Protection rolls around me in an enchanted ring
> Serenity, hope, health, and strength this magick does bring.

Allow your hands to come down to your sides, and let the energy follow the motion of your hands so it grounds itself back into the earth. Take a nice cleansing breath in, hold it for four counts, and then slowly blow it out.

Now open your eyes and close the spell with these lines:

> By the power of the slowly strengthening sun
> As I will, so mote it be, an' let it harm none.

Blessed be.

CHAPTER 7

Vernal Equinox
Ostara
MARCH 20–23

THE FORCE OF Spring—mysterious,
fecund, powerful beyond measure.

Michael Garofalo

As I write this, it is the day of the vernal equinox, and right on schedule my forsythia bushes have bloomed. In my gardens the tulips, hyacinths, and daffodils are all breaking the ground and stretching toward the sky. We have been fortunate for the past week and have had mild temperatures, and the neighborhood saucer magnolias just began blooming a gorgeous candy pink. I guess they are all happy to strut their stuff after a particularly long, tough winter. Today as I ran errands I saw that the willows were hazed with a tender spring green, and I noticed a plum tree had burst into the palest of pink blossoms.

The earliest daffodils are blooming, and the robins are hopping around hunting worms and making a racket just before sunrise. Oh, it's good to see some green and some life return to the gardens!

This sabbat is one of the four solar festivals of the year. In the season of spring the earth's axis is tilted toward the sun, increasing the number of daylight hours and bringing warmer weather that causes the plants to grow.

However, depending on how far north you live, this actual date may not look or feel like spring outside. There have been plenty of times we were hit with a big snowstorm for the sabbat. I live in the Midwestern United States, and for us, the vernal equinox/ Ostara has a fifty-fifty shot of being a snowy one. So if you are still snowed in, hang in there.

I encourage you to go out and to take a careful look at the trees. You will see that the buds are swelling and getting ready to pop. Soon the crocus will be blooming, and the earliest daffodils will follow and be up and breaking the ground. Spring has begun, life is returning to the land—so enjoy it and incorporate all that burgeoning energy and excitement into your craft.

A Little History
THE VERNAL EQUINOX

SPRING IS NATURE'S way
of saying, "Let's party!"
Robin Williams

In some magickal traditions, this is the start of the new year. The Roman year, for example, began the fifteenth of March (the Ides of March). Also, the astrological year begins on the vernal equinox, when the sun enters the astrological sign of Aries the Ram.

The word *vernal* is Latin and means "spring," while the word *equinox* actually comes from the Latin word *aequinoctium*, which means "equal night." Once again, our daylight and nighttime hours are fairly equal. When the sun crosses over the earth's equator, this moment is known as the vernal equinox in the Northern Hemisphere. At the spring equinox we celebrate the midpoint of winter and summer and the renewal of all of nature. There are no shortages of rituals and customs and names for the beginning of the spring, such as Lady Day, the First Point of Aries, and, of course, Ostara.

The name for this sabbat does come from the Norse traditions. Northern Paganism had a strong influence on our ancestors, as they were familiar with the Teutonic lore and customs. In Germanic and English traditions, this festival corresponds to the spring equinox.

The classic seasonal mythology of the vernal/spring equinox revolves around the Germanic goddess Eostre. You will notice that in some texts the goddess is called Ostara or Eostre interchangeably. The Anglo-Saxons hailed Eostre as the Maiden Goddess of spring. Some say that her name means "moving with the waxing sun." Eostre (Old English) and Ostara (Old High German) are both the names of this goddess of the dawn and spring.

Her name was taken for the Christian celebration of Easter, probably due to the fact that in Germanic traditions, the month of April is called *Eostur monath* (Eostre's month). Back in 1882, Jacob Grimm had this to say about the goddess Ostara. Check out this interesting quote from his book *Teutonic Mythology*:

> This Ostarâ, like the [Anglo-Saxon] E*ástre*, must in heathen religion have denoted a higher being, whose worship was so firmly rooted, that the Christian teachers tolerated the name and applied it to one of their own grandest anniversaries.

Eostre, the goddess of spring, was once offered cakes and colored eggs at the equinox. The hare was sacred to her, as is the white rabbit. In many other mythologies, a white animal such as a deer or a horse is often considered a sign of divinity, and it is sacred. Some scholars consider Eostre to be a Maiden Goddess of the east and the dawn, similar to the goddess Eos, who is the Greek Maiden Goddess of the sunrise. Isn't it interesting how these different deities from different cultures have so many similarities? Also, in my opinion, having Eostre associated with both the spring and the sunrise makes sense, as on the day of the vernal equinox the sun rises at true east.

This sabbat honors the fecundity of the land, the sprouting of the seeds within the earth, and the coming of spring's warmth and light from the sun. This time of year is all about balance, renewal, and rebirth. It's a fantastic occasion for new beginnings, starting new projects, clearing out the old to make room for the new, and embracing a fresh start.

Eventually the snow and ice will thaw and melt, and things will be muddy and sloppy for a while. This, too, passes as nature puts all that moisture to good use and it nourishes the plants. To survive the thaw and reblooming of spring, all plants and wildlife have to be hardy and strong. Spring is a season of dramatic change. Even though folks like to romanticize it and say how soft and pretty it is, often the fiercest winter storms happen now. Spring is a brutal season. Only the hardiest of early spring plants endure the wild weather, temperature swings, and severe storms. It is both a challenge and a test of faith to thrive in this season, but spring is all about faith, strength, birth, and growth.

Goddess Magick with Eostre
A Blessing for Your Home

THE ORDINARY ARTS we practice every
day at home are of more importance to the
soul than their simplicity might suggest.

Thomas Moore

The vernal equinox is the launch of the spring season. This festival's familiar symbols of rabbits, pastel-colored eggs, and bright spring flowers are sweet and romantic ones. Look around you: everywhere in nature there are signs of life returning to the land. To bring a bit of this natural magick indoors, pick up a pretty pot of blooming bulbs—try tulips for love or daffodils for chivalry and honor—and take them home to brighten things up.

Perhaps you can jazz them up a little by tucking some moss over the soil or adding a festive bow or tiny colored eggs to the container. Enchant these spring flowers for fresh starts and good luck. Light a soft green votive candle and call on the goddess of spring, Eostre, to work this sabbat spell for new beginnings and to increase the positive things in your life.

> *Ostara begins our season of spring*
> *Good luck, joy, and cheer these flowers do bring.*
> *Eostre, bless my home, family, and friends*
> *May your love and blessings never end.*
> *For the good of all, with harm to no one*
> *By the goddess of spring, this charm is done!*

Allow the green candle to burn until it goes out on its own. Happy spring!

If you care to modify this spell a bit, here are some correspondences for the goddess Eostre/Ostara. Colors employed are all pastel shades and, of course, spring green. Symbols for the goddess include the white hare and colored eggs, birds, feathers, nests, and baskets of spring flowers. The goddess Eostre can be called on in magick for balance, illumination, renewal, new beginnings, fertility, and rebirth.

Ostara's Hare of Fertility and Eggs

"Hallo, Rabbit," he said, "is that you?"
"Let's pretend it isn't," said Rabbit,
"and see what happens."

A. A. *Milne*

The rabbit or hare was naturally associated with the goddess of spring, Eostre. There are also old references about being as mad as a March hare, which comes from folks observing the behavior of hares in the spring during mating season. They chase each other about, jumping and hopping around, and the males are known to box with each other. We all know how quickly rabbits multiply. Rabbits do mate young, and a female may produce several litters in one year. So they really are perfect representatives of fertility in the spring. According to old folklore, the hare was often a Witch's familiar, and it became synonymous with lust and sex.

The hare or rabbit is indeed the "egg bringer" at this sabbat. One story goes that long ago there was a white hare who was also a wizard. This hare wanted to please the goddess Eostre by bringing her a gift, so he gathered up some fresh eggs, charmed the eggs into soft colors, and presented them to her in a nest. The goddess was so impressed that she adopted both the colored eggs and the hare as her symbols.

In old Victorian art the rabbit or hare is shown by a nest or a basket of colored eggs. According to European folklore, the egg-bringing rabbit carried eggs in a pack on his back. This sacred hare of Eostre left the eggs in the cleverest of places.

Depending on the local tradition, the decorated eggs could be tucked inside the home or left scattered in the garden for the children to find—or sometimes they were left in a cache on the ground in a sort of nest created by the hare. This may explain the old German custom of children building soft nests on the ground out of straw, moss, and fresh green leaves in their gardens for the hare to place their colored eggs.

Now, the egg is a natural symbol of spring, as it contains the promise of new animal life, just as a seed contains the expectation of new plant life. The custom of decorating and exchanging eggs as a rite of spring has been handed down through the generations from many cultures since ancient times. The Egyptians and Persians dyed eggs in soft colors in the spring and gave them to friends as gifts and fertility charms. The Pagan Anglo-Saxons, Greeks, and Egyptians all placed eggs in tombs, as a symbol of rebirth.

It is believed that the Druids once dyed eggs red to symbolize the sun and life, and exchanged them at the spring equinox. Why red? Red is a color of magick in many countries. In Romania red eggs were called "love apples," while in China new parents gave gifts of red-dyed eggs to their family and friends if they were blessed with a son. In olden times in France, exchanging red eggs in the spring was thought to ensure abundant crops in the coming autumn harvest.

The Saxons exchanged colored eggs with each other like a talisman to represent new life; the eggs were then ritually consumed in Eostre's honor. Also in Germany back in the day, on the night before Easter, children were told to behave themselves so that the hare would lay eggs for them. So the Pagan Eostre's popular hare of fertility was remade into the Easter bunny.

Folklore states that you can easily balance a raw egg on its end during the actual moment of the equinox. Try it for yourself. I once did this with an entire Girl Scout troop. We all lined up eggs on the garden wall just before the exact time of the vernal (spring) equinox. Then we let the eggs go to balance on their ends. As soon as the moment passed, all the eggs fell over at the same time. It was awesome. And all those girls, who are now grown and graduating from college, still comment to me about the time we "balanced the eggs."

Perfect Eggs for Ostara

I have met a lot of hardboiled eggs in
my time, but you're twenty minutes.

Oscar Wilde

There is a magick trick to cooking the perfect hard-boiled egg. It's simple: put the white eggs in a large stainless-steel or enamel pot filled with cold water; you want at least an inch of water to be completely covering the eggs. (Save the egg cartons to hold the finished dyed eggs.) Bring the uncovered pot up to a full rolling boil, then remove the pot from the heat and place the lid tightly on the pot. Set the timer for twelve minutes. After the time is up, immediately remove the eggs from the pot carefully with a slotted spoon, and set them on a rack or a kitchen towel to cool. Once they are cool, you may now color the eggs and decorate as you choose. These eggs will be perfectly cooked, with no green ring around the yolks. Refrigerate the hard-boiled eggs after you have finished decorating them and the dye is completely dry.

Also, please note that sometimes, no matter what you do, an eggshell cracks while cooking, so I suggest putting a few extras in the pot. If one cracks while cooking, you can save them for a snack later, or dye them anyway.

Natural Egg Dyes

Now when it comes to natural egg dyes, you do have some options. One of the best tricks I have ever seen done is to boil white eggs in a separate pot with red cabbage leaves. Then, when you take them off the heat to cool, gently stir in ½ teaspoon vinegar, then place the lid on the pot for twelve minutes.

After the twelve minutes have passed, remove the lid and allow the liquid to cool. Allow the eggs to stay in the water (with those leaves floating on top of and around the eggs) for a couple of hours. The result is a brilliant robin's-egg blue-green.

To make the more classic dye, where you dip the cooked eggs in the color bath, try these recipes:

> To make yellow—In a pot, mix 1 teaspoon turmeric, 1 teaspoon vinegar, and 3 cups water. Boil mixture for a half hour, cool to room temperature, strain out stray turmeric grains, then add cooked, cooled eggs and soak them in the dye for a half hour.

> To make pink—Mix 1 cup strained juice from canned beets, ½ teaspoon vinegar, and 3 cups water. Soak the cooked, cooled eggs in the dye for a half hour.

> To make a dusky purple—Mix 1 cup grape juice, ½ teaspoon vinegar, and 3 cups cold water. Soak cooked, cooled eggs in the dye for a half hour.

Vernal Equinox Quiche

Egg recipes always seem appropriate to me for the vernal equinox. Here is a reduced-fat spinach and cheese quiche recipe. I made this for my coven's Ostara gathering. It was very delicious and a hit with all the ladies!

> 1 premade pie crust
> 4 eggs
> 1 cup fat-free half and half
> ½ cup reduced-fat mayonnaise
> 2 tablespoons flour
> 1–2 tablespoons dried minced onions (to taste)
> 8 ounces 2% shredded cheddar cheese
> 1 package chopped frozen spinach, thawed and drained
> Pinch of salt

Preheat oven to 375 degrees. Roll out the pie crust and place in a pie plate; crimp the edges and set aside. Whisk together the eggs, half and half, mayonnaise, and flour. Add in minced onion, cheese, spinach, and salt, and whisk until combined. Pour mixture into pie crust and bake 45 minutes or until the top is golden brown.

Be careful not to spill the egg batter out of the pie crust when you place it in the oven. You may want to tuck a cookie sheet on the rack below to catch any spills while it bakes. This quiche, which can be served warm or at room temperature, serves eight.

• • • •

Springtime Decorating
YOUR MAGICKAL HOME

I'D RATHER HAVE roses on my
table than diamonds on my neck.

Emma Goldman

If you are in the mood to decorate your home for the sabbat, hit the stores and look for vernal equinox decorations. In late February the chocolate bunnies and egg-dyeing kits are starting to appear on store shelves. There are also lots of nature-themed springtime decorations out there.

In the past few years, wreaths of pastel-colored eggs have been very popular. I even found candle rings made up of soft-colored speckled eggs and twigs. These types of natural-looking decorations make fabulous accessories for our Pagan holiday of Ostara—after all, the colored egg is a Pagan tradition!

For my own home, I made a large grapevine wreath that is decorated with silk spring flowers and a small faerie, and I wove a yellow pentagram in the center of the wreath. There is a bow in a springtime pattern and artificial vintage-looking decorated eggs also incorporated into this wreath. I hang the wreath up on my front door every year as March begins. After Ostara is over, I remove the eggs and the wreath stays in place through Beltane.

Don't overlook those rabbits you see for spring decorating at this time of year, whether you choose to go with rabbit motifs in your decorating or you just have a hankering for a chocolate bunny. All rabbits, whether edible chocolate or not, can be symbols of the goddess's hare of fertility. Decorated baskets of flowers and eggs are totally appropriate for a Pagan household's sabbat decorations. Go ahead, work up an Ostara basket for your children, family, and coven. These earthy symbols of the hare, the decorated egg, and the flower basket are Pagan in origin. Like the decorated tree at Yuletide, the Christians simply adopted them.

Another obvious option is to pick up a small bouquet of fresh flowers. You can spend a couple of bucks and bring home some fresh flowers for your kitchen table or living room. Let the magick of the blossoms spread a little cheer and charm into your home. This is a joyful springtime celebration, so take pleasure in it and create magick to your heart's content.

Full Moon in March
A Spell for Balance

HAPPINESS IS NOT a matter of intensity
but of balance, order, rhythm, and harmony.

Thomas Merton

The full moon in March is often called the Storm Moon due to the fact that at this time of year we have rain, sometimes snow, and the weather is unpredictable.

The night of the March full moon is the perfect occasion to celebrate the season of spring and to take a moment to reflect on achieving balance and celebrating new beginnings, prosperity, growth, and positive change. Here is a full moon spell for you to perform by yourself or with your group or coven.

Gather these supplies:

- 1 white votive candle
- 1 votive cup to hold the candle
- Fresh, white springtime flowers in a vase (tulips, daffodils, roses, or carnations)
- A moonstone (a small piece of tumbled moonstone would be perfect)
- Lighter or matches
- Your altar or a safe, flat surface to set up the spell components on

Place the votive candle inside of the candle cup. Set the vase of fresh spring flowers off to the side. Set the moonstone in front of the candle. (If you like, you can personalize this spell by scattering a few fresh flower petals on your altar or by adding a drop or two of essential oil to your candle, too.) Once you have things arranged to your preference, begin by lighting the candle and then repeating the spell verse:

On this bewitching night of the full Storm Moon
I call to the Old Ones to grant me a boon.
May I find prosperity and balance today
Leaving room for good luck and joy to come my way.
This small moonstone will act as a talisman true
May I be blessed and steadfast in all that I do.
This March full moon spell now closes up with a rhyme
I will walk in balance and wisdom at all times.

Allow the candle to burn out in a safe place. Pocket the moonstone and keep it with you until the next full moon. Clean up your altar space and enjoy the flowers until they begin to fade. When they do, return them neatly to nature by adding them to your compost pile or into your yard waste so they can be recycled with grass clippings and so forth.

Personal Lesson for the Vernal Equinox
GROWTH AND REBIRTH

I THINK THAT no matter how old or
infirm I may become, I will always plant
a garden in the spring. Who can resist
the feeling of hope and joy one gets from
participating in nature's rebirth?

Edward Giobbi

My coven gathered together to celebrate Ostara on the eve of the sabbat. This year it coincided with the full Storm Moon, complete with a thunderstorm. It was very dramatic and put the whole group in a more witchy mood. The full moon was at perigee that night (at its closest point to the earth), so the moon would have looked extra large if we could have seen it. We did not get to see the full moon during our ritual because of the storm, but no one really minded. What we did have was atmosphere, courtesy of Mother Nature.

We did all have a great time with a simple full moon sabbat ritual, no matter what the weather. We blessed any moonstone jewelry we each owned and also tumbled pieces of moonstones for all of us to keep as talismans. During the equinox ritual we each took white crayons and wrote messages on the hard-boiled eggs—simple words like *strength, prosperity, love, blessed be,* and so on. We were not able to see each other's messages and symbols during the process, which made it more fun. The eggs were all placed in a bowl and mixed up so no one knew which egg was which.

Later, after we had shared our potluck dinner, we would dye the eggs, and then the secret messages and symbols would be revealed. You had to choose an egg and dye it to see what your "Ostara message" would be. It was an enchanted evening, and we all laughed and had a great time.

I got up at 6:30 the morning of the equinox and checked my western-facing kitchen windows, hoping to see that extra-large full moon, and discovered a huge-looking yellow full moon lowering beneath the cloud line and setting in the western sky. It was such a pretty daffodil yellow. I was able to enjoy the full moon and sunrise on the vernal equinox all at the same time.

The morning of the vernal equinox, when I checked the gardens, I discovered that one of my forsythia bushes was in full bloom. I love forsythia in the spring—it's so cheerful after the long winter. In the language of flowers, forsythia signifies that the bearer is "good natured," which makes sense to me, as it's hard to be moping when you've got bright yellow blossoms staring you in the face. Since the weather was so pretty that day, and in honor of the vernal equinox, I planted a few violas in my faerie garden birdbath.

The birdbath had been turned into a little faerie garden…the water dish was way too deep for the birds anyway, so I mounded up the soil and planted perennial creeping plants in it, and every spring I add violas. There are some crystal clusters, a tiny faerie, and a ceramic mushroom or two added to the garden to give it a fairy-tale look. Violas are so cheerful, and they smell terrific!

Violas are a great little flower to plant at this time of year, and they're about the only thing I would consider planting this early in a Midwest spring. Violas can withstand some snow, and they like the chill; even though our temps were in the 70s yesterday and are supposed to be in the 50s and 60s this week, it can still swing back to the freezing point at night for a while.

An enchanting flower, violas are sacred to the goddess Aphrodite/Venus and the god Eros/Cupid. These colorful little flowers have many intriguing folk names, such as Johnny Jump-ups, Kiss-Me-At-the-Garden-Gate, and Heart's Ease. They are rumored to mend a broken heart—hence the folk name—and in the language of flowers they whisper the message "I am thinking of you." According to floral lore, Cupid/Eros accidentally hit the viola/pansy with one of his arrows, and ever after the flower smiled. Take a good look at those happy "faces" on the violas and the pansy. Yup, they are still smiling.

I worked happily away in my gardens and enjoyed the warmer weather. The garden was being reborn all around me, and there is something so uplifting about watching nature come back bigger and better than ever.

A *Spell for March* 31
THE FESTIVAL OF LUNA

SLOWLY, SILENTLY, NOW the moon
Walks the night in her silver shoon.

Walter de la Mare

Since the equinox always falls near the end of March, I thought it would be fun to add a little something different to this sabbat chapter. The final day of March is the festival of Luna, the Roman goddess of the full moon. Here is a spell to celebrate Luna's special day.

Directions and Supplies

Gather together some fresh white spring flowers—tulips, roses, carnations, lilies, or white daffodils—and arrange them in a water-filled vase. Arrange a few moonstones on your work surface. Set white and silver taper candles in tall candlestick holders, and light them with reverence. Take this opportunity to get to know and to honor one of the oldest Mother aspects of the goddess of the moon.

Luna is a powerful deity. She is especially fond of magick users and will gently make her presence known in your life, no matter what the moon phase. If possible, work this spell while outdoors, or at least in a place where you have a view of the moon, no matter what phase she is currently in.

> *On this night I honor Luna, goddess of the moon*
> *In this enchanted time, listen to this Witch's tune.*
> *Grant me illumination and grace, Lady, I pray*
> *May I be respectful of your magick every day.*
> *Bless me now with your gifts and enchantment true*
> *May my magick be blessed in all that I do.*

Now get comfortable; sit in front of your altar and meditate on Luna. See what she has to say to you and to teach you about your path. When you are finished with your meditation, thank Luna in your own words. Extinguish the candles. You may use these again as illuminator candles in any future moon rites. Pocket the moonstones and keep them with you as a reminder of Luna's magick. Enjoy the flowers until they fade, then return them neatly to nature by adding them to a compost pile or to be recycled with your yard waste.

Another idea is to plant white flowers now in honor of Luna. This early in the spring, go for white hyacinths, tulips, and daffodils, or consider adding white varieties of bleeding hearts, pansies, geraniums, petunias, and violas to your gardens.

That way, when darkness falls, your white, pale flowers will brighten up your nighttime spring gardens. Maybe you will even be inspired to plant a moonlight garden filled with pale colors and gleaming white flowers to enjoy for the rest of the year. This way, Luna's magick will stay with you for months. Blessed be.

Ellen's Garden of Witchery Journal
THE APRIL PLANTER'S MOON

DAFFODILS THAT COME before
the swallow dares and take the
winds of March with beauty.

William Shakespeare

As we roll into the month of April, spring is really in the air now! The chilly nights of March are making way for the milder, softer days of April. Now the trees are greening up more each day, the hyacinths and daffodils are blooming in the garden, and the tulips are getting ready to parade their candy colors. The full moon in April is a wonderful time to bless your garden in its earliest days of the growing season.

Take a stroll outside this evening under the light of the rising full moon and bless or consecrate your gardens. (This will still work if your garden happens to be a collection of window boxes and pots on a deck or balcony.) As you walk along the garden, hold your hands above the containers and repeat the following full moon spell to bless the plants that are growing. This charm calls upon the four elements and will mark your garden as an area of magick and power.

Under the beautiful glow of the full Planter's Moon
Elements four, gather now to hear this Witch's tune.
Merge your magick with mine, circle around this space
By earth, air, fire, and water, I bless this place.

This full moon is also the perfect opportunity to magickally enhance any plants, seeds, and seedlings you are preparing to plant into your magickal gardens.

For this blessing, gather together all of your seed packets or young plants and set them in a place where the light of the moon will fall upon them. Hold your hands over the top of the plants or seeds and visualize the magick energy of creation streaming into them. Repeat the following charm three times:

Goddess, bless these seeds/plants with life, health, and vitality
I do enchant these now as the full moon shines brightly.

Happy magickal gardening!

And Now for Something Completely Different
Palm-Reading Sunday

> About astrology and palmistry:
> they are good because they make people
> vivid and full of possibilities.
>
> *Kurt Vonnegut Jr.*

Well, what snarky, twisted individual came up with the "Palm-Reading Sunday" idea? (Ellen raises her hand proudly in the air.) That would be me! My coven started this little get-together about five years ago. One of our full moon celebrations had fallen on a Palm Sunday in April, and I said, "Hey, I know: let's make it Palm-Reading Sunday. We'll get together, do divination, and read each other's palms!"

We all thought it was hilarious, and the ladies in the coven had such a great time with the palm reading and other various divinations that it's become a tradition in our coven every year. So, that is how Palm-Reading Sunday came to be.

Aww, come on—you have to admit it is pretty funny. I think it's only fair, after all; the Christians took a bunch of our holidays and adapted them to *their* celebrations, so why not turn the tables on the situation a bit and have some fun! Wearing flowing black is entirely optional. But I can compromise: you don't have to play Stevie Nicks music or the soundtrack from *Practical Magic* unless you want to.

If you'd like to start your own Palm-Reading Sunday tradition with your friends, study group, or coven, then have each of the people involved choose a type of divination that they can teach to others. Since it was my idea originally, I offered to study up on palmistry and to teach the basics to the rest of the group.

Yes, I said "study up." I have never claimed to be a walking encyclopedia of the occult. Ask me a question about magickal plants or gardens and I'll dazzle you, but palmistry? Well…I had some studying to do.

Many people assume because I am clairvoyant and read the tarot that I can read palms too. It still surprises me when people stick their hands in my face and ask me to read their palms. It must be the whole mentality of "Well, you're a Witch—don't you guys *all* read palms?" I think they may have us confused with the story-book version of the Gypsies. Not every Gypsy reads palms either, and to assume so would be rude.

Now, if I hold a person's hand for a "reading," I would, in fact, be reading the individual psychically—not their palms. Having a psychic take a stroll through their heads can be disconcerting to some folks, but I digress. Anyway, in desperation after coming up with the whole Palm-Reading Sunday idea, I tried to learn some of the palm-reading basics, and that's what I taught my coven sisters. It worked out great, and we all had a fantastic time.

A Few Rules of Etiquette for Divination and Palm-Reading Basics

I should take a moment here and point out a few basic rules when it comes to performing divinatory acts for people. Whether you read the tarot, the runes, tea leaves, or palms, the rules of etiquette and ethical magick still apply.

Rule number one: Never predict death. Why? Because you could be wrong. You are not a god, so don't frighten or upset anyone on purpose—or even as a joke or by accident. To do so would be cruel. Remember: what goes around, comes around, and also you should work to harm none, whether that's through your magick or your divination practices.

Rule number two: If you don't know the answer to a question, then say, "I don't know." Also remind the person whose palm you are reading that this is for fun. The whole idea of this is to learn more about the topic together.

Rule number three: Break out an eyeliner pencil (it washes off easily) and mark the lines on the palm of the hand you are reading so the person knows what you are referring to. When my coven gets together, we all mark our own palms and then compare lines, trying to figure out what it all means. We have a blast and it's funny watching everyone walk around with lines drawn and highlighted on their hands.

Rule number four: Don't ignore your gut instincts when it comes to reading palms. The shape and the "feel" of the person's hand is very important as well. With that thought in mind, let me share a little basic palm-reading information with you.

The Four Main Shapes of the Hand
Often the first thing that is studied is the shape of the hand itself. This is broken down into four basic categories: the conical hand, the spatulate hand, the pointed hand, and the square hand. Interestingly enough, these four types all coordinate with

a magickal element. This is fairly easy to remember, especially since the personality traits match right up with the Witch's classic elemental personality qualities.

Air Hand (Conical) = Square Palm+ Long Fingers: Just as the name implies, the conical hand is wider at the base of the palm than at the top of the fingers. Fingers tend to be long and tapered, with a fine texture to the skin. This type of hand is sometimes called a "feminine hand" because of the shape and texture. These folks are full of thoughts, dreams, and inspirations. A person who possesses an air hand may be a worrier, though, and may have problems dealing with stress in healthy ways. On the opposite end of the spectrum, they may spend a little too much time in their own minds. However, they possess a real hunger for knowledge, have wonderful imaginations, and are witty, romantic, and intellectual. They love tranquility and are family oriented.

Fire Hand (Spatulate) = Oblong Palm + Short Fingers: The spatulate hand is narrower at the base of the palm and the wrist, but the palm is wider at the top where it meets with the fingers. The fingers themselves are shorter and fan out in the form of a spatula. People who posses a fire type of palm are strong, vibrant, and outgoing. These folks are one of a kind, confident, and independent. They are active, impulsive, and like a lot of variety in their lives. They may be prone to bad tempers, lack patience, and get bored very quickly, but they are sexy, warm, and vivacious, so it all balances out. Fire-hand individuals are adventurous, creative, sensual, energetic, and passionate.

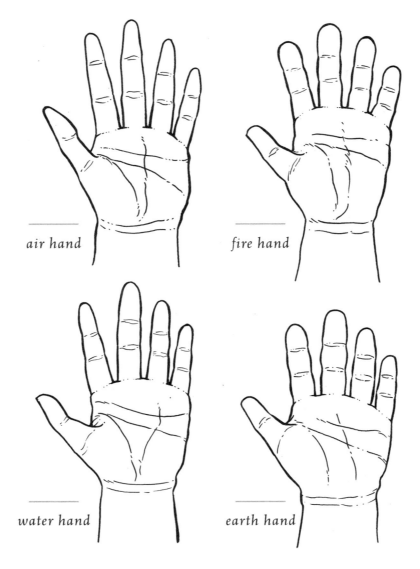

air hand

fire hand

water hand

earth hand

Water Hand (Pointed) = Oblong Palm + Long Fingers: This elemental type of hand has a wide, rounded base that tapers up to more slender, pointed fingers. This is the beautiful and graceful hand of a natural psychic or empath. This shape is classically known as the psychic hand. These perceptive individuals are sensitive, insightful, compassionate, and artistic. They do not hide their feelings and are proud of all of their emotions. Because of this, they can be easily overwhelmed by negative thoughts and bad energy. They truly dislike confrontations and try to avoid them if at all possible, which may make them appear either aloof or withdrawn. Water-hand people may be artists, poets, or musicians, but they have a deeply emotional side and are happiest when their world is calm, tranquil, and serene.

Earth Hand (Square) = Square Palm + Short Fingers: An earth hand is square-shaped, with palms and fingers being of equal length and size. These hands are sturdy and strong and are sometimes described as a "masculine" hand. Earth-hand folks are level-headed, honest, hard-working, and down-to-earth. They tend to be stubborn and can be called a "stick in the mud" when they are confronted with something they do not care for. They do not like change unless they get to think about it and prepare for it first. These individuals love structure and order. They are practical and reliable, and they love the outdoors and are physical, fun, and lusty. They love their family, their pets, and the natural world, and are probably into gardening and plants.

The Four Major Lines of the Palm

The following information is the very least that you need to know about the four main lines on the palm of the hand. In palmistry, the right hand is thought to show the

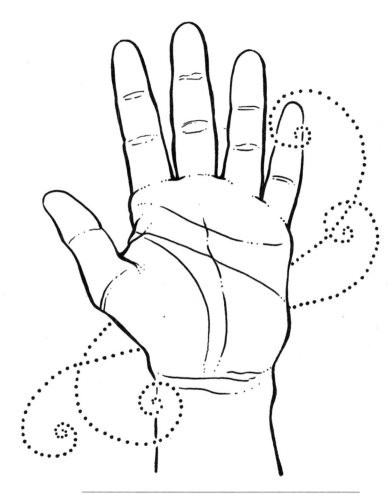

the four major lines of the palm

present and the probable future, whereas the left hand represents potential. However, you should look at both hands while doing a reading. Remember that the lines on the hands do change as time passes. So, without further ado, here are the four main lines of the palm.

HEART LINE: The heart line is the highest horizontal line on the hand. It can be curved or straight, and it starts somewhere between the second and first fingers. This line represents the emotional side of your personality. The more of a curve the heart line has, the more poignant and sensual its owner is thought to be. This line commonly describes the emotions, temperament, and your love life in general.

HEAD LINE: This line starts close to the life line. This is the second horizontal line on the palm. It travels directly across the palm and then toward the outer edge. This line shows our working capabilities, how you deal with problems, and the attitude you possess toward your career. This also shows your mental qualities, such as concentration and ambition.

LIFE LINE: This is the most well-known line on the hand. This line starts between the index finger and the thumb; it curves out and travels down toward the wrist. This line indicates the quality of life, home, and major changes. If the line swoops out far into the hand, it indicates a person who loves to travel. If it hugs closer to the thumb, it represents a homebody.

FATE LINE: The fate line begins its journey at the wrist and moves vertically up toward the middle finger. The deeper the line, the more fate will play a role in your life. If the fate line is separate from the life line, it shows an independent spirit. This line indicates the general pattern one's life will take as well as, interestingly, the relationship you have with your parents.

Divination Is the Theme of the Day
So Have Fun!

PEOPLE RARELY SUCCEED unless
they have fun in what they are doing.

Dale Carnegie

At our Palm-Reading Sunday gathering, divination is always the theme. So with that in mind, have each of your group members decide ahead of time what they will perform for everyone else. It has been my experience that this usually turns out to be a fabulous variety of divinatory techniques. Don't forget to include other forms of divination as well—make it a real party atmosphere.

The second year we did this, I printed up fancy palm-reading handouts with old-time illustrations for my coven sisters. I thought they would be fun for everyone to have as a memento. I found free clip art online of a diagram of the lines of the hand and an old reproduction sepia-toned photo of a woman reading a man's palm. Inspired, I used the clip art to decorate the handouts, then printed them out on parchment paper and used an old-style font to give it some drama.

Basically it was just an excuse to allow the scrapbooking side of me loose to play and be magickally creative. The handouts looked great. Everyone loved the themed pages and added them to their book of shadows. They made a great keepsake of the day.

Reflections on the Spring Season

Life is magic; the way nature
works seems to be quite magical.

Jonas Salk

In the final week of April I took advantage of a unexpected break in the nonstop rains and dove into my water-logged gardens to pull some weeds and to lay down some mulch. Our youngest, our daughter, had moved out a few weeks before to her first post-college apartment, and my husband and I were adjusting to having an empty nest. I kept myself busy working on this book and working in the gardens and enjoyed the peace and quiet of having the place all to ourselves.

By mid-April, the iris bed had starting to bloom, and the battle I had last year with grass growing up between my iris plants made me realize I needed to hit the weeding early and hard. Since the ground was so saturated, the grass and weeds would pull out easier. So I brushed my hair back into a ponytail, put on my grubby clothes and old shoes, and hauled around an old plastic pickle bucket as I pulled weeds and freshened up that iris bed. I filled up that big old pickle bucket several times and dumped it in my compost bin. I was relentless about pulling weeds and other plants that had volunteered.

The lemon balm from a decade ago that I accidentally let reseed it self (all over my lawn) was popping up and trying to cagily hide in my irises. I ripped it out. Some archangel groundcover my husband had added to the back side of the iris bed had volunteered in unwanted spots—out that went, too, not to mention the grass that wouldn't grow when we tried a lawn under that old tree—but now that we had turned it into a flower bed it was only too happy to sprout up everywhere...

The iris bed was a happy accident in my overall garden design plan. What started as a clump of pale purple heirloom iris I had rescued from my husband's family's old farm had been expanded when my neighbor gave me a clump of fancy deep-purple German iris from her gardens. A couple of years later, I found some yellow iris at the end of the blooming cycle that were reduced to 80 percent off, so I grabbed the pot, very happy to get such a good bargain, and took it home and planted it by the other irises and a handful of transplanted tiger lilies.

The following spring, my husband got the idea to make an entire iris/lily garden under our old elm tree. Since iris bulbs sit on the soil the way a duck floats on water, half in, half out—I knew planting iris under that huge old tree would be perfect for the plants.

Delighted at the prospect of a themed flower bed, we went on the hunt for different colors and varieties of irises. I found a black variety called 'Before the Storm' and then found a crimson variety called 'Spartan'. The next year I found a white and purple ruffled variety of iris and winced at the price tag, but it was such a pretty variety that I bought it anyway. The year 2010 was the first year we had an official iris/lily garden, and it was lovely. To jazz it up, we added some big stones to the garden and an accent ornament piece.

So, dodging the rain showers, I pulled weeds, yanked out grass, and spread our homemade mulch—and got sweatier and sweatier, both from the humidity and the exertion. Afterwards the iris bed was looking much better. Inspired, I next tackled the perennial garden that ran along the eastern side of the house. I pulled more weeds and discovered that my marigolds had managed to reseed themselves.

Considering that we had taken a rototiller to that part of the gardens a couple of weeks ago, this was a lovely surprise. Carefully I pulled up the tiny sprouts and trans-planted them in a meandering row at the front of the bed, excited at the prospect of free annuals. Maybe all that snow helped protect them over the winter? I would watch them and let them grow, and by July I'd have pretty little French marigolds all bloom-ing by my soon-to-be-tomato plants.

I was seriously considering snipping some of the blossoms off my snowball bush to bring inside when I realized that it was raining softly. It was a soft, fine mist, so I called it quits for the day and rounded up my gardening tools to get them out of the wet. The light was turning an odd color, as the sun was shining in one part of the sky while another was displaying dark-gray, ominous rain clouds. Considering there had been tornadoes in my area a week before, I decided going inside was the safest move, with the weather being so unpredictable.

As I put away my gardening tools in the shed, a soft roll of thunder announced the rain was going to fall in earnest. Like all Midwesterners, I looked up to check the clouds. To my delight a rainbow was shimmering in the sky to the east, which made me chuckle to myself at the synchronicity.

The iris flower is sacred to the Greek goddess of the rainbow, Iris. She was the messenger of the gods and traveled back and forth from the realm of the gods to earth on a rainbow. How interesting that I had just spent an hour working in the iris garden, and now, like magick, a rainbow had appeared.

In the language of flowers, the iris symbolizes a message, which makes perfect sense considering who the multicolored flower is named after. So I said a quick prayer to Iris, telling her that I was open to receiving any messages she might have for me. I spent the rest of the day working on this book indoors while the rain fell, stopping occasionally to look out my kitchen windows at my now neat and tidy iris bed.

While I longed for some drier days and a blue sky again, I had to admit that the plants looked great. Even though we have had massive amounts of rain this spring, everything was such a lush and vibrant shade of green. I had the rest of the week to tidy up the gardens before my coven and a few guests came over on Beltane to celebrate the sabbat in the gardens.

It was a good week working in the flower beds. My herbs were doing wonderfully and all the foxgloves looked great, but on a rare sunny day I decided to drive by the flower stand just to look and see if there was anything I could not live without.

I was weak…I brought home a big box full of flowers. I grinned the whole drive home, thrilled with the goodies I had purchased. I picked up a huge and gorgeous hanging basket of hot purple-pink petunias and nabbed some more little pots of wave petunias to fill in a spot where my groundcover had died back, plus a few other plants perfect for the garden ritual at Beltane.

I spent that sunny, dry day planting more foxglove. I had found a new variety called 'Carillon'—it's a soft yellowish pink that looks enchanting. I could not stop myself from picking that up just two days before Beltane…besides, foxgloves work very nicely with faerie magick.

I also planted some fragrant heliotrope, which is good for invisibility spells. Finally I planted up a pot of chocolate mint just for fun. The mint encourages prosperity, and chocolate—well, it's basically the food of the gods!

The gardens all looked great. Later in the evening I would trim the boxwood hedges around the formal herb garden while my husband cut the grass. Then all I would have to do on Beltane day would be to sweep the patios and pull any last-minute weeds. My husband set up the fire pit for the coven ladies, and I spent the day before cleaning the house and cooking for the celebration.

With a little luck we would be rain-free and be able to hold our ritual and celebration outdoors in the gardens. I snipped some blossoms off the snowball bush and gathered some irises from the gardens for a casual floral arrangement for the house. Oh, it's good to be back out and working in the gardens, enjoying all the enchanting flowers again!

CHAPTER 8

Beltane

April 30

THE WORLD'S FAVORITE season is the
spring. All things seem possible in May.

Edwin Way Teale

Beltane was once thought of as the beginning of the season of summer. This is believed to have originated with the worship of the Celtic sun god Belenus. His name translates to "bright and shining one." Beltane is one of the greater sabbats, and it is a fire festival. Traditionally, Beltane festivities began at sunset on April 30, and the celebration lasted until sundown on May 1. This is the season of planting and grazing. In Irish Gaelic, the month of May is called Bealtaine.

Being directly opposite the Wheel of the Year from Samhain, they do share some similarities. Both are festivals that were traditionally celebrated by community bonfires. The May bonfires were lit in celebration and to welcome the return of the summer season. To the Celts, Beltane was the beginning of the summer, while for us today it marks the halfway point between the spring equinox and the summer solstice. Traditionally at Beltane there was also the maypole, dancing, and revelry. This is a festive season of celebration, romance, and high spirits.

At Beltane the fae are out in force. While at Samhain the veil between our world and the world of spirit is open, at Beltane it is the veil between our worlds and the world of the fae that is open. This is a festival of the living, so desire, love, play, magick, and rejoicing in the earth are the main themes.

Deities that are popular for this sabbat include the May Queen, the Green Man (who is also known as Jack in the Green), and the Roman goddess Flora, the goddess of flowers and plant life. This sabbat has many variations on the spelling, including Beltaine and Beltine. Of course, many of us are familiar with the American version of the holiday that is simply called May Day. Beltane was and is still celebrated with community bonfires and maypoles in Ireland, Scotland, Wales, Brittany, and Cornwall. Here in the United States, maypoles and May Day have been making a quiet but steady comeback in popularity.

Symbols of the Season
The Maypole and Flowers

> But I must gather knots of flowers,
> and buds of garlands gay, for I'm to
> be the Queen o' the May, Mother,
> I'm to be the Queen o' the May.
>
> *Lord Alfred Tennyson*

Originally the maypole dance was a way to ensure fertility of the land and its people. There is a lot of debate over the symbolism of the maypole and the circular wreath that typically adorns the tip of the pole. Yes, the maypole is a phallic symbol, and the floral wreath that encircles the top of the pole…well, there is no need to be graphic; I am sure you can figure it out.

The pole itself was thought originally to have been made from the trunk of a tall birch or elm tree. The birch was likely chosen for its lovely white bark. Also, as white is the color of the Maiden Goddess, it stood out against the green. Birch was thought to be the wood used for a traditional Witch's broom, which may have also influenced its selection for a maypole. The elm growing in abundance in England was straight and tall, and it was associated with the elves. Either of these trees make fine maypoles.

Spring flowers and greenery play a vital role in this sabbat, as you would imagine. Another popular symbol of this season is the wearing of a chaplet, or garland, of flowers and herbs in the hair. These traditional floral crowns mimicked the one found at the top of the Maypole. Bouquets and garlands of fresh flowers and herbs are decorations that can be incorporated into your modern sabbat festivities.

Young branches of blooming hawthorn and other blooming tree branches were once brought into the home and hung above the doorways to ensure prosperity and health during the year. Small bouquets, or posies, were bound together with ribbons and given as gifts to ensure love and health throughout the growing season.

Deities of Beltane
FLORA THE MAY QUEEN AND THE GREEN MAN

> WILDNESS AND A passionate energy are
> an essential part of the Green Man's character.
>
> *John Matthews*

Flora was a Roman goddess of flowers, fertility, and the spring. Her festival was called the Floralia and was a celebration that lasted for several days. This earliest of May Day festivals was celebrated between April 28 through May 3. From what we know, the Floralia began sometime around 240 BCE. Games, trips to the theater, household animals running amuck through town, beans being thrown to promote fertility, and, of course, drinking were some of the ways the people celebrated. This festival was so popular that it lasted until the fourth century CE. That's a pretty good run for a spring flower and fertility festival.

Flora did have a temple in Rome; rumor has it that it was located next to the Circus Maximus. The Greeks knew Flora as Chloris. Flora's magickal associations are spring flowers, the color green, beans, and bean blossoms. Over time Flora eventually evolved into the May Queen. Her consort for Beltane is, quite naturally, the Green Man.

It is thought that once upon a time this was actually a man disguised by and covered from head to toe in greenery and foliage. It was the folklorist James Frazer who linked the character of Jack-in-the-Green with Beltane—Jack-in-the-Green being a more modern title for the Green Man.

The Green Man is a popular representation of the god of nature. As well as being a standard figure for the festival of Beltane, he is the spirit of the woods and a god of plant life. Representations of the Green Man have been found all over Europe and into Asia and North Africa. This archetypal image goes back to Mesopotamia and the third millennium BCE. Over time, many male deities and woodland spirits were associated with the Green Man. These include Osirus (who was a green god), Dionysus (the god of the vine), Tamuz, Odin, Pan, Puck, Jack-in-the-Green, and John Barleycorn.

Images of the Green Man began springing up in Christian cathedrals and churches all over Europe starting around the eleventh century, probably because the folks they hired to do the work inside the churches were followers of the Old Ways. Either that or the craftsmen decided it would be a good idea to give a nod to the old nature gods of field, stream, and forest while they built the cathedrals to the new religion—just to be on the safe side.

How prevalent are those Green Man faces? Well, for example, there are over one hundred images of the Green Man in the mystical Rosslyn Chapel in Scotland, while there is only one representation of Jesus present. That's pretty interesting when you consider that it was rumored that the Knights Templar built the chapel. Of course, the knights were a pretty mysterious order themselves…

The Green Man has many faces and styles, but you can classify his representations into several types, from frightening to humorous to happy and purely decorative. Some of the titles given to these carved representations are humorous. The most common of the Green Men carvings is, in fact, the Spewing Green Man.

The Spewing Green Man (top center, opposite page, and continuing clockwise) is recognized by the leaves that radiate out from his nose and mouth. The area above the bridge of his nose and his eyebrows all become fans of small leaves.

The Foliated Green Man has leaf accents that take the place of his facial hair. In other words, his eyebrows, mustache, and beard are all leaves. This is one of the most popular versions of the Green Man today.

Next we have the Branched Green Man. His face is made out of leaves that start in the folds of skin on his face. The folds between his nose and cheeks, around his eyebrows, and the crinkles at the corners of his eyes are all branch formations that sprout into leaves.

The Emerging Green Man's face peeps out from around a circle of foliage and greenery. The face is surrounded by the leaves. Architectural scrolls, clusters of fruit, flowers, and leaves are frequent for this variation.

The Green Man or Wood Spirit's face has leaves instead of any type of facial hair on a man's smiling face. In other words, the eyebrows, mustache, and beard are all made of foliage.

The May King or Wood Spirit is a carved figure of a man's smiling face. He has more of a decorative look; you might see twigs, leaves, and berries decorating the man's hair and beard—think of the Holly King or Wizard of the Woods type of look. This version of the Green Man depicts a bearded, smiling man with a wreath of holly and/or greenery in his hair.

A Lusty Beltane Day Spell

It's Beltane day, and we are at the halfway point of spring and summer. Today is a day for lover's trysts, beauty magick, and to commune with the spirits of nature. Gather some flowers and spring leaves from your garden, or pick up a small bundle of flowers from the florist and arrange them in a vase at home.

Share some wine with your lover. Sprinkle the bed sheets with fragrant rose petals. Light a few red and white candles to encourage love and magick, and to bring the energies of the sabbat into your boudoir.

If you like, you can add a Green Man representation to your altar setup. Simply set the candles in their holders on either side of the Green Man's face and then scatter flowers around that. Simple and beautiful. You can keep it simple or go for drama; it's up to you! Just set a magickally romantic and passionate mood. And don't forget to practice safe sex. It is Beltane, you know; fertility magick and all of its energies are at their peak.

Light your candles and repeat the charm:

> *Beltane is a day of magick, ardor, and love*
> *May the Old Ones now bless us all from up above.*
> *With spring flowers I call Flora to bless us here*
> *This lush green foliage calls the Green Man to be near.*
> *A night for enchantment where faeries circle around*
> *Let my magick bring romance and let passion abound.*

I am sure you can figure out what to do next. Allow the candles to burn out in a safe place. Blessed be!

Honor the Green Man
Plant Green Flowers

Simple and sophisticated,
mysterious and elegant: green is beautiful.

Anne Metcalfe

Here is a different idea for your gardens of witchery: plant green flowers to honor the spirit of the Green Man. Green flowers are in vogue at the moment, and green blossoms in a garden are surprising and magickal. When you plant green flowers in the garden, the focus turns to the form and shape of the blossom as opposed to the flashy or brighter colors.

Green flowers are unexpected, unusual, and mystical in gardens and containers. Plant some green varieties of flowers to honor both the Green Man and your practice of green magick this year…you'll be delighted with the results.

Here are a few easy-to-find and charming green flowering plants to try.

Flowering tobacco (*Nicotiana*)—Look for the varieties of this annual called 'Lime Green'. These pale-green varieties tend to be very fragrant at night. The flowers also attract butterflies and hummingbirds. *Astrological correspondence*: Mars. *Element*: fire. *Magickal uses*: moon magick, protection, and may be used as an offering to the nature spirits. US *cold hardiness zones*: 10–11 (grown as an annual for most of the US).

ZINNIA (ANNUAL)—There are new lime-green varieties of zinnias. Look for the 'Envy' variety. This zinnia has semi-double flower heads. It grows up to 30 inches tall, does well in the heat, and will tolerate a bit of shade. There is also a variety named 'Tequila Lime'—this one performs best in full sun. Zinnias are affordable and they are annuals. Plant the seeds once the danger of frost has past and stand back and get ready to enjoy them all summer. *Astrological correspondence:* sun. *Element:* fire. *Magickal uses:* friendship.

TULIP (*Tulipa*)—Try the tulip variety called 'Spring Green'. It is a white- and green-striped tulip that is supposed to have strong stems and staying power in your spring garden. It flowers in May, which is perfect for Beltane. Look for any viridiflora tulip. All viridiflora tulips have a streak of green on each petal, which contrasts with the basic flower color such as white, pink, or yellow. Especially pretty varieties include 'Hummingbird', a yellow and green tulip, and 'Greenland', a soft pink with a green stripe tulip. *Astrological correspondence:* Venus. *Element:* earth. *Magickal uses:* prosperity and love. *US cold hardiness zones:* 3–8.

DAYLILY (*Hemerocallis*)—Daylilies are a garden classic for good reason. Today there are so many delicious and varied colors of daylilies there is no reason to just plant one. For a green variety of daylily, check out the cool 'Lime Frost', 'Green Flutter', and 'Missouri Beauty' varieties. For a more dramatic color, look for a green and burgundy daylily called 'Green Inferno'. *Astrological correspondence:* moon. *Element:* water. *Magickal uses:* protection and to break love spells gone sour. *US cold hardiness zones:* 3–10.

Coneflowers (*Echinacea purpurea*)—Yes, there are green varieties of coneflowers now. Look for 'Green Jewel' and 'Jade'. Both of these new cultivars will grow about 2 feet tall. If you want something a bit more funky in a green coneflower, look for 'Coconut Lime'. It's a new variety with a fuzzy center. *Astrological correspondence:* sun. *Element:* fire. *Magickal uses:* healing and strength. US *cold hardiness zones:* 3–9.

Hydrangeas (*Hydrangea paniculata*)—A green blooming hydrangea shrub. There is a cute 'Limelight' variety and a dwarf version of the shrub called 'Little Lime'. The blossoms on this particular hydrangea start out green but change over to pink in midsummer. *Astrological correspondence:* moon. *Element:* water. *Magickal uses:* protection and warding. US *cold hardiness zones:* 4–8.

Lady's Mantle (*Alchemilla mollis*)—This perennial is a gorgeous blooming herb. The flowers are chartreuse green and have become very popular in floral design. This herb grows in sun or partial shade. *Astrological correspondence:* Venus. *Element:* water. *Magickal uses:* love and beauty. US *cold hardiness zones:* 3–9.

Rudbeckia (*Rudbeckia occidentalius*)—'Green Wizard' rudbeckias are known for their autumn performance in the garden and for their sunny yellow petals, but this variety dares to be different. The plant grows 4–5 feet tall and has no colorful petals but instead gives its show through green bracts that surround its black cone center. It is striking and funky. This flower likes full sun or partial shade. Great for woodland gardens. *Astrological correspondence:* sun. *Element:* earth. *Magickal uses:* honesty and justice. US *cold hardiness zones:* 4–10.

SNOWBALL BUSH (*Viburnum opulus*) 'ROSEUM' OR (*Viburnum macroceph-alum*) 'CHINESE SNOWBALL BUSH'—This is a classic blooming shrub for the spring. The snowball bush's flowers start out as pale green and eventually turn to bright white, round clusters of blossoms. They prefer sun or partial shade and moist, well-drained soils. This shrub may grow up to 12 feet in height. A*strological correspondences:* sun and moon. *Element:* earth. *Magickal uses:* protection from baneful magick. US *cold hardiness zones:* 4–7.

HERBAL BOUQUETS AND TUSSIE-MUSSIES

> I HAVE HERE only made a nosegay of culled
> flowers, and have brought nothing of my
> own but the thread that ties them together.
>
> *Michel de Montaigne*

Here is some information on the traditional Beltane pastime of creating a posy, or a tussie-mussie. The term *tussie-mussie* is derived from the Old English word *tuzzy,* which means "a cluster, posy, or knot of flowers or leaves." The botanicals chosen for the tussie-mussie are traditionally based on the language of flowers. Since the Middle Ages, particular blossoms have held magical meanings based on the symbolism and folklore of plants. The posy, or little floral arrangement, was tied together into a small cluster, typically surrounded by ruffled foliage or lace, and tied off with a beautiful ribbon. Traditionally, this type of bouquet was a fragrant, hand-held clutch of flowers, foliage, and herbs in which specific botanicals were chosen to convey special sentiment. In other words, the recipient was given a romantic, scented, colorful and "secret" message.

During the Victorian era, the language of flowers took on an all-time high. The Victorians developed this art of communicating with flowers into a popular pastime. It was considered an essential part of a lady's education. There are dozens of lists and many variations on the theme—everything from the placement of the bow on the arrangement to the direction the flowers were arranged had a subtle, secret meaning. Leaves in the arrangement signified hope. Thorns warned the recipient of danger, perhaps of discovery. Touching your lips to the bouquet was a signal to let the giver know that you accepted the message and all of the sentiment behind it.

The Language of Flowers and Fragrant Herbs

Want to incorporate the romantic and bewitching language of flowers into your Beltane or spring and summer arrangements and bouquets? Choose your flowers with intention and with an eye for their secret meanings. Here is a primer of garden flowers that will help you learn how to speak the lingo.

ANGELICA—inspiration

APPLE BLOSSOMS—preference

ASTERS—romantic memories

ASTILBE—love at first sight

AZALEA—love and romance

BABY'S BREATH—a pure heart

BASIL—love, fidelity, good luck, and best wishes

BLUEBELLS—constancy

BORAGE—courage

BUDDLEIA (BUTTERFLY BUSH)—wantonness

CARNATION—an enthusiastic and energetic lover

CHAMOMILE—comfort and patience

CHRYSANTHEMUM—cheer and optimism

CLOVER—good luck

COMFREY—happy homes

Coreopsis—cheer

Daffodil—gracefulness

Daisy—innocence

Daylily—flirtatiousness and beauty

Dill—irresistible

Dusty Miller—happiness and industriousness

Echinacea (coneflower)—strength and health

Elderberry (blossoms and foliage)—enchantment and good luck

Fennel—"Worthy of all praise"

Fern—sincerity and fascination, faerie magick

Feverfew—protection and health

Forget-Me-Not—true love and remembrance

Gardenia—ecstasy and love

Geranium—marital love (*red*: protection/health, *pink*: romance, *white*: fertility, *wild*: constancy)

Goldenrod—good fortune

Holly—good wishes and protection

Honeysuckle—prosperity, and a devoted affection

Hosta (leaves)—devotion

Hydrangea—commitment, celebration, true-blue friends

Iris—messages, passion, and promise

Ivy—wedded love and fidelity

Jasmine—joy

Lady's Mantle (foliage and blooms)—love and attraction;
    an alchemist's plant

Lamb's Ears—gentleness, a sense of playfulness

Larkspur—a devoted connection between bride and groom

Lavender—devotion, success, and luck

Lemon Balm—freshness

Lilac—first love and beauty

Lily of the Valley—return of happiness, cheer

Lovage—strength

Magnolia—sweetness, old-fashioned beauty

Mint—prosperity and freshness

Monarda—irresistible

Myrtle—married love

Nigella/Love-in-a-Mist—"kiss me twice"

Oak (leaves)—strength, longevity, steadfastness

Orange Blossoms—marriage and fertility

Orchid—luxury, beauty, and lust

PANSY—loving thoughts, heart's ease

PEONY—beauty

PHLOX—"we are united"

POPPY—comfort

QUEEN ANNE'S LACE—"I'll return home," faithfulness

RANUNCULUS—glowing with charm

ROSE—the main definition is love, and then the color of the rose adds more individualized meanings (*red:* romance, *white:* new beginnings, *yellow:* happiness, *orange:* vitality, *coral:* admiration, *peach:* charmed, *pink:* innocent love, *purple:* passion, *ivory:* romance, *pale green:* fertility, *bicolored red and white:* unity)

ROSEMARY—remembrance, devotion, and fidelity

RUE—grace and virtue

SAGE—wisdom and domestic virtue

SEDUM/STONECROP—"welcome home, husband"

SNAPDRAGON—dazzling and dangerous

SNOWDROP—hope and a symbol of the early spring

ST. JOHN'S WORT—protection from faerie mischief

STEPHANOTIS—a wedding, "let's take a trip"

SUNFLOWER—constancy and respect

TANSY—a safe pregnancy

THISTLE—"Scotland forever" and "I will never forget you"

THYME—courage and strength

TIGER LILY—erotic love

TUBEROSE—voluptuousness

TULIP—love; however, the color of the tulip gives more specific meanings (*red:* a forever love, *pink:* dream lover, *pale green:* a jealous lover, *yellow:* "I am hopelessly in love with you," *white:* "return to me, my love," *variegated:* "you have beautiful eyes," *maroon-black:* a loving enchantment)

VERBENA—faithfulness in marriage

VIOLET—sweetness and modesty

VERVAIN—enchantment

WHEAT—prosperity and riches

WILLOW—serenity, love, and patience

WINDFLOWER—hope and anticipation

WEIGELA (BLOOM)—a heart that's true

WOODRUFF, SWEET—long life

YARROW—health, love, and comfort; a wise woman's herb

ZINNIA—thinking of faraway friends

The Styles of Tussie-Mussies

Tussie-mussies are usually rounded and compact bouquets. They are hand tied or bound together with floral tape and feature dainty, natural garden materials. Flower placement can be formal or ordered, such as the Beidermeier style, or the flower placement may be casual and random, sometimes referred to as Colonial style. The inclusion of fragrant herbs and flowers is very important, and they are chosen for their folklore and their symbolism.

HAND-TIED BOUQUET—Hand tying is a European method for creating bouquets. A hand-tied bouquet is actually a variety of the old and classic tussie-mussie. Hand-tied bouquets are very much the style at the moment. Typically these types of bouquets are rounded-mass arrangements with little to no greenery. To make them, materials are held in one hand while the stems are placed in diagonally, in a spiral fashion, with the other hand. The stems are taped with floral tape as you go along, building one on top of the other, until there's a 4- to 6-inch section of the stems smoothly wrapped in the floral tape. The stems also may be bound at the point where all the stems cross with a plastic cable tie or a zip tie. (This is trickier to do. It may take you a couple of tries if you don't use floral tape.) The zip tie is covered afterwards with a decorative ribbon and most of the stems will show.

THE BEIDERMEIER—This style of bouquet is dome shaped and features larger flowers arranged in concentric rings (see illustration below). This style of flower arranging was popular during the 1800s. Flowers are arranged in concentric rings in these tightly massed bouquets. Each ring features a different type of flower, such as a large rose for the center, marigolds for the next ring, and carnations after that.

MONOCHROMATIC HAND-TIED BOUQUET—These bouquets are currently very popular for wedding flowers and are old and stylish. Imagine a hand-tied rose bouquet all in various shades of pinks and deep mauve, or deep burgundy and brownish-red roses. If you choose to try a monochromatic bouquet for your special day, consider the symbolism of the enchanting colors of the blossoms.

An Enchanting History:
The Bridal Bouquet

It's May, and handfasting and wedding season is in full swing. Maybe you'd like to save some money for your ceremony and do your own bouquet? Carrying flowers by the bride is not a new fad; this idea goes back centuries. There is a lot of enchanting folklore surrounding flowers for the wedding party.

During medieval times, it was believed that bad luck and malicious spirits were common. It was also whispered that using strong-smelling herbs and enchanted flowers would drive these creatures away. Popular herbs in medieval times were rosemary for love and protection, thyme for courage, and varieties of sage for wisdom. Meadowsweet was very popular for weddings too. Its creamy-white, delicate flowers have an almond scent. It was favored to the point that it became known as "bridal wort" (*wort* is an Old English word for "herb").

Historically both the bride and groom wore garlands of flowers to represent new life and fertility. The bride's bouquet, on the whole, symbolizes the maiden in bloom. Flowers carried by the wedding party symbolize possibilities, love, and joy. The bride's bouquet, both fragrant and charming, traditionally signifies happiness and abundant possibilities.

In early times, brides gathered blooming herbs and native flowers and fashioned them into small hand-held bouquets for themselves and their attendants. Herbal foliage or a blossom were also worn by the groom and his men to drive off those spirits or just general bad luck and to promote fertility.

Do you know how the tradition of the bridesmaids and the groomsmen started? The bride was attended by several friends, her maidens, who would dress in a similar fashion as the bride. As they all traveled together to where the ceremony was to take place, it was believed that this confused the more spiteful faeries and malicious spirits into not being sure who was the bride. The men did the same thing, thus keeping the groom safe, which started the tradition of the "groom's men." Therefore, since the spirits couldn't be sure just who was who, they could create no mischief for the couple.

Medieval weddings had earthy and seasonal floral displays. They incorporated whatever was abundant at the time. This could include foliage, twigs, wheat, fruit, and berries. Instead of veils, the medieval bride often wore a crown of flowers, greenery, or flowering herbs in her long and unbound hair.

In more modern times, wedding bouquets evolved. At the beginning of the twentieth century, extravagant bouquets might measure up to 2 feet across. Sophisticated brides in the 1920s carried sheaves of calla lilies or a simple posy of bright colors. Early in the 1930s, brides carried armloads full of large presentation-style bouquets. By the end of this decade, simpler flowers became in style once again, and the Victorian-style tussie-mussie, or "posy," of bright mixed flowers such as azaleas, violets, and pansies became popular.

During World War II when flowers were scarce, brides carried simple and fragrant lily of the valley and garden roses. In the 1950s and early 1960s, bridal flowers became larger and more elaborate, and were often triangular in shape. My mother-in-law's bouquet, circa 1957, had three white orchids in the center that were removed and worn as a going-away corsage—what a cool idea! In the 1950s, all-white, trailing arrangements of orchids, orange blossoms, carnations, stephanotis, and roses were popular choices.

The flower child of the 1960s and '70s preferred natural bouquets such as a clutch of wildflowers or simple daisies. It wasn't unusual to see lots of foliage worked into those bouquets. Floppy hats, floral prints, and flowers arranged on silk fans were a big hit. In the 1980s opulence was the key word, with large arrangements of mostly white or ivory in triangular, crescent-shaped, or large adaptations of the old-fashioned nosegays. While bridal bouquets were mostly white again, baby's breath was added to soften them and some subtle color was also incorporated, such as pale pinks, peaches, or maybe a soft yellow. The more daring bride added touches of brighter pink, red, or purple. I remember that I shocked my floral designer thirty years ago by insisting upon pink roses being added to my round bouquet of white roses and stephanotis. She told me it wasn't done. I told her to get over it. (Hey, I was eighteen and not about to let some floral designer tell me what I could do.)

Today, anything goes. Brides can feel free to choose from any style they like. If you'd prefer to go more old-fashioned and herbal-oriented, then work in a bit of plant folklore with herbs and the language of flowers. Consider creating a nosegay or tussie-mussie bouquet.

When Prince William married Kate Middleton, I was delighted to notice that her bridal bouquet was a small tussie-mussie style, and all of the flowers for her bouquet were rumored to have been chosen for their symbolism—including a flower called Sweet William.

Creating a floral bouquet for yourself, a friend, or a loved one makes those celebratory flowers more personal and enchanting. Whether it's for a wedding, a handfasting, a sabbat ritual, a birthday gift, to celebrate a new baby, a graduation, or for mother's day, a fresh bouquet that you have made yourself adds an extra magickal touch to any special occasion.

The Magick of Color for Floral Bouquets

I often get asked about ways to incorporate both the language of flowers and color magick into floral arrangements and bouquets. So, with that in mind, here is more fun information for you to apply to your floral magick. All-white or ivory bridal bouquets are very popular with brides currently. One modern bridal magazine claims that these all-white bouquets are a symbol of "class, traditional elegance, and style." While that's a lovely thought, the truth is that if you don't add a bit of color to an all-white arrangement, it often blends right into the bride's dress.

If you are creating a bouquet or just plotting one out, then try adding a bit of color to break up all the white. Even adding a touch of celadon green would help. Bottom line? Whether you are making bouquets for fun, for a ritual, or for a wedding party, don't be afraid of color!

Wrap your mind around these enchanting possibilities:

CELADON GREEN—Celadon is often called "the new white" in bridal and floral magazines these days. An elegant and chic color, it is a fabulous neutral tone for floral arrangements and is stunning against white or ivory dresses. Add lime-green button mums and look for the pale green 'Limone' roses to add to a celadon-colored bouquet. *Magickal association:* green encourages prosperity and good luck, just as you would expect.

ORANGE—Passionate and a bold and vivid statement perfect for fall ceremonies. *Magickal association:* orange encourages vibrancy and lots of energy.

Violet/Purple—A royal, dramatic, and daring color. Purple bridal flowers announce that the bride is both mystical and confident. *Magickal association*: power, passion, and enchantment.

Periwinkle—A very popular color for attendants these days. This color is a wonderful shade of purple-blue and brings about peace and serenity on this hectic day. Try working with blue/violet hydrangeas for a natural coordinating flower to go with periwinkle dresses. *Magickal association*: as periwinkle is a mixture of purple and blue, this color gets hope and peace from the blue and power and passion from the purple.

Coral—Another "hot" color for attendants. Coral is a siren's shade. It is a bold and confident color. *Magickal association*: a mix of orange and pink energy from the orange and confidence, laughter, and love from the hot pink.

Hot Pink—Hot pink roses announce passion and are a vogue, cutting-edge color. Hot pink became popular recently as a few celebrities have been adding hot pink trim to their bridal gowns and carrying bright pink flowers. *Magickal association*: humor, love, and cheer.

Bridal Pink—Softer pink roses are old-fashioned and declare a romantic heart and a dreamy first love. This is the ultimate "warm fuzzy" in rose colors. *Magickal association*: romance, gentleness, and affection.

Burgundy—A deeper, darker, more tempestuous love. Deep burgundy flowers add punch and drama. Add some colorful fall foliage and shake things up! Deep burgundy is gorgeous with black attendants' dresses.

Magickal associations: burgundy is a mixture of red and black, so this brings the darkest, most intense aspects of love and passion to the mix.

BLACK—Yes, there are black flowers—calla lilies in the deepest of purples and roses so dark they have a black tone. Also there are black pansies, tulips, and hollyhocks. *Magickal association:* Witchcraft, secrets, and mystery.

SILVER—Try lamb's ears or dusty miller to add a soft, silvery sheen to a bouquet. Silver evokes a touch of magick in your floral arrangements. *Magickal association:* silver is associated with the moon goddess and feminine powers.

Creating Your Own Herbal Tussie-Mussie Bouquet

If there was ever a time to reap the benefits of having your own garden, it's now. Turn your eye toward creating something enchanting with all those blossoms this spring (or any other time of the year your garden is producing lots of flowers)!

Have you ever tried to make a tussie-mussie? I did not just include all that previous information for nothing—give it a whirl! It's fun and easy. You can do this.

I used to teach big, burly landscaper guys how to make these bouquets when I taught flower gardening classes at the community college. At first they'd balk, then they'd really get into it. The funniest part of the experience had to be after the class, when I would suggest that they surprise their wives or partners with the gorgeous bouquet that they had made that night. They would get a certain look in their eye as they headed home. I would try hard not to grin as they left. Flowers speak the language of love for many, many reasons.

Interestingly, during the classes, I found that the guys' bouquets always looked better than the womens'. Why? Because the guys just had a "what the hell" type of attitude—they just jumped in and tried it—while most of the women in the class agonized over each flower they selected. Even though I would encourage the ladies to laugh and experiment with the flowers, the men's bouquets would look more funky and cool and the women's would typically be formal and less casual.

It makes me smile remembering the classes and teaching the students how to work with the floral tape. I would demonstrate first, then walk around and help each of the students. There was a little fumbling until folks got the hang of it, but everyone laughed and had fun. Once I told the class to use floral tape like electrician's tape and to stretch it as they went along. The men immediately got it and handled the floral tape like pros—then *they* would demonstrate to the ladies in class.

They were so cute standing there in tough-guy work boots, with those big hands creating these dainty floral bouquets. It drove a few garden club divas crazy that the bouquets the guys made were so much better than theirs. So: yes, indeed, you bet your striped witchy socks that you *can* do this. Have fun this spring, and experiment!

Directions for Making Tussie-Mussies

Now that I've filled your head with tons of ideas, let's get down to the creation of the tussie-mussie bouquet. Start the arrangement with a large central bloom, such as a rose or a lily, as your focal point. Then encircle it with contrasting foliage and flowers, wrapping the stems together with green floral tape as you go. Leave the floral tape on the roll—just break it off after you wrap the tape around the stem a few times. Stretch the floral tape a bit as you go; it makes it stickier. Break off the tape and smooth the end down before you add the next stem. You will actually only be using about 6 inches of tape per stem; a little goes a long way.

Work out from the center in a circular pattern, taping in the flowers/foliage each time you add a new stem. (This keeps the arrangement tight so things won't be shifting around.) Build up the layers and finally emphasize the outer rim with large-leafed herbs, ferns, or hosta leaves. The fuzzy leaves of lady's mantle are excellent for this purpose, as are variegated ivy, coral bells, and violet leaves. If you use foliage to encircle the outside of the tussie-mussie, you won't need lace trim—the foliage becomes your "lace."

The finished size of the tussie-mussie should be anywhere from 4 to 8 inches across. Remember, they are small. Once you have your outer ring of foliage in place, trim the ends of the stems to an even length and cover the stem's end with the green floral tape. Make sure that the handle is smooth and the stems are completely covered in the tape.

Now wrap the stems in a satin ribbon to create a handle. Start at the bottom, fold the ribbon over the edge, and wrap it up to the top of the stems, right under the flowers. Fold over a bit and secure with a corsage pin. Pins should be pushed carefully down (at an angle), deep within the stems, or, if you prefer, secure the ribbon with hot glue as you wrap the stems. Tie a loose bow and attach or tie this right up and under the flowers. Secure the bow into place with another corsage pin. (Make sure the pin doesn't stick out the side of the wrapped stems!) Push it in almost straight up and down and well into the bundle of stems. Turn the arrangement over and trim up the ribbon if necessary. Store the bouquet in a cool place (like the fridge) in an empty glass or vase until you're ready to use it.

If you have to make the bouquet ahead of time, leave the bottom of the flower stems uncovered by the floral tape and set them in a vase of water. Store the bouquet in the fridge no more than 24 hours (you don't want the flowers to wilt), then pat the stems dry and trim out the ends to one even length. Finally, tape up the bottom and make sure the sides of your stems/handle are smooth. Finish up the stems/handle with the ribbon and bow a few hours before presenting the tussie-mussie to the recipient.

Supplies you will need include:

- A wire cutter
- Scissors
- Green floral tape
- Floral wire or a pipe cleaner to tie the bow
- Leather leaf fern or simple garden-type foliage (see below)
- Foliage from the garden such as ivy, hosta leaves, lady's mantle, or coral bell leaves
- Large flowers such as roses or peonies. Again, it's your choice as to what color and style. Whatever your main flower, go with an odd number—they are always more pleasing in an arrangement. The odd number keeps it from looking like a clock face. Try to arrange your main flowers—be they lilies, peonies, gardenias, or roses—in a triangular pattern within the bouquet.
- 3–4 stems mini carnations (in a pinch they fill out a bouquet, and they smell great)
- 2–3 stems Queen Anne's lace, feverfew, or baby's breath for filler
- 3–7 stems yarrow (fresh or dried)

- Assorted herbs and garden flowers chosen for their symbolism and/or color
- Satin or sheer ribbon in coordinating colors to tie around the stem and to make a bow around the base of the bouquet; try ⅝ inch
- One or two corsage pins
- Imagination and a sense of fun!

Full Moon in May
THE DRYAD MOON

> THE YOUNG MAY moon is beaming, love.
> The glow-worm's lamp is gleaming, love....
>
> *Thomas Moore*

There is an abundance of faerie and nature-spirit activity throughout the entire calendar month of May. Beltane's energies are with us, and the faeries and nature spirits are out in force! One of the titles of this month's full moon is the Dryad Moon. The dryads are female spirits of the woodlands. They are attendants of Artemis, and they are the guardians of the wild places in the forest, the groves, and the woodlands.

The dryads are not typically seen, but their dancing energy can be sensed if you keep an open mind and have a pure heart. However, like many other nature spirits, the dryads are not to be trifled with, so show them the respect and courtesy that they deserve. If you would like the dryads to protect the trees in your yard and the entire garden or your favorite enchanted place in the wild, then the best time to call on them is during the full moon in May.

A Dryad Full Moon Spell to Protect
Your Garden and Favorite Wild Places

For this spell, keep your supplies simple: an offering of milk and honey.

Head out to your gardens or the local park and your favorite place in the wild. Sit quietly on the ground. This may be beneath the trees, at the seashore, along the banks of a spring or creek, or in the mountains. No matter where you are, take a few moments and feel the moonlight filtering down on you.

Stretch out with your intuition and get a real feel for the nature spirits of the place. Leave the dryads an offering of milk and honey—just pour a small bit neatly on the ground to honor them and thank them for their assistance.

Now say the charm out loud:

> *The full moon in May is a time of great power*
> *I call forth the dryads to guard both leaf and flower.*
> *Now weave your protective energy through time and space*
> *With laughter and joy may you guard this natural place.*
> *Whether in grove, hills, plains, woodlands, or by moonlit sea*
> *I do honor your power and leave a gift for thee.*

When you are finished, be sure to take the containers you carried the liquid in home with you. Be responsible, and be sure to leave the area looking better than you found it—no one should be able to tell you were ever there.

Ellen's Garden of Witchery Journal
Secret Gardens

Within your heart
keep one still, secret spot
where dreams may go.
Louise Driscoll

Is there anything more delicious than a secret garden? I don't think so. While I have many garden beds that wrap around the front, sides, and back of my house, one of my favorites is what actually began as a formal herb garden tucked way back at the bottom of my yard. My kids started calling it "the secret garden" when they were teens, and as the years have gone on, the name has stuck. There are stepping stones going down the back yard hill to the entrance, and a brick path begins just outside the curved arbor that leads you into this out-of-the-way garden.

Enchanted with the idea of a secret garden, for several years I kept adding to the formal herb garden as my budget would allow. My husband built slightly raised beds, and I planted them full of magickal herbs such as artemesia, rue, valerian, sage, oregano, rosemary, echinacea, lavender, hyssop, and wolfsbane.

At first it was only the garden shed that closed it in on one side, but over the years we have managed to surround this entire back area of the yard with a privacy fence. It took a few seasons to grow and fill in, but I planted little boxwoods and blooming shrubs, and they now enclose the front entrance of the garden. The boxwoods are now a waist-high emerald-green hedge to the left. A curved arbor in the center has an autumn clematis vine scrambling over the top, and it is through the arbor that you enter the garden. Peony shrubs in the palest of pinks and daylilies guard the other front side of the garden.

Last year I decided to add a large urn to the center of the herb bed and planted even more fragrant herbs and a butterfly bush into those raised beds. I added soft solar lighting last summer and was very pleased with the results. At night those lights beckon you right down into the somewhat hidden and secret garden.

Now as the hedges get taller and with the privacy fence enclosing two sides, it is more secluded and private than ever. So am I finished? Of course not! Eventually I want to figure out a way to add a water feature. I haven't figured out how to pull that off yet, but I'll come up with something.

My goal for this year is to add some seating, like a patio of brick or paving stones where I can place a bench or a fussy little bistro table and chairs. I'll watch for a sale at the end of the summer and see what I can snag at a discount. I also want to figure out a way to add a permanent outdoor altar space or shrine to the Goddess.

The best part about this garden as it's grown over the years is that it is more hidden than ever—it's a garden within other gardens. It is a part of the whole, yet it is separate from the rest of the landscaping. This private sanctuary is an ideal place to dream and create magick, shielded as it is from the neighbors and the rest of the world.

There is an intimate connection to be had when you work with the earth and experience her cycles and seasons in a personal way. The best way I have ever found to accomplish this is by sticking your hands into the soil and growing something in the garden.

If you haven't already, read my *Garden Witchery* or *Herb Magic for Beginners* books and apply a touch of garden magick into your craft. No matter if you live in the city and garden in pots and containers or you have a suburban back yard where you maintain garden beds, stop and notice nature and all of the magick that is around you. (For more ideas for green witchery in the city, I suggest that you refer to my book *Garden Witch's Herbal* and check out chapter 2. There is an entire chapter devoted to gardening in the city.)

Personal Lesson for Beltane
LAUGH, DAMN IT!

SISTERS ARE DIFFERENT
flowers from the same garden.

Author Unknown

The coven and a few guests gathered together this year in my gardens for Beltane. Just to add to the drama, after a week of warm temperatures and sunshine, Beltane day was cloudy, misty, and a bit cold. We did manage to start our ritual outdoors. As we stood there in a circle, I looked around at the women that were present and was so thankful for each of them.

All were Witches united and celebrating together, yet we were all individuals and different. There was a lot of laughter as we tried to begin our Beltane ritual. Ember's high heels kept sinking into the soft lawn, Ruby and I had a terrible case of the giggles, Ravyn was trying to be calm and controlled, our guest was looking at everything all at once, and Noir was trying like hell to be serious, as she had not joined in group magick for a long time. Finally we pulled ourselves together and the ritual began rolling along, and it was lovely.

At the halfway point of the ritual, as we danced a spiral dance and raised energy as a group, the drizzle picked up. The faster we spun, the harder it rained. Finally, as we all tossed our hands into the air in unison, a rumble of soft thunder was heard—and right on cue, it began to pour.

Talk about your special effects! Shrieking with laughter and shivering with cold, I called out "The circle is open!" and we all ran inside. Don't get me wrong, we are not a bunch of sissies squealing at a bit of drizzle. We have done rituals outdoors while thunder and lightning chased each other across the sky, but these were typically just before the rain hit. This year we got dumped on in my gardens, so we ran inside, dried off, and finished up the ritual in my living room.

One of the funniest moments of the night occurred as we stood in the living room to finish the ritual. We were passing a goblet of sparkling cider around for the "cakes and ale" portion of the evening, and as Noir passed the cup to me with a blessing, her cell phone began to ring from her purse.

The ringtone was the song "Raise Your Glass" by Pink. Everyone froze, and Noir said, completely straightfaced, "Ritual fail." She was mortified, but we all laughed until we cried.

Sometimes you have to laugh. All the purses were left inside—we had not expected to end up finishing the ritual inside the house. As her phone began its song again, we all started singing along with the ringtone. It was very appropriate: we were "raising a glass," after all. And as I have said for years, the gods do have a hell of a sense of humor.

Finally once we were finished, the quarters were released, and the circle was opened again, we broke out the wine and the food to celebrate the year we have had as a group of friends, sisters, and Witches.

I think the lesson I have learned this year, with so many changes to our group, has been that magick will have its way, no matter what you plan. What you think you know, you don't. What you plan for rarely happens. People come and go in your life; sometimes they bring sorrow, and sometimes they bring laughter. They always bring lessons. It's up to you as to whether or not those lessons become wisdom.

The trick is to accept these life lessons and not to let them make you bitter. Laugh and keep on rolling—the gods *do* have a plan. We just may not always see it, looking straight ahead. Sometimes your path only becomes clear when you look back and see what has brought you to where you stand now. Time marches on…the Wheel of the Year keeps on spinning. Embrace the wisdom that you receive while on your journey.

Reflections on the Past Year

KNOWLEDGE IS LIKE a garden; if it is
not cultivated, it cannot be harvested.

African Proverb

It has been a year since I began working on this book, and now I am at the end of the month of May, and the Wheel of the Year is turning again toward Midsummer. The temperature is hovering close to 90 degrees today, and my Witch's garden is blooming away in bright colors and fabulous scents and textures.

This morning I discovered my coreopsis, spirea, astilbe, oakleaf hydrangea, foxgloves, fairy roses, lavender, and snapdragons all blooming away. I was inspired to snip some flowers and take them inside to keep me company while I finished up this book. They are now sitting in an antique blue glass canning jar on my office table. It seemed only appropriate that the book end as it began—on a hot, steamy day while I worked in the gardens. I hope you have enjoyed spending the past year with me. I have certainly enjoyed this chronicle of my experiences and traveling the path with you.

Now that summer is close again, be sure to enjoy these bright, warm days. Smile and take pleasure in the magick and the meaning behind those bewitching plants and flowers as spring rolls into summer. Go ahead, plant your gardens and work your seasonal spells and enjoy all of the cycles and seasons of witchery.

The earth has much to teach us, if only we will listen. As Witches, we should stop and take the time to grow our enchanting gardens, to raise our children well, to contribute to our community, and to honor the cycles of nature. We must celebrate each season as it passes, all of us moving together through the cycles of the year.

Let the magick of the sabbats influence your life and your craft in personal and profound ways. Draw strength from the green earth. Stand and face the sun, and turn yourself toward the light with wisdom and hope for the rebirth of our future.

Welcome to the summer; another year has passed! May you and yours be blessed.

Acknowledgments

A few words of thanks here. To my friends Christy, Tess, Jeanne, Shawna, Heather, and to all of the women of my coven (known by their witchy alter egos in the book). I appreciate all of you in so many ways. Thanks for the laughter, the magick, and your friendship.

A special thanks to Wen Hsu for the gorgeous artwork that graces the interior of the book. To Elysia Gallo for her support, and last but not least to Becky Zins, who is, in my opinion, the best damn editor ever.

Sabbat Correspondences

To many people holidays are not voyages
of discovery, but a ritual of reassurance.

Philip Andrew Adams

Here are the magickal correspondences for the sabbats. May this inventory inspire many ideas, both for rituals of your own design and while celebrating the sabbats with coven, family, and friends.

Summer Solstice/Midsummer

THEME—growth, tides of change

ENERGY—enchantment, connection

DEITIES—the Green Man, Tatiana, Aine, Oberon

COLORS—green, white, beach colors

CRYSTALS AND STONES—garnet, fire opal, sunstone, rhodocrosite

HERBS—lavender, yarrow, St. John's wort, valerian, dill, parsley, basil

FLOWERS—hydrangea, roses, daisies, lilies, coreopsis

SCENTS—rosemary, rose, lavender

FULL MOONS—Mead Moon (June), Thunder Moon (July)

DECORATIONS—celestial themes, sun, moon, faeries, starfish, shells

FOODS—strawberries, rhubarb, sugar snap peas, lettuce, fresh spinach, early varieties of tomatoes, cucumbers

Lughnasadh/Lammas

THEME—first harvest, goal setting, creativity

ENERGY—relaxation, reflection

DEITIES—Lugh, Rosemerta

COLORS—gold, yellow, green, golden brown

CRYSTALS AND STONES—ruby, malachite, bloodstone, rutilated quartz

HERBS—rosemary, hyssop, artemisia, wheat, sage, lavender, thyme

FLOWERS—asters, late summer roses, coneflowers, sunflowers, brown-eyed Susans, wild butterfly weed

SCENTS—orange, rose geranium, sage

FULL MOONS—Wort Moon (August)

DECORATIONS—sunflowers, dried wheat, corn, fresh fruit

FOODS—zucchini, green peppers, tomatoes, squash, sweet corn, wheat, blackberries, barley, breads

Autumn Equinox/Mabon

THEME—harvest, abundance

ENERGY—prosperity, thanksgiving, liveliness

DEITIES—Ceres/Demeter, Persephone, Hades, Dionysus

COLORS—red, bronze, yellow, orange

CRYSTALS AND STONES—sapphire, tiger's eye, tourmaline

HERBS—rosemary, sage, basil, thyme, cinnamon, nutmeg, cloves

FLOWERS—chrysanthemums, morning glories

SCENTS—apple, nutmeg, ginger, musk

FULL MOONS—Harvest Moon (typically September)

DECORATIONS—scarecrow, crows, autumn leaves, acorns, grapes, grapevine, pumpkins

FOODS—apple, grapes, squash, oats, corn, barley, pomegranate, pumpkins, pork, turkey

Samhain/Halloween

THEME—completion, the final harvest, Celtic New Year, divination, honoring your ancestors and remembering your beloved dead

ENERGY—mystery and magick

DEITIES—Hecate, Cerridwen, the Morrigan, Anubis, Nepthys, Herne

COLORS—orange, black, white

CRYSTALS AND STONES—topaz, black tourmaline, jet, obsidian, opal

HERBS—apple, oak, acorn, cinnamon, mullein, sage, wolf's bane

FLOWERS—chrysanthemums, marigolds, 'Autumn Joy' sedum

SCENTS—cinnamon, pumpkin, clove, patchouli

FULL MOONS—Blood Moon (October), sometimes the Harvest Moon is in October, Hunter's Moon (November)

DECORATIONS—jack-o'-lanterns, pumpkins, skeletons, Witches, black cats, cauldrons, photos of your ancestors and beloved dead

FOODS—apple, pumpkin (pie and bread), cider, ale, hazelnut, pomegranate, pork, beef

Yule/Winter Solstice

THEME—birth and illumination

ENERGY—wonder, family, peace

DEITIES—Odin, Lucy, Freya, Frigga

COLORS—red, green, white, silver, gold

CRYSTALS AND STONES—diamond, clear quartz, turquoise, amber

HERBS—pine, holly, mistletoe, ivy, sage, thyme

FLOWERS—poinsettias, red and white roses

SCENTS—cranberry, pine, bayberry, cinnamon

FULL MOONS—Oak Moon (December), Wolf Moon (January)

DECORATIONS—evergreen trees, wreaths, kissing balls, ornaments, boughs of holly and pine

FOODS—cranberry, nuts, gingerbread, pork, turkey

Imbolc/Candlemas

THEME—introspection and wisdom

ENERGY—kindness, memories, preparation

DEITIES—Brigid, the Dagda

COLORS—white, purple

CRYSTALS AND STONES—amethyst, moonstone, labradorite, blue lace agate

HERBS—hellebore, pine, juniper

FLOWERS—crocus, snowdrops, hellebores

SCENTS—mint, sandalwood

FULL MOONS—Quickening Moon (February)

DECORATIONS—candles, blooming house plants such as African violets and cyclamen

FOODS—blueberry scones, blackberries, breads, milk, cream, cheese

Vernal Equinox/Ostara

THEME—growth and new opportunities

ENERGY—excitement and rebirth

DEITIES—Eostre, Pan

COLORS—spring green, pastel shades of pink, blue, yellow, purple

CRYSTALS AND STONES—amethyst, pink topaz, peridot, aquamarine

HERBS—clovers, dandelion

FLOWERS—tulip, daffodil, crocus, pansy, violet, fern, hyacinth, forsythia

SCENTS—hyacinth, violet

FULL MOONS—Storm Moon (March), Planter's Moon (April), Hare Moon (April)

DECORATIONS—colored eggs, baskets, rabbits, early spring flowers

FOODS—eggs and egg dishes, lamb, asparagus, spring onions, radishes

Beltane

THEME—unity, partnership

ENERGY—romance, lust, joy

DEITIES—Flora, the Green Man

COLORS—green, white, rose pink

CRYSTALS AND STONES—emerald, rose quartz, aventurine, chrysoprase

HERBS—thyme, oregano, viburnum shrubs, rue, foxglove, chive

FLOWERS—lilac, peony, rose, iris, pansy, viola, snapdragon

SCENTS—lilac, peony, thyme

Full Moons—Dryad Moon (May), Flower Moon (May)

Decorations—baskets of fresh flowers, ribbons, mini maypoles

Foods—berries (raspberries, strawberries), fresh field greens, spring onions

Glossary

Annual—A plant that completes its life cycle in one growing season.

Amulet—A type of herbal charm, ornament, or jewel that aids and protects
its wearer.

Autumn Equinox—A Pagan/Wiccan sabbat also known as Mabon. The
autumn equinox occurs when the sun enters Libra on September 20–23.
This is a time when day and night hours are equal—a time of balance and
change. This sabbat is also known as the Witches' Thanksgiving and is the
second of three harvest festivals and the forerunner of the Harvest Home
celebrations.

Beltane—One of the high sabbats, Beltane is celebrated starting at sundown on April 30. Now is an excellent time to commune with the nature
spirits and the faeries, as the veil between the world of man and faerie is

thin. Wreaths, bouquets, fresh flowers, and the maypole are all part of the celebration.

CHARM—A simple spell or a rhyming series of words used for specific magickal purposes.

CHARM BAG—Similar to a sachet, a charm bag is a small cloth bag filled with aromatic herbs, charged crystals, and other magickal ingredients. Charm bags may be carried for any magickal purpose: health, safe travel, protection, to increase your confidence, and so on.

CHARGE—To fill or imbue an object with magickal energy.

CORRESPONDENCE CHART—A listing of which items are compatible in magickal use and will work in harmony with each other. For example, deities, the days of the week, sabbats, herbs, colors, and crystals all have magickal correspondences. (See the appendix for a correspondence chart for the eight sabbats.)

CRAFT, THE—The Witches' name for the Old Religion and practice of Witchcraft.

COVEN—A group of Witches or Wiccans who worship and celebrate the sabbats and esbats together. Covens may be formal traditions that include ranks, titles, and degrees or informal eclectic groups that draw from many magickal traditions and styles.

CROSS-QUARTER DAY—These four days are known as the four major sabbats. They occur at the halfway point between the seasons. They are Lughnasadh, Samhain, Imbolc, and Beltane.

CURSE—A magickal working intended to bring bad luck, sickness, or injury to its target.

DECIDUOUS—A tree or shrub that loses its leaves annually in the autumn. The plants go dormant during the winter months and regrow their foliage the following spring.

DOG DAYS—The scorching weeks that begin in July and continue throughout early September; typically the hottest time of the year in the Northern Hemisphere.

DRYAD—The mighty spirits of nature, or tree spirits. A dryad is typically associated with one specific tree.

ELEMENTALS—Nature spirits or energies that coordinate with each element. Earth elementals are brownies and gnomes. Air elementals are faeries and sylphs. Fire elementals are dragons, drakes, and djinns. Water elementals are undines and sirens.

ELEMENTS—The four natural elements are earth, air, fire, and water. These are the components of reality; without any one of these natural elements, human life would not be possible on our planet.

ENCHANT—The classic definition is to "sing to." To enchant something means that you load, or charge, the object with your personal power and positive intention.

ENCHANTMENT—An act of magick. This word is often used interchangeably for the word *spell.*

ESBAT—A full moon celebration.

FAERIE—A nature spirit, usually an earth or air elemental. May also be the spirit of a particular plant or flower.

FIRE MAGICK—Work with the element of fire to bring a quick and dramatic transformation into your life. Fire is the element of transformation.

FLORIGRAPHY—The language of flowers.

FLOWER FASCINATION—*Fascination* is the art of directing another's consciousness or will toward you—to command or bewitch. Flower fascinations are elementary flower spells and floral charms used for various magickal purposes.

GARDEN WITCH—A practical, down-to-earth type of magickal practitioner. A Witch who is well versed in herbal knowledge and its uses, and who is a magickal gardener.

GREEN MAN—The spirit of nature, an aspect of the god of the green world, typically depicted as a man's face made up of leaves and foliage.

GREEN MAGICK—A practical, nature-based system of the Craft that focuses on a reverence for the natural world, the individual's environment, and the plants and herbs that are indigenous to the practitioner's area. Herbal and natural magicks are essential to green magick.

HERB—A plant that is used for medicine, food, flavoring, or scent. Any part of the plant—the roots, stem, bark, leaves, pits, seeds, or flowers—may be used for such purposes. An herb may be a tree, shrub, woody perennial, flower, annual, or fern.

HERBAL ALLY—A plant that has a complementary vibration that is harmonious with an individual's personal magickal energies, allowing them to "link up" and to work well together. Sometimes referred to as a plant familiar or plant totem.

HERBALISM—The use of herbs in conjunction with magick to bring about positive change and transformation.

HEX—Classically this word has been defined as practicing Witchcraft. Today, if someone is talking about a hex, they are typically referring to affecting another person by means of a baneful spell.

IMBOLC—A Pagan/Wiccan sabbat. A cross-quarter day and the halfway point of winter and spring. The light is returning, and spring is not far away. This sabbat is celebrated on February 2 and is also known as Brigid's Day, Candlemas, and Oimelc.

LITHA—A popular name created by novelist J. R. R. Tolkien for the summer solstice sabbat.

LUGH—A Celtic solar god of many skills.

Lughnasadh—Also known as Lammas. Celebrated August 1, it is a festival of the first harvest, celebrating the gathering of fruits, grains, and veggies from the garden and the fields.

Mabon—A title for the sabbat of the autumn equinox.

Magick—The combination of your own personal power that is used in harmony with natural objects such as herbs and crystals and the elements. Once these are combined and your goal is focused upon, typically by the act of repeating the spell verse and the lighting of a candle or creating an herbal charm, the act of magick then creates a positive change.

Midsummer—A title for the sabbat of the summer solstice. One of the best times of the year to work with the faeries and the plant spirits in the garden. The point of the year when the sun is at its highest in the sky, Midsummer is the longest day. The summer solstice date will vary from year to year, but the sabbat always is celebrated when the sun enters the astrological sign of Cancer on June 20–23.

Ostara—Another title for the vernal (spring) equinox. This is a spring celebration that honors the Norse goddess Eostre. A fertility festival, the vernal equinox date also varies from year to year, but the sabbat always is celebrated when the sun enters the astrological sign of Aries on March 20–23.

Plant Familiar or Plant Totem—see Herbal Ally.

Perennial—A perennial plant is one that lives three or more years. Herbaceous perennials are plants that are nonwoody and whose aboveground parts usually die back to the ground each winter. They survive by means of their vigorous root system.

PSYCHIC PROTECTION—This is an active way to protect yourself from other people's thoughts, feelings, and psychic energy.

SABBAT—One of the eight holy days of the Witch's year. The sabbats are divided into two categories: the high sabbats (the cross-quarter days—Imbolc, Beltane, Lughnasadh, and Samhain—whose dates do not change from year to year) and the low sabbats, which are the equinoxes and the solstices (Ostara, the spring equinox, in March; Midsummer, the summer solstice, in June; Mabon, the autumn equinox, in September; and Yule, the winter solstice, in December). The dates of the solstices and equinoxes vary from year to year depending on when the sun enters a certain astrological sign, typically between the 20th and the 23rd of those months.

SACHET—A small cloth bag filled with aromatic herbs and spices.

SAMHAIN—Also known as Halloween, the Witches' New Year, this is the day when the veil between our world and the spirit world is at its thinnest. This greater sabbat is celebrated at sundown on October 31. A popular holiday for children and adults, this is the time of year to honor and to remember your loved ones who have passed and to celebrate the coming year.

SPELL—A spell is a series of rhyming words that verbally announces the spellcaster's intention. When these spoken words are combined with specific actions such as lighting a candle, creating an amulet, or gathering an herb, this is then worked in harmony with the tides of nature and, combined with the spellcaster's personal energy, makes it a magickal act endowed with the power to create positive change.

TUSSIE-MUSSIE—A small handmade bouquet also known as a posy or a nosegay. These bouquets rely on the language of flowers to convey an enchanting message.

VERNAL EQUINOX—The spring equinox that occurs in March in the Northern Hemisphere. A day when the night and daylight hours are equal, it is a time of balance and new beginnings. Another title for this sabbat is Ostara. It occurs when the sun enters Aries on March 20–23.

WICCA—The contemporary name for the Witches' religion. Wicca takes its roots from the Anglo-Saxon word *wicce*, which may mean "wise." It is also thought to mean "to shape or to bend." Wicca is a Pagan religion based on the cycles of nature and the belief in karma, reincarnation, and the worship of both a god and a goddess.

WICCAN REDE—A guiding principle that states "Do as you will, but harm none."

WISE WOMEN—The first Witches and the custodians of the old herbal knowledge of benevolent spells and charms.

WITCH—A practitioner of magick. A Witch may not necessarily be a Wiccan. That being said, most Witches will work their magick from a place of neutrality. Witches know and accept that they are fully accountable and responsible for all of their actions on both the mundane and the magickal levels.

WITCHCRAFT—The Witches' Craft.

WORT—An old Anglo-Saxon word that means "herb."

WORT CUNNING—Herbcraft.

WORT OR WYRT MOON—Wort or Wyrt is an old word for "herb," a title ascribed to the full moon in August. Now is a time for gathering and then drying magickal herbs from the garden for use in spells for the coming year.

YULE—A title for the sabbat of the winter solstice. This is the longest night and shortest day of the year. From this point on, the daylight hours will increase. Traditionally, this is a time when Pagans celebrate the return of light and the birth of the Sun God from the Mother Goddess. The winter solstice occurs when the sun enters Capricorn on December 20–23.

Bibliography

AS MAN THINKETH, so he is.

Gladys Taber

Allen, Linda. *Decking the Halls: The Folklore and Tradition of Christmas Plants.* Minocqua, WI: Willow Creek Press, 2000.

Altman, Nathaniel. *Palmistry.* New York: Sterling Publishing Company, 1999.

Andrews, Ted. *Animal-Speak.* St. Paul, MN: Llewellyn, 1994.

Bremness, Lesley. *Herbs.* New York: Dorling Kindersley, 1994.

Cabot, Laurie, and Jean Mills. *Celebrate the Earth: A Year of Holidays in the Pagan Tradition.* New York: Dell Publishing, 1994.

Campanelli, Pauline. *Ancient Ways: Reclaiming Pagan Traditions.* St. Paul, MN: Llewellyn, 1993.

———. *Wheel of the Year: Living the Magical Life.* Woodbury, MN: Llewellyn, 2008.

Conway, D. J. *Maiden, Mother, Crone.* St. Paul, MN: Llewellyn, 1994.

———. *Moon Magick.* St. Paul, MN: Llewellyn, 1995.

Crippen, T. G. *Christmas and Christmas Lore*. Detroit, MI: Omnigraphics, 1990. (Facsimile reprint of 1923 edition first published by Blackie & Son Limited, London.)

Cunningham, Scott. *Cunningham's Encyclopedia of Magical Herbs*. St. Paul, MN: Llewellyn, 1996.

———. *Magical Herbalism*. St. Paul, MN: Llewellyn, 1993.

Danaan, Clea. *Voices of the Earth*. Woodbury, MN: Llewellyn, 2009.

Denison, Edgar. *Missouri Wildflowers*. Jefferson City, MO: Missouri Department of Conservation, 2001.

Dugan, Ellen. *Autumn Equinox*. St. Paul, MN: Llewellyn, 2005.

———. *Book of Witchery*. Woodbury, MN: Llewellyn, 2009.

———. "Faeries in the Herb Garden." *Llewellyn's 2006 Herbal Almanac*. Woodbury, MN: Llewellyn, 2005.

———. *Garden Witchery*. St. Paul, MN: Llewellyn, 2003.

———. *Garden Witch's Herbal*. Woodbury, MN: Llewellyn, 2009.

———. *Herb Magic for Beginners*. Woodbury, MN: Llewellyn, 2006.

———. "Midsummer." *Llewellyn's Sabbats Almanac*. Woodbury, MN: Llewellyn, 2009.

———. "Palm Reading Sunday." *Llewellyn's Magical Almanac*. Woodbury, MN: Llewellyn, 2010.

———. "Yule." *Llewellyn's Sabbats Almanac*. Woodbury, MN: Llewellyn, 2010.

Dunwich, Gerina. *The Pagan Book of Halloween*. New York: Penguin Putnam, 2000.

Ellis, Peter Berresford. *The Druids*. Grand Rapids, MI: William B. Eerdmans Publishing Co., 1995.

Farrar, Janet, and Stewart Farrar. *Eight Sabbats for Witches*. Custer, WA: Phoenix Publishing, 1981.

Ferguson, Diana. *The Magickal Year*. London, England: Labyrinth Publishing UK, 1996.

Franklin, Anna. *Midsummer: Magickal Celebration of the Summer Solstice*. St. Paul, MN: Llewellyn, 2002.

Gallagher, Anne-Marie. *The Spells Bible*. Cincinnati, OH: Walking Stick Press, 2003.

Grant, Ember. *Advanced Crystal Magic*. Woodbury, MN: Llewellyn, 2012.

Greer, John Michael. *Natural Magic: Potions and Powers from the Magical Garden*. St. Paul, MN: Llewellyn, 2000.

Hoblyn, Alison. *Green Flowers: Unexpected Beauty for the Garden, Container or Vase*. Portland, OR: Timber Press, 2009.

Hopman, Ellen Evert. *A Druid's Herbal for the Sacred Earth Year*. Rochester, VT: Destiny Books, 1995.

Illes, Judika. *The Element Encyclopedia of Witchcraft*. London, England: HarperElement, 2005.

———. "The Spirits of Yuletide Lecture." Lecture notes, December 2010.

Irish, Lora S., Chris Pye, and Shawn Cipa. *Wood Spirits and Green Men: A Design Source Book for Woodcarvers and Other Artists.* Petersburg, PA: Fox Chapel Publishing, 2005.

K, Amber, and Azrael Arynn K. *Candlemas: Feast of Flames.* St. Paul, MN: Llewellyn, 2003.

Krasskova, Galina. *Exploring the Northern Tradition.* Franklin Lakes, NJ: New Page Books, 2005.

Laufer, Geraldine Adamich. *Tussie-Mussies: The Victorian Art of Expressing Yourself in the Language of Flowers.* New York: Workman, 1993.

Matthews, Caitlin. *Celtic Devotional: Daily Prayers and Blessings.* New York: Harmony Books, 1996.

Matthews, John. *The Winter Solstice.* Wheaton, IL: Godsfield Press, 1998.

Miles, Clement. *Christmas in Ritual and Tradition, Christian and Pagan.* Rockville, MD: Wildside Press, 2008. (Originally published by T. Fisher Unwin, 1912.)

Muller-Ebeling, Claudia, Christian Ratsch, and Wolf-Dieter Storl. *Witchcraft Medicine: Healing Arts, Shamanic Practices & Forbidden Plants.* Rochester, VT: Inner Traditions, 2003.

Muller-Ebeling, Claudia, and Christian Ratsch. *Pagan Christmas: The Plants, Spirits and Rituals at the origins of Yuletide.* Rochester, VT: Inner Traditions, 2006.

Nahmad, Claire. *Earth Magic: A Wise Woman's Guide to Herbal, Astrological and Other Folk Wisdom.* Rochester, VT: Destiny Books, 1994.

————. *Garden Spells: An Enchanting Collection of Victorian Wisdom*. Philadelphia, PA: Running Press, 1994.

Patterson, Jacqueline Memory. *Tree Wisdom*. London, England: Thorsons, 1996.

Rogers, Nicholas. *Halloween: From Pagan Ritual to Party Night*. New York: Oxford University Press, 2002.

Rowinski, Kate, ed. *The Quotable Cook*. New York: Lyons Press, 2000.

Sams, Jamie, and David Carson. *Medicine Cards*. Santa Fe, NM: Bear & Company, 1988.

Siden, Jan. *The Handbook of Palmistry*. Rozelle, Australia: Sally Milner Publishing, 1993.

Siefker, Phyllis. *Santa Claus, Last of the Wild Men*. Jefferson, NC: McFarland & Company, Inc., 1997.

Stewart, R. J. *Celtic Gods, Celtic Goddesses*. New York: Sterling Publishing Company, 1990.

Telesco, Patricia. *A Victorian Grimoire*. St. Paul, MN: Llewellyn, 1993.

Valiente, Doreen. *An ABC of Witchcraft*. Custer, WA: Phoenix Publishing, 1973.

Vitale, Alice Thoms. *Leaves in Myth, Magic & Medicine*. New York: Stewart, Tabori & Chang, 1997.

Whitaker, Hazel. *Palmistry: Your Highway to Life*. New York: Barnes & Noble Books, 1997.

Websites

Elderberry research (July 2010):

    http://www.killerplants.com/herbal-folklore/20030203.asp

Julenisse research (December 2010):

    http://www.ricksteves.com/plan/destinations/scan/norwayxmas04.htm

Candlemas research (February 2011):

    http://www.twilightbridge.com/hobbies/festivals/groundhog_day/world.htm

Imbolc research (February 2011):

    http://paganwiccan.about.com/od/imbolcfebruary2/p/Imbolc_History.htm

Index

Acorn, 75, 280

Air, element of, 12, 18, 46–48, 108, 153, 156–157, 225, 287–288

Angelica, 11, 27, 250

Anglo-Saxon, 38, 52, 204, 292–293

Annual, 8, 11, 15, 44, 233, 245–246, 285, 289

April, 175, 204, 220, 222, 231, 237, 240, 282, 285

Aphrodite, 113–114, 217

Apple, 95, 113–118, 128, 156, 250, 279–280
Apple muffin recipe, 117

Artemisia, 278

August, 27, 35–40, 45–47, 51–53, 55–56, 60, 62–64, 71, 74, 105, 125–126, 278, 290, 293

Autumn equinox, 35, 51, 64–69, 73–77, 89–91, 95, 113, 208, 279–280, 285, 290–291

Bacchus, 137, 154

Balance of energy, 190, 285

Balance, spell for, 213

Balder, 141, 156

Balsam fir, 152

Baneful magick, 184, 248, 289

Banishing evil, 184

Baskets, hanging, 9, 51, 234

Beach, 3–4, 194–198, 277

Bees, 4, 8, 13, 27, 47–48

Belenus, 237

Beltane, 35, 99, 212, 234–235, 237–238, 240–241, 244, 246, 248, 250, 266, 270, 282, 285, 287, 291

Berries, 8, 21–22, 150, 154–156, 189, 243, 258, 283

Bertcha, 146

Birds, bird feeder, xxii, 8, 9, 49, 50, 92, 94, 206, 217

Black (color), 14, 47, 54, 61, 72–74,
    86, 105–107, 126–128, 174, 183,
    222, 232, 247, 261–262, 279–280

Blackberry, 128, 189
    Blackberry wine, 128, 189

Blessing, home, 79, 205–206

Blue moon, 3, 7, 31, 261, 281–282

Blueberries, 41, 185
    Blueberry scone recipe, 186

Bonfire, 99–100, 105, 146, 177

Bread, 36, 38, 40–43, 95, 117, 181, 185, 280

Bridal flowers, 14, 257–261

Brigid, 171–172, 177–183,
    189–190, 281, 289
    Brigid's cross, 180–181

Brown-eyed Susans, 8, 278

Butterfly, 44–48, 250, 269, 278

Cancer, astrological sign of,
    1, 3, 32–34, 290

Canada, 59, 103

Candles, xx, 145, 171–172,
    174, 212, 214–215
    Candle magick, 34, 63–64, 73, 79,
        108, 147, 180, 206, 290–291

Candlemas, 169, 172, 174–175, 281, 289
    Candlemas Queen and King, 177

Capricorn, 136, 293

Carnations, 181, 214, 218, 256, 258, 265

Cauldron, 2–3, 34, 106–108, 116
    Cauldron-blessing ritual, 108

Celtic, 37, 99, 102, 110, 114, 171,
    178–179, 237, 279, 289

Chamomile, 11, 125, 250

Chocolate, 189, 212–213, 235

Christmas eve, 146

Chrysanthemums, 50–51, 66, 90,
    98, 119–121, 131, 279–280

Clover, 10–11, 250

Coffee, 145, 159

Coneflowers, 14, 27, 45, 50–51, 247, 278

Coven, xx, 3, 23, 28–34, 53–56, 59–60,
    71, 79–80, 87, 91–92, 102, 106,
    124, 126, 128, 134, 149, 166, 169,
    187–191, 211, 213–215, 222–224,
    230, 234–235, 270, 275, 277, 286

Coven sisters, 23, 28, 31, 54–55, 128,
    149, 187, 189–191, 222–223, 230

Cornstalks, 69, 75, 95, 105

Craft, the, xvii, 82, 172, 269,
    274, 286, 288, 293

Crocus, 181–182, 202, 281–282

Crone, 21, 106–107, 295

Crystal, 18–19, 55, 58, 149, 217

Cupid, 217

Daffodil, 216, 251, 282

Dandelion, 10, 12, 282

Daylily, 26, 246, 251

Day of the Dead, 88, 101–102,
    126–127, 131

Death, 22, 98, 100–102, 224

December, 2, 124, 133–139, 141,
    144–147, 165, 280, 291, 293

Decorating, xx, 69, 74, 101, 104–105,
    127, 149, 152, 208–209, 212, 243

Demeter, 63, 66–67, 279

Dionysus, 75, 154, 241, 279

Divination, 38, 116, 175, 222–224, 230, 279

Dog days of summer, 38–39

Dogwood, 8, 61, 150

Dragonflies, 4, 58–60

Druid, 158

Dryad, 22, 266, 283, 287
    Dryad Moon spell, 267

Earth, element of, 19, 63, 246, 248, 287

Eclipse, lunar and solar, 7

Eggs, 204, 206–213, 216, 282
    Egg bringer, 207

Egyptians, 39, 208

Elderberry, 20–21, 23, 251

Elderflower, 21

Elder tree, 21–22

Elfin ear loss, 87

Elements, 20, 108, 156, 165, 221, 287, 290

Elementals, 7, 9, 47, 287

English customs, 110, 156, 177, 203

Eostre, goddess, 204–208, 282, 290

Equinox, autumn, 35, 51, 64–69,
    73–77, 89–91, 95, 113, 208,
    279–280, 285, 290–291

Equinox, vernal, 201–204, 206, 209,
    211–212, 215–216, 281, 290, 292

Eros, 217

Etiquette, 223

Fairy, 6, 119, 121, 143, 149, 273

Fae, faerie, 2–19, 21, 46, 50, 86–87,
    102–103, 144–145, 153, 179, 212,
    216–217, 235, 238, 244, 251, 253,
    258, 266, 278, 285, 287–288, 290
Faerie garden, 5–9, 10–18, 12, 50,
    216–217, 235, 266, 288
    Faerie garden blessing, 18
Falcon, 92–94
February, xvii, 35, 169–172, 175–177,
    180, 194, 196, 198–199, 212, 281, 289
Fertility, 13, 38, 75, 114, 137, 141, 143,
    155–156, 158, 188–190, 206–208, 213,
    239–240, 244, 251–253, 257, 290
Fire, element of, 18, 32, 139, 154,
    160, 181, 245–247, 288
Fire magick, 1–2, 18, 28–32, 61, 99–100,
    105, 108, 112, 130, 154, 160, 179,
    181, 183, 221, 237, 245, 287–288
Fire ritual, 2, 28–31, 108, 130, 235
Fireflies, 4
Fireworks, 2, 28, 30
Fishing, 56–58, 61
Flora (goddess), 238, 240–241, 244, 282
Floral bouquets, 239, 247, 255,
    258–260, 262–263
    Floral bouquets and color, 260
Floralia, 240

Flowering tobacco, 245
Foliage, 16, 21, 74, 91, 98, 105, 114,
    120, 145, 154–155, 192, 241,
    243–244, 249, 251–252, 257–258,
    261, 263–265, 287–288
Forsythia, 201, 216, 282
Foxglove, 12, 23, 235, 282
Freya, 94, 113, 143, 146, 280
Frigga, 141–142, 156, 280
Full moon, 7, 12, 50–52, 55, 76–77, 79,
    108, 190, 213–216, 218, 220–222,
    246–247, 266–267, 278–283, 288, 293
    Full moon spell, 51–52, 79, 108,
    213–214, 218, 220, 266–267

Garden, xvii, xix, xxii, 2–3, 5–10, 12–20,
    23–27, 34, 36, 38, 43–45, 47, 50, 52–53,
    55, 66, 68, 84–85, 88–89, 92, 95, 109,
    111, 114, 119–120, 151, 182, 184,
    191–193, 208–209, 215–218, 220–221,
    232–235, 244–247, 250, 255, 258,
    262–263, 265–270, 273, 288, 290, 293
    Garden container, 8–9, 120, 296–297
    Garden herb, 9–10, 12–17, 23–24,
    184, 234, 246, 268–269, 288
    Garden magick, xvii, xix, 2, 5–7, 10, 12,
    17–20, 24–25, 27, 34, 36, 38, 45, 52,
    55, 66, 92, 95, 109, 114, 119–120,

151, 182, 184, 192–193, 208–209, 218, 220–221, 234, 244–245, 247, 250, 269–270, 273, 288, 290
Gardening, summer, 5–6, 8, 26, 48–49, 52, 55, 119, 274
Garden of Hesperides, 114
German, 136, 143, 204, 208, 232
Ghosts, 101–102, 105, 110, 121, 123, 131
Ginger, 159–161, 279
Gingerbread, 159, 161, 281
Gnomes, 146, 287
Goddess magick, 12, 21, 62–63, 66, 94, 108, 113, 115, 154, 179–180, 182–183, 189, 204–206, 213, 218–219, 234, 269, 292
Goldfinches, 4, 8, 14–15, 50
Golden bough, 4, 155, 157–158
Gothic Halloween party, 91, 126–127, 130
Greeks, 39, 121–122, 155, 208, 240
Green (color), 2–3, 12, 24, 25, 31, 35–36, 66, 69, 71–73, 79, 91, 98, 100, 120, 149, 152–153, 155–156, 158, 182–183, 192, 193, 202, 206, 208–210, 234, 239, 241, 244, 245–248, 253, 260, 263–264, 265, 268, 274, 278, 280, 282, 288
Green flowers, 98, 100, 120, 149, 154, 182–183, 192, 206, 234, 238–240, 243–248, 254, 260, 263–265, 270, 277–278, 280, 282, 288–289

Green knight, 153–154
Green magick, 2, 5, 245, 270, 288–289
Green Man, the, 79, 238–241, 243–245, 277, 282, 288
    Types of, 243
Groundcover, 16, 232, 234
Greenhouse therapy, 191
    Greenhouse therapy charm, 193
Groundhog, 175
Guadalupe, Lady of, 173–174
Guisers, 103

Hand, lines of the, 230
Halloween, 70–72, 74, 91, 97, 99–101, 103–105, 107, 109–112, 115–116, 123–127, 129–131, 279, 291
    Halloween stress, 123–125, 131
Hare, 204, 206–208, 213, 282
Harvest, 5, 35–38, 41, 52, 67–69, 75–77, 79, 95, 99, 109–110, 113, 208, 278–280, 285, 290
    Harvest Moon, 76–79, 279–280
    Harvest Moon blessing spell, 79
Hawks, 4, 94
Hellebores, 181–183, 281
    Hellebore spell for protection, 183–184

Heliotrope, 235

Hera, 113–114

Herb magick, 10–13, 17, 24, 52, 113,
153, 182, 185, 247, 269, 289, 292

Herbal bouquets, 248, 257, 262, 285

Herbal familiar, 22–25, 288–290

Holda/Hulda (goddess), 143, 146, 154

Holly, 137, 143, 147, 149–151, 153–155,
157–158, 167, 243, 251, 280–281

Holly King, 153–155, 243

Honeysuckle, 21, 251

Hummingbird, 8, 49–50, 246

Hungary, 145

Hyacinth, 282

Hydrangea, 48, 150, 247, 251, 273, 278

Idunna, 113–114

Imbolc, 35, 99, 169–172, 174–176,
180–183, 185–189, 194, 198,
200, 281, 287, 289, 291
Imbolc spell, 180–181, 183,
198, 200, 287, 289, 291

Iris, goddess, 12, 234

Iris, flower, 10, 12, 231–233, 235, 252, 282

Irish, 36, 103, 110, 177, 237

Isis, goddess, 62

Ivy, 57, 137, 149, 151, 153–155,
158, 252, 264–265, 280

Ivy Queen, 154–155, 252, 265

Jack in the Green, 238

Jack-o'-lantern, 73, 110–112
Jack-o'-lantern spell, 110–112

January, 170, 194, 280

July, 27–28, 30, 39–40, 51, 53,
74, 126, 233, 278, 287

June, 1, 4–5, 16, 26–27, 278, 290–291

Julenisse, 164–165

Jupiter, 39

Labor day, 68

Lady's mantle, 12, 70, 247, 252, 264–265

Lammas, 35, 37, 278, 290

Language of flowers, 114, 153–155,
157, 216–217, 234, 248–250,
259–260, 263, 288, 292

Lavender, 13, 27, 48, 252,
268, 273, 277–278

Leo, 38

Libra, 68, 77, 285

Lightning bugs, 3–4

Lingonberry, 145

Lilac, 13, 252, 282

Litha, 1, 4–5, 289

Loki, 156

Love, xvii, 11, 13–16, 18, 20, 34–35, 41,
    45, 52, 55, 100, 104, 113, 115–117,
    121–122, 126, 128, 131, 133, 148–149,
    156, 160, 165–166, 169, 190, 195, 206,
    208, 216, 225, 227, 229, 238, 240, 244,
    246–247, 250–254, 257, 261–263, 266

Lughnasadh, 35–36, 38, 53, 62,
    99, 278, 287, 290–291

Luna, festival of, 218

Lussinatten, 146–147

Maiden, 63, 173, 178–179, 204, 239

March, 201, 203, 207, 212–214,
    218, 220, 282, 290–292

Mars, 153–154, 160, 245

Marjoram, 13

May, 12, 27, 35, 100, 238, 240, 246,
    257, 266, 267, 273, 283
    May Day, 17–18, 27, 59, 66, 68, 77,
        80, 96, 100, 135, 143, 145, 172,
        184, 208, 219, 237–240, 243,
        255, 272–273, 286, 289, 292
    May King, 243
    Maypole, 238–240, 286
    May Queen, 143, 237–241

Meadowsweet, 14, 257

Mercury, 37

Midsummer, xix, xxi–xxii, 1–6, 10–11,
    13, 16, 18–19, 25–26, 28–30, 32,
    151, 247, 273, 277, 290–291

Mint, 16, 235, 252, 281

Mistletoe, 139, 151, 155–158, 280

Moon, 1, 3, 6–7, 12, 31–34, 44, 51–53,
    55–56, 76–77, 79, 108, 173–174, 190,
    193, 213–216, 218–222, 245–248,
    262, 266–267, 278–283, 288, 293
    Moon magick, 1, 6–7, 31, 33–34, 51–52,
        55, 76–77, 79, 108, 190, 218–221,
        245, 247–248, 278–279, 288

Mother, 21, 37, 62–64, 66–67, 71,
    109, 141, 143, 156, 173–174, 179,
    197, 215, 218, 239, 259, 293

Native plant, 8

Nature spirits, 6–9, 11, 17, 46, 109, 146,
    157, 241, 245, 266–267, 285, 287

Norse, 94, 113–114, 136, 138, 155–156, 203, 290

November, 68, 74, 99, 101–102, 111, 120, 159, 280

Nut-Crack Night, 99

Oak, 23, 72, 75, 121, 156, 280
Oak leaves, 2, 72, 75, 97, 150, 252

October, 35, 71, 73, 76–77, 80, 90, 97–98, 100, 102, 104–105, 111, 115, 117, 119, 124–126, 128, 130–131, 280, 291

Odin, 138, 140–143, 146, 241, 280

Old Ones, Old Gods, 2, 100, 214, 244

Old Path, Old Ways, 151, 241

Orange (in color magick), 90, 105–106, 120

Oregano, 13, 268, 282

Ostara, 201–204, 206–207, 209, 211–213, 215–216, 281, 290–292

Pagans, 4, 80–81, 103, 135, 138, 149, 178, 293

Pagan Pride Day (PPD), 80, 86
Rules for PPDs, 80–88

Palm-Reading Sunday, 222–223, 230

Palm shapes, 224

Pansy, 14, 217, 253, 282

Peony, 14, 253, 269, 282

Perennial, 11–12, 30, 45, 49, 119–120, 184, 217, 233, 247, 289–290

Persephone, 66, 279

Petunias, 45, 119, 219, 234

Phlox, 27, 45, 47, 50, 253

Pine, 75, 137, 147, 149–153, 158, 280–281
Pine cones, 75, 149

Pink (color), 12, 17, 119, 122, 201, 202, 210, 234–235, 246–247, 251, 253, 254, 256, 259, 261, 269, 282

Plant ally, 22–25, 288–290

Planter's moon, 220–221, 282

Popcorn, 104, 150

Poppy seeds, 146

Practical Protection Magick, xvii, 60

Prosperity, 2, 11, 68, 75, 77, 148, 152, 158, 160, 177, 189–190, 214, 216, 235, 240, 246, 251–252, 254, 260, 279

Protection, 11–13, 16, 75, 99, 106, 112, 122, 125, 141, 153–155, 160, 183–184, 199–200, 245–248, 251, 253, 257, 286, 291
Psychic protection, 125, 199–200, 291

Public Witches, 125

Pumpkin, 43, 63, 73, 75, 79, 95, 103, 106, 110–112, 280

Puritan, 173–174

Quarters, the, 17–20, 30–31, 271–272

Queen Anne's lace, 27, 253, 265

Quiche recipe, 211

Rabbit, 204, 207, 212

Raisins, 145

Recipes

    Apple muffin, 117

    Blueberry scones, 186

    Gingerbread cookies, 161

    Quiche, 211

    Sangria, 30

    Zucchini bread, 41

Red (color), 11, 17, 29–31, 61, 77, 90, 98, 119, 122, 127–128, 139, 144, 150, 154, 163, 181, 208, 210, 244, 251, 253–254, 259, 262, 279–280

Robins, 202

Romans, 39, 136–137, 153

Rose, xxi, 4, 13, 15, 39, 114, 150, 183, 244, 253, 256, 261, 263, 278, 282

Rosemary, 15, 253, 257, 268, 278–279

Rudbeckia, 247

Rue, 253, 268, 282

Sabbat, xix–xxi, 2, 4–5, 7, 28–29, 35–37, 40, 67–69, 75, 99, 102, 105–106, 109, 113, 136, 142, 171–172, 176, 189–190, 202–203, 205–207, 212–213, 215–216, 218, 234, 237–240, 244, 259, 274, 277, 285–287, 289–293

Saffron buns, 145

Sage, 15, 253, 257, 268, 278–280

Saint Brigit, 179

Saint Nicolas, 139

Samhain, 35, 73–74, 91, 97, 99–105, 109–113, 115–117, 121, 123–124, 126–131, 237–238, 279, 287, 291

Sangria recipe, 30

Santa, 138–140, 149, 162–164, 166

Saturn, 137, 153–155, 183

Saturnalia, 136–137, 149, 153–154

Scarecrow, 69–74, 89, 95, 119, 279

Scorpio, 31, 102

Scottish customs, 103, 110, 238, 241, 254

Seashells, 3, 197

Secret gardens, 216, 268–269

September, 8, 39, 45, 48, 50, 60, 62–63, 65–70, 74, 76–77, 80, 88, 90–91, 117, 119, 279, 285, 287, 291

Shadow work, 170–171

Shaman, 138, 140

Shrubs, blooming, 8, 68, 247–248, 268

Sidhe, 102–103

Silver bough, 114

Sinterklaas, 139–140

Sirius, 39–40

Snap-Apple Night, 99, 115

Snow, 98, 134, 138, 143, 151, 166, 170, 176, 181, 189, 192–196, 198–200, 205, 213, 217, 233

Snow Queen, 143

Snowball bush, 233, 235, 248

Solitary magick, 131

Solstices, 291

Spring, season, xvii, 7, 14–15, 23, 25–27, 67–68, 88, 119, 169, 175–176, 182, 191–193, 198–209, 212–220, 231–232, 234, 237–240, 244, 246, 248, 250, 253, 262–263, 267, 274, 282–283, 287, 289–292

Spells, xx, 2, 5–6, 13, 15, 17, 21, 25, 74, 103, 106, 111, 114–115, 131, 160, 189, 235, 246, 274, 288, 292–293

St. Lucy, 144, 163

St. John's wort, 16, 253, 277

Star, 31, 39–40, 61, 114, 116, 142

Steampunk, 127

Summer, 2–6, 8, 16, 21, 24–26, 28, 32–36, 38–40, 43–45, 47–52, 55–56, 58, 61–62, 64–66, 90–91, 99, 119–120, 126, 194, 203, 237–238, 244, 246, 250, 269, 274, 277–278, 289–291

Summer solstice, 1–5, 11, 16, 20, 32–35, 237–238, 277, 289–291

Summer vacation, 51–52, 55–56, 61–62, 194

Sun, the, xxi, 1–3, 10, 13–14, 19, 30, 32–35, 38–39, 49, 61, 68, 77, 91–94, 105, 114, 135–137, 144, 146, 151–152, 157–158, 165, 167, 174, 178, 193, 196–197, 199–200, 202–205, 208, 233, 237, 246–248, 274, 278, 285, 290–293

Sympathetic magick, 152

Tarot, 28, 60, 83, 125, 170, 223

Thanksgiving, 67, 72–74, 159, 279, 285

Thistle, 8, 15, 51, 254

Thyme, 16, 254, 257, 278–280, 282

Tombstones, 129, 131

Totem, 22–23, 289–290

Transformation, 28–29, 31–32,
46, 100, 102, 190, 288–289

Trick-or-treaters, 100–101,
103–104, 107, 111, 130

Tussie-mussies, 248, 255, 263

Valerian, 16, 268, 277

Variegated, 155, 254, 264

Veil between the worlds, 98, 238

Venus (goddess), 113–114, 217

Venus (planet), 39, 59, 113, 114, 246, 247

Vernal equinox, 201–204, 206, 209,
211–212, 215–216, 281, 290, 292

Viburnum, 8, 248, 282

Viola, 14, 17, 217, 282

Violet, 10, 23, 254, 261, 264, 282

Virgo, xxi, 62–64

Warding off ghosts, 110, 121, 123

Water, element of, 18, 75,
110, 113, 246–247

Weather, xxi–xxii, 14, 36, 67, 80, 86–87,
91, 119, 125, 130, 164, 175–176, 189,
194–195, 202, 205, 213, 216, 218, 233

Welsh, 67, 149

Wheel of the Year, xix–xx, xxii,
2, 61–62, 112, 131, 136, 165,
170, 175, 237, 272–273

White (color), 11–12, 17, 21, 23, 34, 36, 58,
71, 73–74, 79, 122, 134, 138–141, 144–
145, 147, 149, 156, 163, 167, 181, 186,
190, 195, 204, 206–207, 209–210, 214,
216, 218–220, 232, 239, 244, 246, 248,
251, 253–254, 258–260, 277, 279–282

Off-white (color), 3, 73, 74

Wildflowers, 56, 184, 258

Wild Hunt, 141–144, 146

Window boxes, 9, 26, 220

Wine, 21, 28–30, 43, 54–55,
83, 128, 189, 244, 272

Winter, 2, 13, 15, 25, 37, 66, 91, 99,
119–120, 131, 133–139, 141–144,
149, 151–153, 157, 159, 161, 166–167,
169–170, 172, 175–176, 178, 181–182,
184–185, 189, 191–195, 198–201, 203,
205, 216, 233, 280, 287, 289, 291, 293

Winter solstice, 2, 15, 91, 133–137,
139, 142, 144, 151–153, 159,
166–167, 175, 280, 289, 291, 293

Witch, xvii, xix–xx, 5, 10, 17, 20–21, 37, 41, 52, 56, 64, 67, 73, 85, 95, 107–108, 111, 121, 125–126, 130, 144, 149, 158, 162, 165, 169, 172, 175–176, 182, 184, 207, 219, 221, 223, 225, 239, 270, 273, 288, 291–292

Witches' Ball, 91, 125–126

Witchcraft, 82, 113, 145–146, 156, 182, 262, 286, 289, 293

Witchery, xvii, xx, 2, 10, 26, 43, 68, 88, 119, 151, 184, 191, 220, 245, 268–270, 274

Wizard, 121, 138, 207, 243, 247

Wizard of the woods, 243

Wodin, 140

Wolfsbane, 268

Wort Moon, 51–53, 56, 277–278, 293

Wreath, 75, 145, 156, 163, 212, 239, 243

Yarrow, 17, 23, 27, 50, 254, 265, 277

Yellow (color), 2, 12, 17, 27, 34–36, 45, 47–48, 50–52, 61, 90, 98, 119–120, 122, 210, 212, 216, 232, 246–247, 253–254, 259, 278–279, 282

Yule, 133–136, 141–142, 144, 147, 149, 152, 163–166, 176, 190, 280, 291, 293

Yule log, 133–134, 141, 152

Yuletide, 15, 139, 141–142, 144–145, 147–151, 153–155, 158–159, 162, 165, 213

herbal charm, 158

Yuley the goat, 164–165

Zeus, 114

Zinnia, 246, 254

Zodiac, 3, 32–33, 38, 62, 136

Zone, US Hardiness, 10, 16, 245–248

Zucchini, 41–43, 278

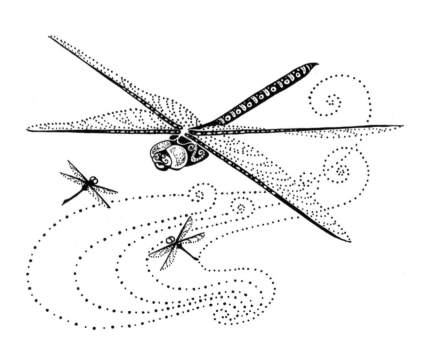